Praise for The Great Surge

"Powerful, lucid, and revelatory, *The Great Surge* makes a vital argument and offers indispensable prescriptions about sustaining global economic progress into the future."

—George Soros, chairman of Soros Fund Management

"Steven Radelet's brilliant new book demonstrates how the world has actually gotten better in recent years, not by a little but by a lot. This is a careful antidote to today's fashionable pessimism and should be read by everyone."

—Francis Fukuyama, author of *The End of History*

"With the airwaves filled with news of insurrection, desperation and stubborn diseases, this book jars you out of a cliched response. With his typical care and detail, Steve describes humanity's greatest hits over the last twenty years—never have we lived in a time when so many are doing so well. The job surely isn't done, but these pages provide the evidence the job can be done, if we choose to do it."

—Bono, cofounder of ONE and (RED)

"Steven Radelet is one of the leading development thinkers and practitioners in the world today. This captivating book shows that progress for the world's poor is not just possible, it is happening right now all around the world."

—Ellen Johnson Sirleaf, president of Liberia

"Human nature is evolutionarily wired to notice bad news much more than good news. But good news there is, for billions of people on the planet. Using compelling stories and data, Steve Radelet shows us just how far developing countries have come and makes a convincing case that understanding this positive history is essential for future decision-making."

—Anne-Marie Slaughter, president and CEO of the
New America Foundation, director of Policy Planning,
US Department of State 2009–2011

"You won't see this in the everyday news headlines, but our world is making historic progress. Extreme poverty and disease are declining while school enrollment and self-government are on the rise. Georgetown professor Steven Radelet has written an uplifting, spirited and compelling book on what he calls The Great Surge—an ongoing global transformation we're privileged not only to witness but to help bring about. An effervescent roadmap to the recent past and what comes next!"

—Muhtar Kent, chairman and CEO of The Coca-Cola Company

"At a time when doom, danger, and disaster dominate analysis of global trends, Steven Radelet pushes back against the pessimists with mountains of evidence and breathtaking vision. *The Great Surge* tells the other side of the story of global change over the past two decades, a story of unprecedented human progress in reducing poverty, hunger, illiteracy, oppression, childhood deaths, and even (despite the headlines) violent conflict. This is far from a naïve book. A leading development economist with deep policy experience, Radelet readily acknowledges the enormous work still to be done, and the tenacious obstacles that persist. But in lucidly exposing the factors that have delivered transformative development progress, he shows us how leadership and cooperation at the global and developing country levels, combined with continued investments in technology, can continue to bring reductions in human misery that were once nearly beyond imagination. This is a stunning, wise, and deeply hopeful book that anyone concerned about global development must read."

—Larry Diamond, senior fellow at the Hoover Institution &
Freeman Spogli Institute, director of the Center on Democracy,
Development and the Rule of Law, Stanford University

"The Great Surge is one of the most optimistic and compelling looks at global development of our time. It challenges us to rethink both economic progress and environmental sustainability, especially when they come in conflict. While this dilemma has mystified many development experts for decades, Radelet charts a path forward that is not only possible, but imperative."

—Howard W. Buffett, lecturer in International
and Public Affairs, Columbia University

"A must read. The strong optimism about global development brings up the key questions about how the momentum of progress from 1990 to about 2010 could be renewed in the post-2015 period."

—Kemal Dervis, vice president and director of the Global Economy
and Development program at the Brookings Institution, former
administrator of the United Nations Development Programme,
former minister of economic affairs for the government of Turkey

THE GREAT SURGE

*The Ascent of the
Developing World*

STEVEN RADELET

SIMON & SCHUSTER

New York   London   Toronto   Sydney   New Delhi

Simon & Schuster
1230 Avenue of the Americas
New York, NY 10020

First Simon & Schuster hardcover edition November 2015

SIMON & SCHUSTER and colophon are
registered trademarks of Simon & Schuster, Inc.

For information about special discounts for bulk purchases,
please contact Simon & Schuster Special Sales at 1-866-506-1949
or business@simonandschuster.com.

The Simon & Schuster Speakers Bureau can bring authors to your live event.
For more information or to book an event, contact the
Simon & Schuster Speakers Bureau at 1-866-248-3049
or visit our website at www.simonspeakers.com.

Interior design by Ruth Lee-Mui

Manufactured in the United States of America

10 9 8 7 6 5 4 3 2 1

Library of Congress Cataloging-in-Publication Data is available.

ISBN 978-1-4767-6478-8
ISBN 978-1-4767-6480-1 (ebook)

For Carrie—
my partner, inspiration, best friend,
and the love of my life

CONTENTS

PART THREE: THE FUTURE

PROLOGUE

November 9, 1989

ON NOVEMBER 9, 1989, THE PEOPLE OF NAMIBIA IN SOUTHWEST AFRICA GATHERED IN droves to wait under a sweltering sun and claim a prize for which they had fought for decades: the right to vote. A remarkable 98 percent of registered voters turned out over five days to select delegates to a constituent assembly that would draft a new constitution and set the stage for presidential elections and the formation of a new government.[1]

The Namibians lining up that day had no way of knowing it, but their actions would reverberate far beyond their borders and mark the beginning of a slow but steady sweep of democracy across Africa.

They could not know that exactly as they were voting, forces were under way that would bring about some of the most important changes in world history. Far to the east that same day, Deng Xiaoping was resigning as chairman of China's Central Military Commission, his last formal post in the Communist Party leadership. Deng had transformed the Chinese economy by abandoning Mao Tse-tung's rigid Communism and adopting a more mixed, market-based economy. His resignation marked a key political change: It effectively ended the tradition of Chinese leaders ruling like emperors until death.[2] It also shifted power from a single supreme leader to the group leadership of the party and effectively marked the beginning of de facto term limits. Imperial strongman rule in China was over.

Meanwhile, that very afternoon, five thousand miles away in Berlin, the government of East Germany capitulated to overwhelming upheaval and threw open the country's western borders for the first time in twenty-eight years. The Berlin Wall was coming down. Political relationships and systems around the world were about to undergo seismic changes—most obviously in Eastern Europe, but also in Namibia and in developing countries around the world. Dictators supported by the United States and the Soviet Union would fall. Proxy wars and conflict that had wreaked havoc in developing countries would decline. Communism as both an economic and political system would lose its last shreds of credibility. Ideas and ideologies would change. Trade would expand and technology would spread. Dozens of developing countries would adopt more vibrant and accountable political systems and more market-based and open economic strategies.

The greatest surge of progress in developing countries in world history was about to begin.

PART ONE

THE SURGE

ONE

A GREAT TRANSFORMATION

What is happening in Liberia is but a microcosm of the transformation that is sweeping across many countries. Dictators are being replaced by democracy. Authoritarianism is giving way to accountability. Economic stagnation is turning to resurgence. And most important, despair is being replaced by hope—hope that people can live in peace with their neighbors, that parents can provide for their families, that children can go to school and receive decent health care, and that people can speak their minds without fear.

—*Ellen Johnson Sirleaf, president of the Republic of Liberia*

WE LIVE AT A TIME OF THE GREATEST DEVELOPMENT PROGRESS AMONG THE GLOBAL POOR in the history of the world. Never before have so many people, in so many developing countries, made so much progress in so short a time in reducing poverty, increasing incomes, improving health, reducing conflict and war, and spreading democracy.

If you find that hard to believe, you are not alone. Most people believe the opposite: that with a few exceptions such as China and India, the majority of developing countries are stuck in deep poverty, led by inept dictators, and living with pervasive famine, widespread disease, constant violence, and little hope for progress.

The old story is no longer true. A major transformation is under way—and has been for two decades now—in the majority of the world's poorest countries, largely unnoticed by much of the world. Since the early 1990s, 1 billion people have been lifted out of extreme poverty. The average income for hundreds of millions of people in dozens of poor countries has more than doubled, 6 million fewer children die every year from disease, war and violence have declined significantly, average life expectancy has increased by six years, tens of millions more girls are in school, the share of people living in chronic hunger has been cut nearly in half, millions more people have access to clean water, and democracy—often fragile and imperfect—has become the norm rather than the exception in developing countries around the world.

To be sure, the surge of progress in health, income, poverty, education, and governance has not reached everyone: many poor countries remain mired in poverty and conflict, and even in the countries moving forward, millions of people are still left behind, even if their numbers are shrinking. Rapid progress has brought new challenges, especially around urbanization, environmental degradation, and climate change, that raise critical questions about long-term sustainability. Nevertheless, the majority of poor countries—and hundreds of millions of individual people living in those countries—are now making greater progress in a wider range of development indicators than ever before.

This book tells the story of this remarkable economic, social, and political transformation among the global poor. The pages that follow show how the end of the Cold War, the demise of Communism, groundbreaking new technologies, increased global integration, local action, courageous leadership, and in some cases, good fortune, have combined to improve the fate of hundreds of millions of people in poor countries around the world. How did these extraordinary changes come about? Why have some countries moved forward, while others have remained behind? What do these changes mean for the rest of the world? And most important, can the gains continue? Or will climate change, resource demand, demographic pressures, economic and political mismanagement, or possible war conspire to derail the great surge in development progress?

The story of the dramatic progress in developing countries begins in the 1960s. In the immediate post–World War II era, several countries in East and Southeast Asia (alongside a few others like Botswana and Mauritius) began to make remarkable advances that continue today. China began its rapid resurgence in 1980, in many ways setting the stage for the broader transformation that followed in other countries. Some other developing countries started to move forward, only to see progress halt in the late 1970s and 1980s following the global oil shocks and subsequent debt crises. However, most developing countries made little headway—that is, until the early 1990s, when progress accelerated and dozens of developing countries around the world began to move forward.

My central focus is on four critical dimensions of development progress: poverty, income, health and education, and democracy and governance (although I will touch on many others). Global poverty is falling—fast. In 1993 almost 2 billion people around the world lived in extreme poverty on less than $1.25 per day.* Then, for the first time in history, the number began to fall. Astonishingly, in just eighteen years, the number was cut by almost half: by 2011, it was down to just over 1 billion, meaning that *almost 1 billion fewer people were living in extreme poverty*. The proportion of the population of developing countries living in extreme poverty has fallen even faster, from 42 percent in 1993 to just 17 percent in 2011. The opening of China accounts for a large share of the change, but the fall in extreme poverty goes well beyond China and includes dozens of countries in every region of the world, including many in sub-Saharan Africa.

At the same time, incomes have been rising. People living in developing countries today have incomes that are nearly *double* those of their parents from two decades ago, on average (in "real" terms, after

*Consumption of $1.25 a day is the World Bank's definition of "extreme" poverty, with all figures in purchasing power parity terms and adjusted for inflation, as described in chapter 2.

controlling for inflation). This improvement is remarkable, especially when one considers that in the previous generation, there had been essentially zero change in average incomes in the majority of developing countries. The acceleration in growth has been relatively widespread. Whereas in the 1980s only around 20 developing countries were achieving even modest growth, since the mid-1990s, 70 developing countries (out of 109) have done so. The surge in growth reaches far beyond China and India to countries in every region of the world, including Mozambique, Ghana, Rwanda, Bangladesh, Indonesia, Mongolia, Brazil, Chile, the Dominican Republic, Moldova, Macedonia, Turkey, Morocco, and many others. New markets are emerging, businesses are opening, trade and investment are soaring, and jobs with better wages are more plentiful.

Meanwhile, health and education have improved dramatically. In 1960, twenty-two out of every hundred children born in developing countries died before their fifth birthday; today it's only five. Out of one hundred children born, seventeen more live today who would have died just a few decades ago. In 1990 almost 13 million children died from preventable diseases; by 2013, it was down to 6.3 million (and falling). Because of both the reduction in child deaths and progress in fighting a range of diseases (such as malaria), life expectancy is now much longer. Whereas in 1960 the typical person born in a developing country could expect to live around fifty years, today his or her grandchildren will live sixty-six years. People born in developing countries live fully one-third longer, on average, than they did two generations ago. More children are enrolling in and completing primary education, especially girls. In 1980 only half of all girls in developing countries completed primary school; today four out of five do so. More people than ever before have access to clean water, basic sanitation, and some electricity.

The changes go further, and include personal freedoms and political systems. Around the world, dictatorships have been replaced by democracies. There are fewer wars and less violence, and basic rights and liberties are far more likely to be upheld. In 1983 seventeen developing countries were democracies; by 2013, the number had more than tripled to fifty-six (excluding many more developing countries with populations less than 1 million, which I do not count here). Meanwhile, there are far fewer dictatorships and autocracies. While the spread of democracy has slowed in recent years and even reversed in some countries, the difference from the 1980s to today is astonishing. This change is *not* just about perfunctory elections: it includes improvements in basic political rights and personal freedoms, stronger legislatures, more robust civil-society organizations, and other institutions of democracy alongside more free and fair elections. Many of the new democracies are imperfect and fragile, but the change is unmistakable. Equally remarkable, violence is declining sharply. Since the 1980s, the incidence of civil war in developing countries has been cut in half, and battle deaths in war have fallen by more than 75 percent.

The dramatic shift in political systems has upended some old ideas about democracy and development. Until recently, most people believed that the best way to make progress in poor countries was to put a benign dictator in charge. The East Asian "miracle" countries seemed to provide the evidence, with Singapore's former prime minister Lee Kuan Yew as the prime example. But since the end of the Cold War, the pattern has changed: in most cases the improvements in economic well-being have gone together with a shift toward democracy. While there are important exceptions such as China, Ethiopia, Rwanda, and Vietnam, increasingly they are exactly that—exceptions. India, South Korea, Indonesia, Mongolia, the Philippines, Brazil, Costa Rica, Chile, the Dominican Republic, Bulgaria, Hungary, Moldova, Turkey, Tunisia, Botswana, Ghana, Liberia, Senegal, South Africa, and dozens of other developing countries are showing that democracy has become the new norm, and that it complements and supports economic and social progress.

What is remarkable about these changes is not so much the progress in any one area but the dramatic improvements in *all* of these areas at the same time. The simultaneous improvement in so many aspects of development in so many of the world's poorest countries in such a short period of time is unprecedented. There have been spurts of economic growth in developing countries before (such as in the 1960s and early 1970s), and there have been improvements in global health for several decades. But never before have we seen such substantial improvement in income, poverty, health, education, and governance at the same time.

By this point, you're probably thinking, Wait a minute. It can't be *that* good. Just about everything in the newspapers is bad news. What about Afghanistan, Iraq, and Syria, all entangled in major conflict? Or Somalia, which has not had a functioning government for several decades? How about Sudan and its unconscionable treatment of its own people in Darfur? Or Haiti, where weak leadership and deep corruption made the country both more vulnerable to the deep destruction of the 2010 earthquake and unable to respond effectively in its aftermath? Or the ineptness in North Korea? What about despots like Robert Mugabe in Zimbabwe and Islam Karimov of Uzbekistan?

All true. Unfortunately, not all developing countries are making progress. Some countries remain stuck in conflict, dictatorship, and stagnation, just as in the old days. However, while they still capture the headlines, they have become the minority, and their numbers continue to shrink. In the 1980s, there were more than sixty developing countries that had both authoritarian governments and little or no economic growth, accounting for well more than half of all developing countries. Today that group is down to around twenty, accounting for less than one-fifth of developing countries. They are the exceptions, while most developing countries are now on the move.

Nor do I argue that the progress that has been achieved so far is enough, that it is guaranteed to continue, or that all is well in developing countries. Such claims would be misleading and naïve. There are still 1 billion people living in extreme poverty, and even those whose incomes now exceed that basic standard of $1.25 a day are hardly well off. Every year, 6 million children still die of preventable disease. Many countries, especially the poorest, remain vulnerable to the effects of devastating shocks, such as the sharp rise in global food prices in 2007 or the Ebola outbreak that swept through West Africa in 2014. There is still a long way to go in creating well-functioning democracies in which basic rights are respected and leaders are held accountable. In many countries, especially India and China, rapid economic growth has come with a high price in terms of environmental degradation, air and water pollution, and biodiversity loss (as it has for much longer in today's rich countries). Rising greenhouse gas emissions and accelerating climate change are serious threats. These issues are central to the prospects for both sustaining and spreading the recent progress in developing countries. Nevertheless, the changes over the last two decades are a big start—the strongest and most promising start ever—in improving the well-being of millions of people in many of the world's poorest countries.

Throughout this book, my analysis will focus on a core group of 109 developing countries. A list is provided in the appendix. There is no standard definition of a developing country, but this group includes all countries in which per capita incomes were below $3,000 (in constant US dollars from the year 2000) at some point between 1960 and 2013. This income line corresponds roughly with the World Bank's classification of low- and lower-middle-income countries, although its income definitions change each year. The group includes countries such as Panama, Botswana, and Thailand, where incomes now exceed the $3,000 benchmark, since they were below the threshold for most of the period (the alternative of excluding these countries would eliminate developing countries that have been successful in achieving sustained growth). The group excludes several countries for which there are insufficient data, such as Myanmar, North Korea, Somalia, and Afghanistan. I also exclude all countries with populations less than 1 million people. Since many small countries have achieved economic progress and become democracies during the last two decades, by excluding them I am erring on the side of understating the actual number of countries in transition, and avoiding including a large number of countries that contain a relatively small number of people. Also, throughout the book, all data are drawn from the World Development Indicators (the World Bank's primary public database), except where noted otherwise.

PERVASIVE PESSIMISM

The transformation in the world's developing countries during the last two decades is difficult for many people to believe. Stories of poor countries are typically tales of gloom and doom. Newspapers, television, and movies are filled with war, violence, disease, corruption, and failure. The emphasis on the negative reflects human nature: for whatever reason, we are drawn to stories of tragedy and failure. What most people around the world know about developing countries is what they see in the media: war in Afghanistan, famine in Darfur, stolen elections in Zimbabwe, earthquake destruction in Haiti, terrorist bombings in Indonesia, Ebola in West Africa, and so on. Charitable organizations don't help when they emphasize tragedy and deprivation as a means of soliciting donations.

Of course, war, disease, and famine are all critical issues that should receive serious attention. But our strong attraction to them creates a deep pessimism about the potential for progress, and their domination in the media overshadows the larger truths about human advancement. Steady gains do not make for good copy. World Bank reports showing the largest decline in poverty in history hardly get mentioned. Successful democratic elections—those without riots, shootings, or claims of fraud—can go unnoticed. War and conflict get (justifiable) attention, but evidence that there are fewer wars and less violence does not. Outbreaks of disease command understandable attention, while the huge reductions in deaths from malaria and diarrhea do not. Stories of bungled foreign aid programs make the front page; those that achieve their goals are ignored.

That nearly 1 billion people have been lifted out of extreme poverty during the last two decades surely ranks as one of the greatest achievements in human history, yet few people know about it. In fact, people think the opposite is true. A recent survey showed that 66 percent of Americans believed that the proportion of the world's population living in extreme poverty had doubled during the last twenty years, and another 29 percent thought it had stayed roughly the same. Combined, that means that 95 percent of Americans got it wrong. Only 5 percent knew (or guessed) the truth: that the proportion of people living in extreme poverty had fallen by more than half.[1]

Widespread pessimism about development is not just the result of misperception or our attraction to bad news. In the decades before the early 1990s, most developing countries *were* filled with bad news and failure. The oil crises of the 1970s, the deep global recession of the 1980s, economic and political mismanagement, right-wing totalitarian rule, leftist dictatorships, failed experiments with militarism and Communism, and turbulence from the Cold War sparked two decades of disaster. Outside of the Asian miracle countries and a few others, there was little progress, and many countries went backward. Debts mounted, inflation soared, and growth stagnated. The average rate of economic growth per person across all developing countries between 1977 and 1994 was *zero*.*

Millions of families saw their incomes fall. With populations growing, the number of people living in extreme poverty rose. For the most part, the initial experiments with democracy that followed the independence movements of the 1960s failed. Dictatorship was pervasive, from Ferdinand Marcos in the Philippines, to the Duvaliers in Haiti, to the generals across Latin America, to the notorious Mobutu Sese Seko in what was then Zaire. Wars raged in Cambodia, Sri Lanka, Mozambique, Liberia, Nicaragua, and dozens of other countries. The overall story for most developing countries was misery and failure.

That period is over, and has been for two decades. Yet the pessimism born from those years pervades. Twenty years ago, as the Cold War ended, almost anyone writing about poor countries predicted disaster as the quasi stability and order imposed by the superpower standoff disappeared. Journalist and author Robert Kaplan wrote famously in 1994 about *The Coming Anarchy: How Scarcity, Crime, Overpopulation, Tribalism, and Disease Are Rapidly Destroying the Social Fabric of Our Planet*, just as most of the world was embarking on a turn in the opposite direction. While conflict and disease have not disappeared, most developing countries have experienced improved governance, less violence, better health, and a steady rise in prosperity. While a few astute observers have recognized and written about some of these changes—such as the Center for Global Development's Charles Kenny, the author Matt Ridley, and Johns Hopkins University's Michael Mandelbaum—most people continue to portray a world of failure and catastrophe.[2]

---

*This figure was calculated as a simple (unweighted) average, counting each country the same. A weighted average yields a higher growth rate due to the impact of China and a few other fast-growing countries with large populations.

Every time a major crisis has emerged during the last two decades, naysayers have declared that development was doomed, and that reversal of economic progress and democracy would follow. After financial crises ripped through Southeast Asia in the late 1990s, the pessimists pounced and claimed that the Asian miracle was over; instead, the countries rebounded fast. When the global food crisis struck in 2007, many analysts predicted that poverty and famine would rise sharply, but developing countries showed their resilience, and poverty continued to fall. The 2008 global financial crisis brought fears that growth in developing countries would end, but while the pace of progress slowed, developing countries rebounded faster than rich countries.

Pessimism is particularly pervasive about Africa. The writer Paul Theroux declared recently, "I can testify that Africa is much worse off than when I first went there fifty years ago to teach English: poorer, sicker, less educated, and more badly governed."[3] The easily obtainable evidence shows the opposite: Africa today, on the whole, is less poor, less sick, better educated, and better governed. Much of the ire is aimed at foreign aid. The writer Dambisa Moyo charges that "evidence overwhelmingly demonstrates that aid to Africa has made the poor poorer, and the growth slower. The insidious aid culture has left African countries more debt laden, more inflation prone, more vulnerable to the vagaries of the currency markets and more unattractive to higher-quality investment, [and] increased the risk of civil conflict and unrest."[4] The facts are rather different: poverty is falling, incomes are growing, debt levels have plummeted, inflation is at its lowest level in decades, investment is pouring in as never before, and civil conflict has fallen. The evidence shows that on the whole, foreign aid (for all of its shortcomings) has helped bolster development progress.

BREAKING OUT OF TRAPS

This progress mostly has been overlooked by people working in and researching development. With a few exceptions, debates about development have been dominated by three strands of research and thinking in recent years. While each of them contributes to our understanding of development in different ways, they have all missed the major transformation under way, and they do not explain why it is happening.

The first strand takes a long historical perspective: it examines country characteristics and critical events from long ago to explain why some countries today are rich and others poor. The late Harvard professor David Landes argued in *The Wealth and Poverty of Nations: Why Some Are So Rich and Some So Poor* that Europe's ascendancy had much to do with its culture, work ethic, attitudes toward science and religion, and social organization, and that these centuries-old differences reverberate today. Jared Diamond, in *Guns, Germs, and Steel: The Fates of Human Societies*, reached a different conclusion, finding that Europe's prosperity was largely the result of differences in geography, demography, and ecology that can be traced back to the beginnings of the domestication of plants and animals. Economists Daron Acemoglu, Simon Johnson, and James Robinson argued that where European colonizers faced serious health threats from disease (think the Belgian Congo in the late nineteenth century), they set up repressive institutions to extract resources through violence, and that these tactics and institutions established hundreds of years ago are central to understanding institutions in developing countries today.[5] Other researchers suggest that differences in income today date back to inventions from three thousand years ago, or even further to the timing of the migration of different groups out of Africa to form new societies around the world.

These hotly debated studies are helpful in understanding the historical origins of the large differences between rich and poor countries today. But their conclusions provide little help for people in today's developing countries, as they suggest that their fate is tied to decisions and actions taken centuries ago or factors outside their control. They do not help us understand the recent acceleration of development progress or the reasons why so many developing countries began to turn at roughly the same time in the 1990s.

The second field of research has been the opposite: microlevel studies on the effectiveness of specific actions and programs in particular contexts, often evaluated through rigorous randomized controlled trials

(RCTs).* These studies focus on questions such as the impact of pricing on the uptake of insecticide-treated malaria bed nets, whether identity cards reduce theft and improve the delivery of subsidized rice to the poor, and the impact of shouting at bus drivers to get them to drive more safely. (It turns out that it helps, a lot.) RCTs have been brought to prominence through the pathbreaking work of Abhijit Banerjee and Esther Duflo at the Massachusetts Institute of Technology (MIT), among others.[6] These studies offer insights into the nature of poverty at the individual and family levels, the constraints and incentives people face, and the reasons they make the decisions they do. They also help guide the design and implementation of specific policies and programs aimed at helping the poor. But they can't help explain why a country that was stagnating for years turns the corner, or why so many developing countries began to make progress at the same time.

A third major focus has been on the idea of "poverty traps," in which low-income countries are trapped in poverty at least in part because of poverty itself. Families (or societies) with low incomes have difficulty saving, so they can't invest as much in schools, technology, and infrastructure, so incomes don't grow, and they are stuck in poverty. This idea has a long pedigree in both research and pop wisdom. But as a general proposition, a poverty trap focused on income alone doesn't hold up. If it were true for everyone, since the whole world was poor five hundred years ago, we should all still be poor. If there are these kinds of poverty traps, many people, and many societies, have been able to escape them. That doesn't mean that traps don't hold in some countries or in some contexts. Just because some people have the opportunities and capabilities to break out of poverty traps doesn't mean that everyone does.

The basic poverty trap idea has been refined in recent years by economists Jeffrey Sachs and Paul Collier, among others, each of whom introduced additional factors that interact with income and savings—such

---

*In RCTs, two groups of people are randomly selected from a population. One group (the treatment group) receives the product, policy, program, or action that is being studied (e.g., a new malaria medication, or free school lunches), and the other group (the control group) does not. This approach provides the basis for a more precise measure of the impact of the treatment.

as health, geography, conflict, and governance—to explain why some families, regions, or societies remain trapped. Sachs shows that developing countries are more prone to endemic disease such as malaria, which reduces worker productivity and scares away investors, keeping people poor. In turn, poverty makes people even more susceptible to disease, creating a vicious cycle (a trap). Collier, of Oxford University, argues that poor countries are more vulnerable to conflict and war, which undermine growth and increase the odds for additional conflict, trapping countries in a self-reinforcing negative cycle. Similarly, bad governance keeps countries poor because leaders steal resources and undermine economic opportunities, and poverty itself makes it harder to build the legal, government, and political institutions necessary to improve governance. Both Sachs and Collier conclude that while it is not impossible for a country to escape these traps, it is tough.[7]

The recent work on these broader development traps is compelling, and corresponds with what I have seen up close living and working in developing countries for the last thirty years. Most people in developing countries *have* been trapped in one way or another for much of the last several centuries, with various economic, political, and social forces preventing them from moving forward. That some have escaped does not mean that the traps are not real for those left behind. Violence, oppressive governments, disease, conflict, isolation from markets, and adverse geography have obstructed opportunities, prevented people from accessing technologies and education, and otherwise blocked people and societies from progress.

One of the basic ideas of this book is that starting in the 1960s, then accelerating markedly in the 1990s, hundreds of millions of people in dozens of the world's poorest countries began to break out of these development traps. Not all countries have broken out, and clearly not all people have broken free of extreme poverty. A few countries, such as South Korea, Singapore, and Botswana, began to move forward in the 1960s and 1970s. China began to surge in the 1980s. Several forces then came together in the 1980s and 1990s to create the circumstances that facilitated a much broader surge. By the mid-1990s, millions of people and the majority of developing countries were beginning to move forward on multiple fronts: poverty reduction, income growth, improvements in health and education, reductions in conflict and violence, more effective institutions, and a shift toward greater freedoms and democracy.

THE WINDS OF CHANGE

So what happened? In my view, widespread development progress requires three factors to work together in concert: the creation of favorable *global conditions* conducive to development, the formation of meaningful *opportunities* for individuals and communities to make economic and social progress, and the development of the right *skills and capabilities* to take advantage of those opportunities—one of the most important of which at a national level is *leadership*. To a large extent, development is about creating new opportunities for the poor, both globally and locally, then building the capacities and capabilities to enable people to take advantage of those opportunities. That's what began to happen to a much larger degree in the 1980s and 1990s.

Three major catalysts sparked the great surge. First, major geopolitical shifts created *global conditions* that were much more favorable for development. The big spark came with the end of the Cold War, the demise of Communism, and the collapse of the Soviet Union. Global power structures, strategic relationships, and powerful ideas about governance and economics all changed. Some of the biggest obstacles to development melted away—many of which dated back hundreds of years to colonialism and other forms of autocratic rule. The United States and the Soviet Union cut their unquestioned support for some of the world's nastiest dictators, and one by one they began to fall. Proxy wars and political violence related to the Cold War came to an end. Communism, strong state control, and right-wing totalitarian dictatorship lost credibility. A new consensus began to form around more market-based economic systems and—at least in the majority of countries—more accountable, transparent, and democratic governance, alongside greater respect for individual freedoms and basic rights. Developing countries around the world introduced major economic and political reforms and began to build institutions more conducive to growth and social progress. The doors opened to new possibilities.

Second, globalization and new technologies provided the key *opportunities* through which people could begin to move toward prosperity. Deeper global connections through trade, financial flows, information and ideas, movement of people, and access to technologies provided the vehicles through which people in developing countries could begin to earn higher incomes, reduce poverty, improve health, and strengthen governance. Exports from developing countries are *five times* larger today than just twenty years ago (in constant prices). Financial flows to developing countries now top $1 trillion per year, fully *twelve times* larger than they were in 1990 (in constant prices). A significant portion of the increase in trade and financial flows is between developing countries themselves. The rises of China and India have been important drivers of growth in dozens of other developing countries. Perhaps most important, deeper global integration has allowed a range of technologies to spur development progress: vaccines, medicines, seeds, fertilizers, mobile phones, the internet, faster and cheaper air travel, and containerized shipping. To be sure, globalization has brought challenges, risks, and volatility, not least the 2007 food and 2008 financial crises. But it also has brought investment, jobs, skills, ideas, and markets, and has been an important part of the great surge in development.

Third, the surge required the right *skills and capabilities*, and in particular it required *leadership* to begin to bring about institutional transformation. Developing countries began to achieve significant progress primarily because of the choices, decisions, and actions of the people in those countries themselves. Where new leaders at all levels of society stepped forward to forge change, developing countries began to build more effective institutions and make progress. Where old dictators stayed in place, or new tyrants stepped in to replace the old, political and economic systems remained rigged. Strong leadership, smart policy choices, and committed and courageous action at the village, local, and national levels made all the difference in beginning to build the institutions needed to ignite and sustain progress. New national leaders such as Nelson Mandela of South Africa, Cory Aquino of the Philippines,

Oscar Arias of Costa Rica, Lech Wałesa of Poland, and many others worked to build new and more inclusive political systems while introducing stronger economic management. Civil-society and religious leaders like Rigoberta Menchú Tum of Guatemala, Desmond Tutu of South Africa, Muhammad Yunus of Bangladesh, Jaime Sin of the Philippines, and Wangari Maathai of Kenya gave greater voice to everyday citizens and pushed for expanded economic opportunities for the poor. Less famous local leaders opened schools, clinics, microfinance organizations, and businesses to support the turnaround. As effective leadership began to emerge in some countries, it spread to others by creating new models and growing peer pressure for better governance.

Geography also shaped opportunities for progress in ways that differed across countries and influenced which countries began to advance and which did not. Countries with more favorable geography—such as easy access to global shipping routes, higher-quality soils, and better climate—had more options and opportunities and tended to make more progress, especially where it was paired with effective leadership. It's far more difficult to make progress if you live in a remote desert, or someplace where the disease burden is particularly high. It's not impossible, but it's much harder.

Foreign aid played a supporting role in bolstering development progress. Too often discussions about developing countries become polemic arguments about aid, and some high-profile writers have claimed that aid has failed. While the critics make several legitimate points, and some aid has been ineffective, they underplay the successes. The bulk of the evidence shows that, on the whole, foreign assistance had a moderate positive impact on development progress. Its influence varies across countries and sectors. It has had a particularly strong effect on improving global health, fighting disease, mitigating the impacts of natural disasters and humanitarian crises, and helping to jump-start turnarounds from war in countries like Mozambique and Liberia. Aid efforts have been strengthened by global campaigns such as the Millennium Development Goals (MDGs), a United Nations initiative in which countries around the world agreed to specific targets for progress between 1990 and 2015 (many of which have been achieved). Aid is not the most important driver of development, but it has played an important secondary role in the development surge over the past two decades.

In his classic work *Development as Freedom*, Nobel laureate Amartya Sen defined development as "a process of expanding the real freedoms that people enjoy." He argued that "development requires the removal of major sources of unfreedom: poverty as well as tyranny, poor economic opportunities as well as systematic social deprivation, neglect of public facilities as well as intolerance or over-activity of repressive states."[8]

In essence, my basic argument is that beginning in the 1980s and 1990s, many of the "unfreedoms" that had inhibited development began to be removed. The combination of huge geopolitical shifts, changing economic and political systems, deepening globalization, access to new technologies, stronger leadership, and courageous action created the conditions, opportunities, and drivers necessary for progress. The result was the great surge.

THE BENEFITS TO THE WEST

The unprecedented progress in the world's poorest countries is ultimately good for the richest countries, and for the whole world. Some people in advanced countries fear the rise of competitors, and while there will be new political and economic competition, the advances by the world's poor are central to a future of enhanced global prosperity and greater security. The United States, Europe, and Japan face major challenges and opportunities in the decades to come, and their futures are now linked inextricably to the futures of the rest of the world. Global threats such as climate change, pandemic disease, and terrorism know no boundaries; at the same time, continued economic growth in the world's leading countries will increasingly depend on growth and prosperity in developing countries.

Continued progress in developing countries is good for traditional Western powers for three basic reasons.[9] First, development and increased prosperity in the world's poorest countries enhance global security. Higher incomes, improved health, and stronger governance all reduce the threat of violence within developing countries, and reduce the potential for these countries to be used as launching points for violence and terrorism. The biggest threats to global security in recent years have come from groups operating in failed and failing states. Development brings stronger institutions, greater capacity for effective governance, less violence, and fewer security threats. As progress has accelerated in the last two decades, the number of civil wars in developing countries has been cut in half. This reduction in conflict makes the world a safer place for both rich and poor countries, and reduces the need for international military intervention. As former US secretary of defense Robert Gates put it, "Development is a lot cheaper than sending soldiers." Development also strengthens the global capacity to fight and limit pandemic disease and other threats. As poor countries grow wealthier and strengthen their institutional capacities, they become better equipped to fight diseases that can spread beyond their borders, such as the Ebola virus, the H1N1 flu virus, and HIV/AIDS.

Second, continued development is good for trade, investment, business, and ultimately global income growth. Economic growth in developing countries creates huge markets for US and European businesses, from China to South Africa to Brazil. The growing global middle class creates new opportunities for manufacturers of aircraft, automobiles, semiconductors, medical equipment, and pharmaceuticals, as well as consultancy services, financial services, and the entertainment industry. In 1990 low- and middle-income countries accounted for 32 percent of the global economy; by 2013 the share was 49 percent. Some of the largest and fastest-growing markets for Western goods and services are in today's emerging countries. US exports to developing countries now account for 53 percent of its total exports, up from 40 percent in the mid-1990s. In Japan the share is now 65 percent.[10]

To be sure, the rise of emerging countries creates competition for US and European businesses, and hardship for workers who lose their jobs because of foreign competition. But deeper global integration and larger emerging markets also create jobs in the United States and Europe, both because of Western firms expanding abroad and because of increased investment in the West by companies from emerging countries. In addition, developing countries are increasingly becoming sources of new innovations and technologies that help advance progress everywhere, from medicine, to food security, to alternative sources of energy. Japan's economic rise in the 1970s and 1980s created widespread concerns in the West, but ultimately its progress has been enormously beneficial as a major trading partner, a source for innovation and ideas, a trusted global partner, and a force for stability and peace.

Third, development helps spread and deepen shared values of openness, prosperity, and freedom. The surge of progress in developing countries has included greater respect for basic rights, increased personal freedoms, enhanced international cooperation, and the spread of democracy. Continued development in the world's poorest countries will mean a greater global extension and deepening of the core values that Western countries have championed for decades. Ultimately, those changes make the world a better and safer place.

WILL THE TRANSFORMATION CONTINUE?

The surge progress in developing countries is remarkable. But for most countries it has been under way for only around twenty years, which, from a development perspective, is not very long. The key to development is sustaining advancements over time, and there is no guarantee that the surge of progress that started two decades ago will continue. We've seen spurts of economic growth in developing countries before (although not as long, and not accompanied by massive reductions in poverty and such large shifts to democracy), only to watch them falter. So far, the turnaround is incomplete: while the fates of hundreds of millions of people in poor countries are improving, many others have been left behind. Big risks lie ahead, including population pressures, climate change, resource demand, environmental degradation, changing demographics, disease threats, terrorism, and tensions from the rise of China and India, to name just a few. With these risks comes uncertainty about the future of development progress.

One scenario is that the development transformation continues: sustained economic growth, smart investments and policy choices, continued advances in technology and ideas, stronger health and education systems, and deepening democracy lead to growing prosperity and improved welfare in the coming decades. China, India, Brazil, and other middle-income countries continue their ascendancy (with gradually slowing growth rates), followed by Turkey, Indonesia, Colombia, South Africa, Ghana, and many others. Trade among developing countries continues to grow, mobile phones expand their reach, and the internet extends to more people in poor countries. New technologies lead to increased agricultural productivity, cleaner and more efficient energy sources, reduced environmental damage, and further advances in health. Although progress does not reach everywhere and some countries stagnate or face tragic setbacks, others, such as Myanmar and Cuba, eventually join the widening circle of development. Democracy spreads further and deeper, perhaps in different forms and new variations, with more countries embracing accountability, transparency, and good governance. The number of people living in extreme poverty falls quickly.

A second future is one in which development progress slows considerably. China's rapid economic expansion decelerates, the US and European economies remain sluggish, and economic growth and job creation begin to weaken across many developing countries. More nations follow Thailand and Venezuela and step backward in democracy. Rich and poor countries alike fail to make critical investments in infrastructure, education, health, and technology. As global competition grows, countries erect new barriers to trade and choose to protect aging industries rather than support newer, more dynamic ones. Resource mismanagement and environmental degradation begin to undermine progress. Advancements in health continue, but at a much slower pace as antimicrobial resistance expands and new epidemics strike, as with Ebola in West Africa. A backlash against democracy takes shape, opening doors to authoritarianism. Poverty continues to decline, but less quickly.

A third scenario is that development progress is derailed: population pressures, resource demand, climate change, environmental degradation, and growing conflict and war combine to halt and in some countries reverse development progress. Rising urban populations and increasing incomes create much greater demand and growing shortages of water, food, energy, and minerals, while climate change significantly destabilizes food production and worsens health conditions. Both rich and poor countries fail to take the actions necessary to introduce sound policies and smart investments in new technologies to slow climate change, increase agricultural productivity, and develop new energy supplies. Food and commodity prices increase and become even more volatile. Growing tensions from an ascendant Asia and a declining West—coupled with greater competition over scarce resources, or growing global religious and ideological hostilities—spark increased conflict, both within and between countries. Western countries increasingly turn inward, creating a global leadership void that allows security threats to grow as trade and investment suffer. International organizations lose legitimacy and effectiveness. Democracy is seen as an unsuccessful experiment, and dictators rise again. Economic growth decelerates sharply, much as it did in the 1970s and 1980s, and the declines in global poverty slow significantly. Development progress largely ends, and some countries go backward.

Any of these futures, or shades between them, is possible. It is easy to be pessimistic, and to conclude that the obstacles to continued progress are just too great, and that progress will falter. For hundreds of years, people have predicted at one point or another that global progress would halt. However, they have always underestimated the world's growing abilities to work cooperatively, meet new challenges, and expand global prosperity and basic freedoms. While we can picture many of the future difficulties facing developing countries, it is much harder for us to envision the new ideas, innovations, technologies, governance structures, and leadership that will emerge to tackle them. These ideas and innovations will not happen automatically. They will depend on human choices, sacrifice, cooperation, leadership, and action.

I believe that in the coming decades, development progress can and will continue to expand and endure in most developing countries. We are in the early stages of a new age of global prosperity in which, with many setbacks and challenges along the way, extreme poverty will continue to decline, incomes in developing countries will grow, health and education will improve, and democracy and basic freedoms will expand—haltingly, unevenly, but unrelentingly.

TWO

BREAKTHROUGH
FROM THE BOTTOM

> . . . the life of man, solitary, poor, nasty, brutish, and short.
>
> —*English philosopher Thomas Hobbes, 1651*[1]

FOR MOST OF HUMAN HISTORY, HOBBES HAD IT RIGHT. UNTIL THE DAWN OF THE INDUSTRIAL revolution, the vast majority of people around the world lived in what today we would consider extreme poverty, eking out little more than subsistence living on the equivalent (in today's dollars) of only $1 or $2 per day. They had feeble housing, poor health, and little education. Major cities, such as Paris and London, were jammed with impoverished people living in squalor with little access to clean water or basic sanitation. Outside of cities, most people lived in rudimentary huts that barely kept out the weather as they struggled to survive from one harvest to the next. Few ever went to school or saw anyone resembling a doctor. Many died young: more than one out of three children died before they reached five years of age, and life expectancy averaged fewer than thirty-five years.

According to the best estimates we have, as assembled by economists

François Bourguignon and Christian Morrisson, in 1820 about 94 percent of the world's population, or around 1 billion people, lived on less than $2 a day (in 1985 prices).[2] That's almost nineteen out of twenty people around the globe living on meager incomes. It's not because $2 went further back then, or that $2 buys you more in some countries than others. The data are adjusted to account for these differences (as best we can with the data we have). Most people were living on far less: 84 percent were living on less than $1 a day. What we now consider extreme poverty was not just widespread; it was the norm, for just about everybody.

Human welfare and average incomes began to improve slowly, in some parts of the world, starting in the twelfth and thirteenth centuries, but progress was incremental and not widespread. That pattern began to change rapidly in the nineteenth century, as the impacts of the industrial revolution took hold, and increasing numbers of people began to escape the ravages of extreme poverty. James Watt's invention of the steam engine in the 1770s ignited a surge of new innovations and technologies, including the transformation from hand to machine production, the introduction of mechanized cotton spinning (and with it the mass production of textiles), Jethro Tull's (earlier) development of the horse-drawn seed drill (which helped increase food and agricultural production), the shift in energy sources from wood and charcoal to much cheaper coal, and the large-scale production of chemicals and iron. The beginnings of modern manufacturing and industrialization helped create millions of jobs for poor, low-skilled workers. While the wages they earned seem paltry by today's standards, they were better than the low and highly volatile farm income that most left behind. As manufacturing grew more sophisticated and workers learned more specialized skills, which took several decades, wages began to grow. By the middle of the nineteenth century, incomes were rising faster than at any previous time in world history.

As important as these changes were, they were concentrated in Western Europe, North America, and a few other places, such as Australia and New Zealand, and later Japan after the Meiji Restoration of

1868.* In most of the rest of the world, and most especially in today's developing countries, deep poverty continued unabated. So, as global population grew, the total number of people living in extreme poverty continued to rise. And rise. And rise.

POVERTY: DEFINITIONS AND TERMINOLOGY

The incidence of poverty is typically measured by estimating the number (or percentage) of people with consumption or income below a specified poverty line. For developing countries, the most widely used poverty line is consumption of less than $1.25 a day in 2005 prices, which the World Bank defines as "extreme" poverty. (The World Bank also regularly tracks two other poverty lines: $1 a day and $2 a day.) The $1.25-a-day figure may seem arbitrary, and to some extent, it is. Any poverty line is arbitrary, since we deem those with consumption just below the line to be in poverty and those just above it not to be. But the $1.25 figure is not just picked out of the air: the World Bank uses it because it is roughly equal to the average of the national poverty lines constructed by governments in the poorest fifteen countries in the world. That is, the figure is based on poverty lines derived in some of the poorest countries themselves. As countries become better off, they typically draw the poverty line at higher levels. The median poverty line for all developing countries is around $2 a day. The official poverty line in the United States is around $16 a day, more than twelve times higher than the "extreme" poverty line.

Are these figures of $1 or $1.25 or $16 comparable over time and across countries? The answer is yes, at least as well as can be done with the data we have. The figures are adjusted in two ways. First, they are corrected for inflation over time within countries by using the prices in a set base year. (That is, the data are measured in "constant" prices, or "real" terms.) Most of the data are measured in 2005 prices, although the

---

*The Meiji Restoration was a political revolution that ended the Tokugawa shogunate and consolidated control of Japan under the emperor Meiji, resulting in enormous political, social, and economic changes in Japan in the decades that followed.

Bourguignon and Morrisson data mentioned earlier are measured in constant 1985 prices. Second, the estimates are based on purchasing power parity (PPP) prices, sometimes called international prices. PPP prices account for the differences in price levels across countries. Anyone who travels knows that the cost of living varies widely across countries, and that the prices of the same goods can be very different. Fruits, vegetables, haircuts, and taxi rides are cheap in Tanzania, but expensive in Switzerland, so $1 converted at the local exchange rate goes a lot further in Dar es Salaam than it does in Zurich. According to the latest estimates, the price level in Tanzania is only about 25 percent of the price level in Switzerland. To account for these differences, consumption and income figures are adjusted by a PPP exchange rate so that all goods and services are valued with the same prices across countries—that is, the figures are adjusted so that $1 has the same purchasing power across countries. As a result, the figures are comparable both over time and across countries, at least as much as is possible. With constant price PPP figures, $1 in country A in 1990 is roughly equivalent to $1 in country B in 2010.

My primary source of poverty data is the World Bank's PovcalNet database, put together over the years by a team led by Martin Ravallion (now at Georgetown University) and Shaohua Chen.[3] These estimates are based on a rich data set of hundreds of household income and consumption surveys from around the world. Some analysts argue that the World Bank's standard of $1.25 a day is too low, and others see it as too high, and still others are critical of the bank's estimation methodology. The World Bank's data are not perfect, but they are by far the most widely used and accepted around the world. Modestly changing the poverty line or using other estimation techniques does not change the broad outlines of the dramatic story of the decline in global extreme poverty during the last two decades.

THE UNPRECEDENTED DECLINE IN GLOBAL POVERTY

Beginning in the nineteenth century, as the impacts of the industrial revolution began to take hold and incomes began to rise, the *share* of the world's people living in extreme poverty began to decline steadily for the first time in history. But global population was growing even faster, so the *total number* of extreme poor continued to grow rapidly. This distinction between the percentage of the world's people living in poverty and the absolute number is crucial. The percentage has been declining for two centuries, and the speed of the decline has accelerated in recent decades. As world population grew, the total number of extreme poor continued to grow, seemingly inexorably, from the beginning of human history. However, that pattern changed dramatically beginning in the 1980s, and especially in the 1990s.

FIGURE 2.1: THE RISE AND FALL OF GLOBAL POVERTY, 1820–2011

Total Number of People with Income Less Than $1 a Day

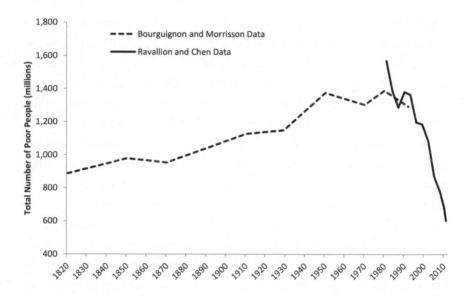

Source: Bourguignon and Morrisson, "Inequality Among World Citizens"; World Bank, PovcalNet database; Ravallion and Chen, "Update to the World Bank's Estimates of Consumption Poverty."

Let's start by looking at the total numbers, beginning with the deepest level of abject poverty: those with consumption of less than $1 a day. According to Bourguignon and Morrisson, in 1820 around 900 million people were living on less than $1 a day (in 1985 PPP prices). Because of population growth, by 1950 that number had risen to about 1.4 billion, as you can see in figure 2.1. Then a transition began: as Japan and Europe recovered from World War II, and as a few developing countries (like South Korea and Taiwan) began to register more rapid economic growth, the number of people living on less than $1 a day stopped rising, and remained relatively unchanged for about forty years. That might not sound important, but it was. No change was a big change, as the continuous historical rise in the number of global poor had come to a halt, despite the continued growth in world population.

Then a dramatic turn began in the early 1990s. *For the first time in world history, the total number of people living in extreme poverty began to fall*, and it fell fast.

To see this change, we have to switch to the Ravallion and Chen (World Bank) data set, since the Bourguignon and Morrisson data set ends in 1992. While the two data sets do not match exactly, they tell a similar story.

According to Ravallion and Chen, the number of people living on less than $1 a day in 1993 was just over 1.3 billion, roughly comparable to the earlier data set. Then the number dropped. Astonishingly, by 2011—just eighteen years later—the number of people living on less than $1 a day had fallen to 600 million. Try to grasp the enormity of the change: *after rising relentlessly from the beginning of human history, the number of people around the world living in abject poverty dropped by more than half in just eighteen years*.

Of course, $1 per day is an especially low poverty line, drawn at a level of consumption just barely above what is needed for basic subsistence. So over the last decade, most analysts have focused on the somewhat higher poverty line of $1.25 a day. The pattern of change is similar, although, of course, the number of poor is larger with the higher poverty line, as shown in figure 2.2. The number of extreme poor remained steady at just under 2 billion people from 1981 until 1993, when it started to drop—fast. By 2011, the number had fallen to 1 billion—*a drop of almost half in just eighteen years*. Although data are not yet available after 2011, all indications are that the trend continues, with something like 50 million or more people being lifted out of extreme poverty each year.

FIGURE 2.2: THE DECLINE IN GLOBAL EXTREME POVERTY SINCE 1981

Total Number of People and Percentage of Population Living in Extreme Poverty ($1.25-a-day Poverty Line)

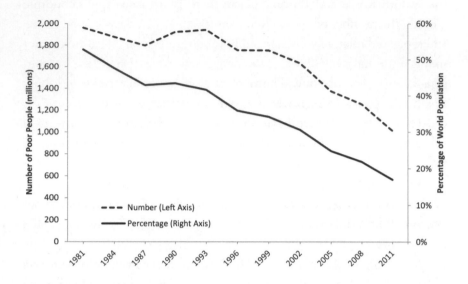

Source: World Bank, PovcalNet database, http://iresearch.worldbank.org/PovcalNet/.

Meanwhile, the *percentage* of the world's population living in extreme poverty has been falling even faster. In 1981, 53 percent of people in developing countries lived in extreme poverty. But by 2011, the share had fallen to just 17 percent—a 36 percentage point drop in thirty years, a remarkable achievement. Whereas one out of every two people lived in extreme poverty just three decades ago, today it is down to one out of six. At a poverty line of $2 a day, the pattern is similar, with the key turning point in 1999. Since then, the number of people living on less than $2 a day has fallen from 2.9 billion to 2.2 billion, and the population share has fallen from 57 percent to 36 percent.

Never before in human history has extreme poverty fallen as quickly as it has in the last few decades. No other time is even close. The UN Millennium Development Goal of cutting in half the share of the world's people living in extreme poverty between 1990 and 2015—established by UN member countries at the Millennium Summit in 2000—was achieved five years early. The decline in extreme poverty ranks as one of the most important achievements in global economic history, a seismic shift that continues to unfold today, with far-reaching economic, political, and security implications.

LIVING IN EXTREME POVERTY

The news is not all good. That 1 billion people still live on less than $1.25 a day is sobering, even if it is half the number it was a few decades ago. Too many people still live at or close to the minimum level of subsistence, going days without a meal and not having enough income to buy basic medicines, much less decent shelter or education for their children. Clearly, even for those who have shifted from consumption of $1.25 a day to $1.50 a day or $2 a day, life remains difficult, even if it is better than it once was.

The lives of the extreme poor vary, both across countries and within countries from urban to rural areas. Most are poor because of the lack of opportunities to work full-time and earn a decent living. There is not enough demand for their labor. As a result, many tend to earn small amounts of income from multiple sources. They do not specialize in one skill or have one "job," but rather undertake a variety of activities, if they can find them, to earn money. Most of the rural poor farm their own land, but since a small plot of land typically is not enough to support a family, farming is not their only (or even major) source of income. MIT economists Abhijit Banerjee and Esther Duflo describe women in the southern Indian city of Guntur who make and sell *dosa* (a rice and bean pancake that is a breakfast staple) in the morning and later in the day earn additional money by collecting trash, making and selling pickles, gathering fuel wood to sell, working as laborers, selling fruits and vegetables, or selling saris.[4] Poor men work their own land but also hire themselves out as day laborers or as rickshaw drivers, or they might own or work in a small shop. Many men will leave their families for a month or two to migrate to find temporary work. One survey from twenty-seven villages in the state of West Bengal showed that the median family had three working members with seven different occupations.

The poor face manifold risks day after day. Too much reliance on farm income runs the risk that drought or flood leaves you with nothing. Too much time trying to find day jobs or selling *dosa* puts you in direct competition with dozens of others doing the same thing, with no certainty you will get much, if anything, out of it. Any kind of illness means a direct loss of income from lost work. Building up some small savings, to the extent that is possible, to spend on fertilizer, a sewing machine, or a small shop is taking a big step into uncertainty.

To complicate matters, there are enormous variations during the year in opportunities to earn money. Having an income of $1.25 a day is an average for the year, but the poor don't actually get that amount every day. Some days (such as during the harvest) there is much more work and income, and other days there is far less.

As a result, one of the biggest risks that the world's poor face, as described by Daryl Collins and his colleagues in the book *Portfolios of the Poor: How the World's Poor Live on $2 a Day*, is that they won't have the funds they need for a sudden emergency at the wrong time of the year, even though they might (barely) have enough to afford it over the course of the year.[5] The problem is not only that incomes are small but that they are also highly irregular and unpredictable. *Portfolios of the Poor* shows how many of the extreme poor use basic financing tools to make it through: a little savings here, a loan from a relative there, borrowing some salt or other provisions from a neighbor, joining a rotating savings-and-loan club, or perhaps a bit of credit from the local shop or money-lender. As creative as these schemes are, they are often not enough. They are not always available when they are needed, they can be expensive, they are time consuming and inefficient, and they come with their own risks and stresses.

Rickshaw drivers in India have some of the toughest work you can imagine. While they are pedaling, their earnings fluctuate with weather conditions, police harassment, the level of economic activity, and just plain luck. But it's extremely demanding even for the most fit; consequently, few people can do it for more than four days a week—and that is only if the rickshaw is available. Many drivers try to find other work as street cooks or garbage collectors or construction workers. Other members of the household will try to take on work cleaning homes, sewing, or picking rags—if they can find the work—or taking in boarders. Because there are so few opportunities for steady work, poor families often need multiple sources of small amounts of income to get by.

Standard economics teaches the benefits of specialization—greater skill, speed, quality, and efficiency—but for the extreme poor, these gains are outweighed by the risks of not being able to find full-time specialized work or by being too dependent on the weather or the vagaries of the markets. They don't specialize, because they need to make use of what otherwise would be wasted time—selling *dosa*, even if they are the best in town, can occupy you for only so many hours in the morning.[6] Farmers have lots of downtime between planting and harvest. Even if they wanted to specialize, they often face financing constraints, which may be the biggest barrier of all. It is difficult enough to get small loans to help smooth out the cycles during the year, and much harder to raise the amount of capital necessary to build a business that would occupy them full-time. Even if it made financial sense to expand their storefront or irrigate a larger piece of land, they might not have access to the necessary funding.

Adding to the difficulties of full-time work, the extreme poor also tend to be frequently sick or undernourished. In the Udaipur district in the state of Rajasthan, India, for example, Banerjee and Duflo found that only 57 percent of the members of each household had enough to eat throughout the year. Many people have a low body mass index, and more than half of the adults are anemic. About half of adults report having difficulty carrying out at least one of their activities of daily living, such as working in the field, walking, or drawing water from a well. Diarrhea is common, especially among children.[7] In nearly half of the extreme poor households in Udaipur, adults had to cut down the size of their meals at some point during the year, and in one out of eight households, children had to reduce the size of their meals. In more than one-third of households, adults went without food for an entire day at some point during the year.

Consider the challenges faced by Dinesh and his wife, Shikha (as told by Daryl Collins and his coauthors in *Portfolios of the Poor*), who at one time owned four acres of fertile land in rural India. But Dinesh fell ill. He was coughing up blood and could not work. The family needed money to pay for treatment. So they started selling their land. Within a year, the land was gone. They had to start borrowing money from a local moneylender, who was charging them the equivalent of an annual interest rate of 180 percent. Through working hard in other farmers' fields, Shikha and her sons cleared the debts, but the farm was gone. So they moved to Delhi to find work. But soon one of their sons fell ill with tuberculosis, and the cycle started again. Their debts soon totaled more than $1,200, an enormous sum that would take years to repay—if they were lucky enough to earn the income to do so. Because of two illnesses, they went from moderate security to near destitution.[8]

All of these challenges together create one more: the extreme poor report being under a great deal of stress, much more so than those with higher levels of income. Surveys from India and South Africa show much higher levels of both financial and physiological stress among the extreme poor compared with people at higher incomes.

For those moving out of extreme poverty, the changes are palpable. Increasing incomes from, say, $1.25 a day to $2 a day per person may seem small, but that 60 percent increase for a (typical) family of six is the difference between $2,700 per year and $4,400 per year. It means much lower risk of catastrophe, less volatility in income, and less daily stress wondering how to provide for a family. It means an extra meal each day, perhaps a tin roof rather than thatch to keep out the rain, or, in time, maybe a house made of cement block. It means a bit more money to put another child in school, have an extra change of clothing, and buy medicines when needed. It means getting a bicycle, or maybe a sewing machine, which may help provide a bit more income. It means being able to save just a bit more when income comes in so that the family can get by when times are lean. It means being able to splurge more and buy better-tasting food, a piece of candy or cake, additional beer and cigarettes, or a better wedding for your son or daughter. Most important, moving out of extreme poverty goes a long way toward reducing the risk of death: it's the difference between living on the edge, where a prolonged drought means that people die, and having enough to eat and a little extra seed or food to put away to safeguard against calamity.

Let's not romanticize it: moving to $1.50 a day or $2 a day hardly means an escape from poverty altogether. Life is still difficult and stressful. There are still 1 billion people with incomes less than $1.25 a day that haven't even made it this far. At the same time, there has been a remarkable breakthrough from the bottom, and hundreds of millions of people who were living in destitution are much better off than they were just two decades ago.

WHAT HAPPENED?

The biggest force behind the decline in poverty is clear: China. The changes in China since the 1980s have been so vast, the country is so big, and the rise in incomes is so substantial that it should come as no surprise that it is the major driver behind the decline in the global poverty numbers. Indeed, the impact of China is so large that some people have concluded that the decline in poverty is *exclusively* about China. That claim is incorrect, since dozens of other countries are also reducing poverty. But China is the largest contributor.

Poverty was widespread during Mao Tse-tung's rule in China, as it had been for centuries under the emperors before him. While there were improvements in living standards and health in the 1950s, Mao's drive for rapid industrialization and collectivization in the notoriously misnamed Great Leap Forward (1958–1961) led to widespread famine that killed upward of 40 million people. Poverty only deepened during the violent days of the Cultural Revolution (1966–1976). In 1976 Mao single-handedly and dramatically changed the direction of global poverty with one simple act: he died.

While Mao had overseen some economic growth alongside dramatic improvements in health, he left China a poor country. In 1981 there were 838 million Chinese living in extreme poverty—fully 84 percent of its population. But as Deng Xiaoping began to introduce wide-ranging economic reforms in the 1980s, starting with the decollectivization of agriculture, economic growth accelerated and the number of extreme poor began to fall. By 1993—just twelve years later—the number of extreme poor had dropped to 646 million, and the share of the population in extreme poverty had dropped to 55 percent. Incredibly, following that fast start, the pace accelerated even more, so that by 2011, the number of extreme poor in China had dropped to 84 million, and the share had plummeted to just 6 percent. It is hard to express how astonishing it is for the most populous country in the world to move from 84 percent of its population living in extreme poverty to 6 percent in three decades.

China accounts for about 60 percent of the decline in extreme poverty between 1993 and 2011, or about 560 million of the global decline of 955 million people. What about the other 395 million? Where are they?

The decline in extreme poverty is now reaching dozens of developing countries in every region around the world. Between 1981 and 1993, seventeen developing countries saw the number of extreme poor reach its historical peak and begin to decline. Since 1993, an additional sixty-four countries have done so. In just the last thirty years, eighty-one developing countries reached their historical turning point and began to reduce the total number of people living in extreme poverty—despite continued population growth.

Let's take a quick global tour. In East Asia (excluding China), the number of people living in extreme poverty peaked in 1987 at 281 million; by 2011, it had fallen to 77 million, with declines in Cambodia, Timor-Leste, Indonesia, South Korea, Vietnam, Thailand, and several other countries. In some of these countries—especially South Korea, Taiwan, Indonesia, and Thailand—poverty had begun to fall in the 1970s and 1980s. In Eastern Europe and Central Asia, the number of extreme poor has been declining since 1996, with falls in countries as diverse as Kazakhstan, Macedonia, Moldova, Poland, Romania, and Turkey. In Latin America and the Caribbean, the number has been falling since 1999, with declines in Brazil, the Dominican Republic, Ecuador, El Salvador, Guatemala, and Nicaragua, among others. In the Middle East and North Africa, the total number has been falling gradually since 1987, with declines in Algeria, Jordan, Morocco, and—yes—Egypt, where the number of people living in extreme poverty fell from 6.3 million in 1981 to 1.3

million in 2011. In India, the number of extreme poor peaked in 2002 at 476 million; nine years later, it had fallen by more than one-third to 300 million. As for the rest of South Asia, extreme poverty has been declining in Bangladesh, Nepal, Sri Lanka, and Pakistan. Yes, Pakistan, where the number of extreme poor fell dramatically from 74 million in 1993 to 22 million in 2011. Sub-Saharan Africa is the only region in the world in which the total number of extreme poor is not yet falling, but even there, the number has essentially leveled off since 2002. The *percentage* of people living in extreme poverty in sub-Saharan Africa declined from 59 percent in 1999 to 47 percent in 2011. The number of extreme poor is already falling in Botswana, Ghana, Mauritius, Namibia, Senegal, South Africa, and several other countries across Africa. Around the world, in country after country, the number of people living in extreme poverty is falling for the first time in history.

To illustrate the extent of the change, consider the following thought experiment about what the global poverty numbers might look like today if they had continued their earlier upward trend. Let's exclude China, since its size and extraordinary changes dominate the numbers. According to the World Bank's data, between 1981 and 1993, the number of extreme poor grew from 1.1 billion to 1.3 billion, or a rise of about 14 million people per year. Had that trend continued, by 2011, the total number of extreme poor would have reached 1.55 billion. Instead, the number fell to 930 million.

The difference: 600 million people. *More than a half billion fewer people in the world, excluding China, are extremely poor than would have been the case had the 1981-to-1993 pattern continued.* This is obviously just a crude calculation, and the assumption of continuing the previous trend is overly simplistic. Nevertheless, it illustrates roughly the magnitude of the change from continuous rise, to leveling off, to sharp decline in the number of extreme poor during the last several decades. It also shows that the improvements go well beyond China.

In country after country, the major, but not exclusive, force behind the rapid decline in poverty has been a revival in economic growth. In most cases, growth has meant new economic opportunities for the poor in agriculture, construction, retail trade, hotels and restaurants, basic manufacturing, and other similar activities. However, growth alone does not tell the whole story. Developing countries began to invest more in health and education, providing the poor with greater opportunities to earn a decent living. At the same time, there has been a major reduction in conflict and violence, with direct benefits to the livelihoods of the poor. Few things are worse for poverty than war.

In addition, many countries are actively introducing social safety net programs designed to support the poor. The programs come in a variety of forms: pension and social insurance programs aimed at the elderly; job training and unemployment benefits for workers; and, of particular importance to the poor, a variety of direct assistance programs such as disaster relief, food assistance, subsidies, and cash transfer programs. Many countries have introduced conditional cash transfer programs, such as Brazil's Programa Bolsa Família (Family Benefit Program), which provides cash grants to poor families on the condition that their children go to school and get vaccinated. Researchers at the World Bank estimate that upward of 150 million people have been lifted above the extreme poverty line because of social protection and safety net programs.[9]

Indonesia provides a good example of these forces. Today it is the world's fourth most populous country, with 250 million people. Poverty began to fall in the 1970s, and continued to do so through the mid-1990s until the Asian financial crisis erupted in 1997. At that point, the number of extreme poor rose for about three years, but it has been falling ever since. Like so many other countries, Indonesia's poverty reduction was ignited in the rural areas. The government introduced deliberate strategies to support agriculture, including distributing new varieties of seeds and fertilizers as part of the Green Revolution, ensuring favorable prices for small rice farmers, and building an extensive network of rural roads to connect markets. Farm productivity rose quickly, and as a result, so did rural incomes. Nonfarm rural incomes also played a role, with people finding employment in small businesses making farm tools, building furniture, processing food, and selling goods in small retail shops. In the 1980s, Indonesia began to promote urban-based, labor-intensive manufacturing of shoes, textiles, garments, toys, jewelry, and many other goods for the export market. These enterprises created millions of jobs for low-skilled workers—many of them poor or near poor. All along, Indonesia complemented these strategies with efforts to invest in basic education, make primary health care available, and introduce one of the first (and largest) profitable microfinance programs in the world. The combination of sound macroeconomic management, political stability, and sensible economic policies promoted growth and helped create new economic opportunities for the poor. Following the financial crisis of the late 1990s, the government introduced a variety of safety net programs, including subsidized rice for the very poor, labor-intensive work programs, cash transfers for poor families with children in school, free health services for the poor, and a community empowerment program. The impact of these strategies has been huge: between 1981 and 2011, the share of people living in extreme poverty fell extraordinarily fast, from 82 percent to 16 percent.

Or consider El Salvador, where rapid poverty reduction coincided with the end of the brutal civil war in 1992. El Salvador consolidated peace, introduced democratic rule, and ushered in wide-ranging economic and structural reforms. Economic growth accelerated to more than 6 percent per year in the 1990s, school enrollments jumped, and many more people gained access to basic health care and clean water. New firms began to export a wide variety of manufactured products to the United States. Although growth has slowed in recent years, extreme poverty fell from 15 percent of the population in 1990 to just 3 percent in 2011.

SHIFTING FORTUNES

As hundreds of millions of people have been lifted out of extreme poverty, how much have their standards of living risen? Do they now live on $1.26 a day? Or $1.50 a day? Or more? For many people, the rise in incomes has been modest. For many others, the gains have been larger. The changes go beyond people who were living on less than $1.25 a day. Many other people who lived on $1.50 or $2 a day in the 1990s have seen their levels of consumption rise as well.

Figure 2.3 summarizes these shifts. Since 1993, the number of people living on less than $1.25 a day has fallen by half. At the same time, the number living on between $1.25 a day and $2 a day rose, but by much less. The biggest increases came at higher consumption levels: The number of people living on between $2 a day and $5 a day has nearly doubled. The number living on more than $5 a day has almost tripled. *For the first time in world history, there are more people in developing countries living on more than $5 a day than there are living on less than $1.25 a day.*

FIGURE 2.3: SHIFTING FORTUNES

Total Number of People in Developing Countries with Consumption in Each Bracket

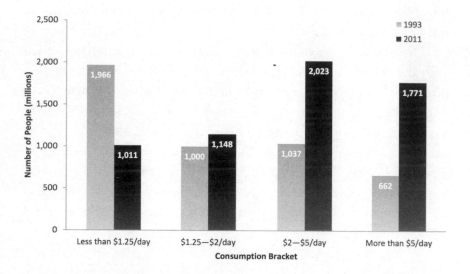

Source: Author's calculations, based on data from the World Bank's PovcalNet database. http://iresearch.worldbank.org/PovcalNet/.

What has happened to the 1 billion people who are still living on less than $1.25 a day? Obviously life remains difficult, and for many millions, income has changed little. But research indicates that for many of those living under the extreme poverty line, income and consumption levels are beginning to rise, at least to some extent, even if they have not yet crossed the basic poverty line. World Bank researchers have compiled estimates of the average consumption levels of people living on less than $1.25 a day, based on detailed household surveys, and examined what has happened to consumption over time. In 1981 the extreme poor lived on an average of just $0.74 a day. Bear in mind that this is the average figure, so around half of the extreme poor were living on even less than this paltry amount. By 2010, the average was $0.87 a day.[10] (Both figures are in constant 2005 prices, so the increase is after controlling for price inflation.) This change is hardly a huge increase—about 18 percent (in real terms)—but neither is it stagnation. Of course, for some, incomes have not changed much, if at all. But for others, income has risen even more. So even *within* the group of extreme poor, average consumption is rising.

FIGURE 2.4: MOVING ACROSS THE EXTREME POVERTY LINE

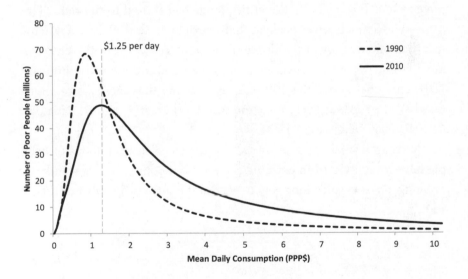

Source: Laurence Chandy, Natasha Ledlie, and Veronika Penciakova, "The Final Countdown: Prospects for Ending Extreme Poverty by 2030," policy paper 2013-04, Global Economy and Development at Brookings Institution, Washington, DC, April 2013.

People are not yet rich. While millions of people no longer live in *extreme* poverty, they are still poor by global standards. Nonetheless, for the majority of people in most developing countries, along almost the entire range from poor to rich, consumption levels are rising. We can see the increase across the full range in figure 2.4, which is derived from research conducted by Laurence Chandy and others at the Brookings Institution.[11] The two curves represent the population of developing countries arranged by levels of daily consumption in 1990 and in 2010. The figure includes a vertical line representing extreme poverty, at $1.25. The height of the curves at that point shows the number of people with consumption equal to *exactly* $1.25 a day. The full area to the left of the line shows the total number of people living in extreme poverty; the area to the right represents the people living above the extreme poverty line.

The shape of the curve shifted dramatically between 1990 and 2010. The 1990 curve peaks sharply at around $0.80 a day, showing a huge number of people living at or near this meager sum just two decades ago, and the large number of people living under the $1.25-a-day poverty line. But by 2010, the entire range had shifted to the right. The peak—and a much lower peak, at that—is right around $1.25 a day, with less than one-quarter of the distribution now to the left of the extreme poverty line. Notice that everywhere to the right of the poverty line, the 2010 curve lies above the 1990 curve, meaning that there was a larger number of people at every consumption level greater than $1.25 a day in 2010 than there was in 1990.

No matter how you look at it, the message is clear: millions of people have been lifted from extreme poverty to modestly higher standards of living. There is still a long way to go, but it is an enormously important start.

THREE

THE WEALTH OF A
NEW GENERATION

To get rich is glorious.

—*Deng Xiaoping*

WHEN MOZAMBIQUE'S CIVIL WAR ENDED IN 1992, THE COUNTRY WAS IN RUINS.[1] *ARMED* rebellion against Portuguese colonial rule started in the 1960s, but conflict intensified significantly after the 1974 coup in Lisbon led to Portugal's withdrawal. When the Portuguese pulled out, "they did so with spite, sabotaging vehicles and pouring concrete down wells, elevator shafts, and toilets, leaving the country in disarray," according to David Smith of the *Guardian*.[2] The new government in Maputo established one-party rule, aligned itself with the Soviet Union, and provided support to the liberation movements in South Africa and Rhodesia, while the governments of South Africa and Rhodesia countered by financing an armed rebellion to fight the Mozambican government. Sporadic conflict escalated into all-out war. More than 1 million people died in the conflict out of a population of 13 million. Another 1.7 million became refugees.

The government's economic policies made a bad situation worse. It nationalized corporations, ran large budget deficits, printed vast amounts of money to finance its spending, stifled farmers by manipulating agricultural prices, and undermined private business. Investment and trade collapsed, and poverty soared. By the early 1990s, Mozambique was one of the poorest countries in the world. The combination of colonialism, the Cold War, apartheid, gross economic mismanagement, and protracted war had created a disaster. Mozambique was a poster child for all that had gone wrong in sub-Saharan Africa.

But all of that began to change in the early 1990s. The government stabilized the economy by cutting the budget deficit, reducing inflation, and improving exchange-rate management to eliminate the black market for currency. It privatized more than twelve hundred state-owned enterprises, lowered import tariffs, streamlined customs management, and improved incentives for farmers. Strong financial support from major donors helped reduce a crippling debt burden; rebuild roads, schools, and clinics; and otherwise support Mozambique's recovery. The country has attracted significant new private investment, led by the Mozal aluminum smelter and more recently around coal mining and oil- and gas-extraction projects. Alongside larger businesses, farmers, shopkeepers, construction workers, market women, and many others have found growing economic opportunities.

The results have been impressive. Gross domestic product (GDP) per person has grown at nearly 5 percent per year for twenty years, one of the highest growth rates in the world. Average income has more than doubled (after accounting for inflation) and far surpassed its prewar levels. Primary school enrollment has jumped from 42 percent to 90 percent, child mortality has been cut by half, and the debt-to-GDP ratio has dropped from 330 percent to 40 percent. Poverty rates have plummeted from 82 percent in 1990 to 55 percent in 2011.

People have noticed. Gabriel Fossati-Bellani, a Mozambican-American entrepreneur, puts it this way: "People are expecting a lot from Mozambique—and they should. Business is growing, the middle class is growing, the level of professionalism and service delivery has gone up in leaps and bounds. Maputo is a metropolis now. It functions like a city should in this day and age."[3]

Mozambique is still a poor country. Poverty, while falling, remains high, especially in rural areas. Violence sometimes flares, rekindling old tensions from the civil war. The political system has improved, but has not transformed into a full-fledged democracy, and the quality of governance and the protection of individual rights and freedoms remain weak. Nonetheless, the turnaround since the end of the war has been remarkable, with much greater progress than most people could have imagined.

Mozambique is a relatively small country, so from a global perspective, its turnaround may not seem important. But Mozambique was not alone. It was part of a much bigger transformation.

THE GROWTH RESURGENCE

For two decades now, economies have been growing—and incomes have been rising—faster in more developing countries than ever before. Since 1995, real GDP has increased by an average of 4.7 percent per year across all developing countries, and GDP per person has grown at an annual rate of 3 percent. As a result, *real GDP per person increased by an average of more than 70 percent between 1995 and 2013* (figure 3.1). Dozens of developing countries—indeed the majority— are now enjoying steady growth, including China and India alongside countries as far-flung as Mongolia, Bangladesh, the Dominican Republic, Jordan, Ghana, Chile, Rwanda, Brazil, Vietnam, Tanzania, and many more.

Far more people are finding better jobs and earning higher income from agriculture, retail trade, construction, tourism, manufacturing, finance, and industry. On a population-weighted basis, *real income per person has increased 90 percent since 1994*—and that figure excludes China. Hundreds of millions of people in the world's poorest countries—in fact, several billion people—have much higher incomes than twenty years ago. The increased income is not just concentrated among the rich in these countries. In most countries (although not all), the incomes of the poor, middle class, and rich are growing at roughly the same pace.

FIGURE 3.1: GROWTH IS SURGING

GDP per Capita, 109 Developing Countries (Unweighted Average)

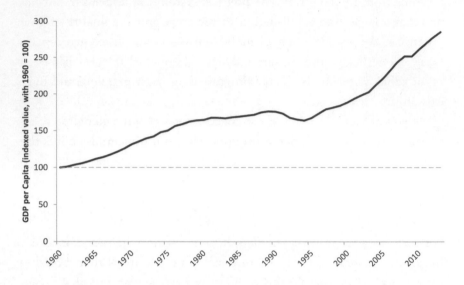

Source: Author's calculations, based on an unweighted average of GDP per capita in constant prices, with the data drawn from the World Bank's World Development Indicators. The figures in the graph are indexed values, with the original GDP per capita figures recalculated to equal 100 in the base year of 1960 for all countries.

Business is booming, large and small, local and international. More than 16 million smartphones were sold in Latin America in the first quarter of 2013 alone, and in Brazil, smartphone sales jumped 89 percent in one year. Apple opened its first retail outlet in Rio de Janeiro in early 2014.[4] Coca-Cola recently opened its forty-third bottling plant in China, bringing its total employment there to more than fifty thousand people. Coca-Cola has invested $4 billion in China in just the past three years and is planning for another $4 billion during 2015–17.[5] Walmart spent $2.4 billion in 2011 to acquire a controlling share of Massmart Holdings Ltd., which operates 350 retail stores in South Africa and eleven other countries across sub-Saharan Africa.[6] That a major corporation like Walmart would drop more than $2 billion to gain access to the consumer retail market in sub-Saharan Africa would have been unfathomable two decades ago.

It's not just businesses from rich countries investing in developing countries. Firms in developing countries are becoming much more competitive and increasing their revenues both locally and around the world. In 1980 trade *between* developing countries accounted for less than 6 percent of the global total; by 2010 it accounted for more than 21 percent.

In 1994 Ecuador's Florecot (Flores del Cotacachi SA) began producing summer flowers for export. It was a tiny firm with ten employees and four hectares of farmland. But the company has grown, and Florecot has become one of Ecuador's largest summer flower producers. By 2008, the company employed seven hundred field workers covering forty-seven hectares and earned $8 million in annual revenue through sales to the United States, Canada, the Netherlands, Italy, France, England, Russia, Chile, Venezuela, the Dominican Republic, and Kuwait.[7]

Safaricom is East Africa's largest mobile telecommunications provider, and is widely considered one of the most innovative companies in sub-Saharan Africa. In 2007 Safaricom launched M-Pesa, Africa's first text-message-based money transfer service, which, since then, has become one of the most sophisticated mobile payment systems in the world. M-Pesa (the *M* is for "mobile," and *pesa* is a Swahili word for "money") allows users with a national ID card or passport to deposit, withdraw, and transfer money with a mobile device. For a small fee, users can deposit money into an account stored on their cell phones, send balances through short message service (SMS) text messages to other users (including shops and businesses), and redeem deposits for cash. In just five years, more than 17 million M-Pesa accounts were registered in Kenya.

There are hundreds of similar examples of growing businesses in dozens of developing countries around the world—in countries that most casual observers would not think of as promising places for economic growth.

One way to understand the breadth of the changes is to examine the number of countries in which economic growth has accelerated in the last two decades. More specifically, let's look at the number of developing countries for which growth in GDP per capita has exceeded the benchmarks of 2 percent and 4 percent per capita, and how the patterns have changed over time. (Note that these are *per capita* growth rates, so that in countries where populations are growing by 2 percent, they are roughly equivalent to GDP growth rates of 4 percent and 6 percent, respectively.*) Why these benchmarks? Economists often use 2 percent per capita growth as a standard for a respectable rate of moderate growth for two reasons: it is roughly equal to the average long-term growth rate for the United States and other leading economies since the industrial revolution, and it is roughly equal to the world average growth rate since 1960. The reasoning is simple: if a country is doing as well as America has done for two hundred years, and if it is growing at least at the world average rate, it is making reasonable progress. It turns out that 2 percent per capita growth is fairly powerful if it is sustained over time. At that rate, average income doubles every thirty-five years, or basically every two generations. Sustained growth of 4 percent per capita is fast by any historical standard; much faster than most Western economies have ever been able to sustain. At that rate, average incomes double in eighteen years—less than a generation.

So how have developing countries fared against these standards?

Out of 109 developing countries with complete data and populations greater than 1 million, between 1977 and 1994, only 21—fewer than 1 out of 5—achieved per capita growth exceeding 2 percent per year (figure 3.2). But between 1995 and 2013, that number more than *tripled* to 71 countries. Economic growth has changed from being the rare exception to the predominant rule: almost two-thirds of developing countries are now achieving moderate or better economic growth. If we think in terms of people and not countries, 4.6 billion people— nearly two-thirds of the world's population—now live in developing countries in which growth has exceeded 2 percent per person since the mid-1990s.

---

*Here is the quick math: If GDP = Y, and population = N, then GDP per capita = Y/N. If GDP grows 4 percent and population grows 2 percent, then GDP per capita will increase to $(Y*1.04)/(N*1.02)$, which is equal to $Y/N*(1.0196)$, or an increase in Y/N of approximately 2 percent.

Many countries are doing even better. For instance, 30 developing countries have recorded growth of at least 4 percent per person per year or higher since 1995, compared with just 10 in the earlier period. And this is not an inconsequential group—these 30 countries are home to more than 3.2 billion people. In these countries, which include more than 40 percent of the world's population, *average incomes have far more than doubled in real terms since 1995.*

We can also look at growth rates at the other end of the spectrum: the number of countries with negative per capita growth, or falling average incomes. Between 1977 and 1994, there were 51 developing countries that recorded negative growth. Almost half of all developing countries were moving in the wrong direction. However, since 1995, that number has fallen to just 10: Burundi, Central African Republic, Democratic Republic of Congo, Eritrea, Gabon, Guinea-Bissau, Haiti, Jamaica, Madagascar, and Zimbabwe.

FIGURE 3.2: GROWTH INCLUDES MANY MORE COUNTRIES

Number of Countries with Annual GDP per Capita Growth

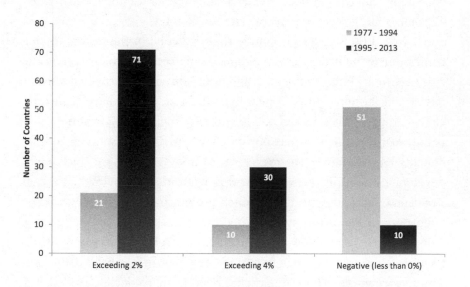

Source: Author's calculations, based on data from the World Bank's World Development Indicators.

So where are the 71 countries that have achieved 2 percent per capita growth? All over the world, it turns out. It's no surprise that 15 are in South Asia and East Asia, but 19 are in Eastern Europe and Central Asia, all still in the midst of a rebound from Soviet occupation, including Georgia, Romania, and Albania, among others. In Georgia, growth has averaged 6.5 percent per person per year, and average incomes have tripled. There are 8 in Latin America, including the Dominican Republic, Panama, and Costa Rica, and 8 more are in the Middle East and North Africa, including Tunisia, Morocco, and Jordan. In the Dominican Republic, growth has averaged 4.2 percent per person; and in Morocco, growth has averaged a solid 2.7 percent per year for the last two decades. In Brazil, average household income increased by more than 50 percent (after accounting for inflation) in just *six years* after 2003.[8]

The biggest surprise to most people is that seventeen of the growing economies are in sub-Saharan Africa, including Botswana, Ethiopia, Ghana, Liberia, Mauritius, Mozambique, Namibia, Rwanda, Sierra Leone, Tanzania, Uganda, and several others.[9] Ghana began to reverse its economic decline in the mid-1980s, and its growth rates have accelerated steadily ever since. Rwanda's income has doubled since 1994. Tanzania's has grown 70 percent. The list goes on.

It would be wrong to conclude that everyone in the faster-growing countries is benefitting or that all developing countries have turned the corner. China, India, Indonesia, and Vietnam are all growing quickly, but several hundred million people in those countries have seen little change in their incomes and still live in extreme poverty. In some other countries, the growth is fueled by oil or other natural resources, and the benefits are accruing to a small elite. Moreover, there are thirty-eight developing countries in which growth has remained below 2 percent per capita, including the ten in which growth has been negative. Some countries remain just as stuck as they have been for decades. Burundi, Congo, Haiti, Papua New Guinea, Paraguay, Yemen, and many others have seen almost no change in average incomes. In Zimbabwe, the bottom has fallen out. The economy has been in sharp decline since 1998, and average income today is far below what it was in the 1980s. Many millions remain left behind.

The differences in growth experiences across groups of countries is evident in figure 3.3, which shows changes in average GDP per capita (indexed so that 1960 = 100 for all countries) for all developing countries, as well as the twenty-five with the fastest growth rates and the twenty-five with the slowest growth rates. The middle line—the average GDP per person for all developing countries—replicates what we saw in figure 3.1. The top line shows that for the twenty-five fastest-growing developing countries, average GDP per person is more than five times higher than it was in 1960, after accounting for inflation. Over this time, some of these countries have experienced economic growth at rates unprecedented in human history. The bottom line shows that for the twenty-five slowest-growing countries, GDP per person has hardly changed in fifty years.

FIGURE 3.3: MOST COUNTRIES ARE GROWING FASTER, BUT SOME ARE STILL LEFT BEHIND

Average GDP per Capita in Fast-, Average-, and Slow-Growing Countries

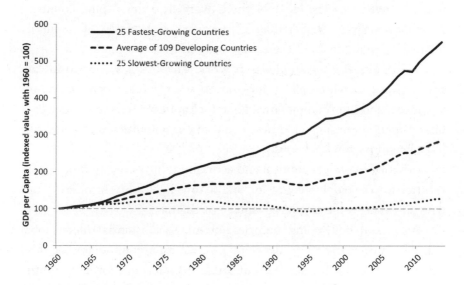

Source: Author's calculations, based on an unweighted average of GDP per capita in constant prices, with the data drawn from the World Bank's World Development Indicators. The figures in the graph are indexed values, with the original GDP per capita figures recalculated to equal 100 in the base year of 1960 for all countries.

WHAT SPARKED THE GROWTH RESURGENCE?

Why did economic growth begin to accelerate in so many different countries at about the same time? I'll discuss the major forces of change in more detail in chapters 6 through 9, but three stand out.

First, with the end of the Cold War, political and economic systems changed dramatically in many countries, which led to improved governance, a substantial reduction in violence, less repression, and more economic opportunities. During the colonial period, and continuing through the era of the Cold War, most people in today's developing countries were shut out of opportunities for economic advancement. Thirty years after the wave of independence movements, more open and effective political and economic institutions took root.

Second, new leaders came to the fore and introduced much more sensible economic policies that encouraged trade and investment, closed down dysfunctional state-owned enterprises, removed exchange-rate distortions, and changed policies that had undermined agriculture and manufactured exports. In 1994 there were fifty developing countries with inflation rates higher than 20 percent—a clear sign of economic mismanagement. In 2013 there were only five.

Third, global integration was at work. The 1990s saw a worldwide shift toward increased global integration with much greater trade, investment, and information flows. New technologies reduced trade costs, linked markets, and created new economic possibilities that could not have been imagined previously.

In short, major geopolitical and economic shifts created new opportunities for developing countries, and astute leadership in many countries allowed people to take advantage of them.

As a result, developing countries now play a substantial role in global markets. In the early 1990s, developing countries accounted for about 30 percent of the global economy, but today they account for half, and the share is rising rapidly. Excluding China, they account for one-third of the world economy.

The rapidly growing importance of developing countries to the global economy became clear during the 2008 global financial crisis. Growth in Europe and North America ground to a halt, and the emerging countries kept the global economy moving forward. In 2009, rich-country economies contracted sharply, with GDP growth averaging a dismal -4.2 percent. Many thought the impact on developing countries would be disastrous. It wasn't. Developing-country GDP growth remained a relatively buoyant 3.1 percent, helping to moderate the impact on the global economy. Trade plunged sharply, reflecting the abrupt slowdown in global economic activity. But within two years, trade was back to near its peak. The same is true with investment, lending, and other financial flows: they peaked in 2007, fell rapidly in 2008 and 2009, but by 2010, they were back to their previous high. This rapid recovery contrasts with the global recession that started in 1980, when it took developing countries fourteen years to return to the same trade levels. Not only are developing countries more important to the global economy, but it is clear that economic policy makers in developing countries today are much more astute and skilled than their predecessors.

IS IT JUST A COMMODITY BOOM?

Where has all of this economic growth come from? What are developing countries producing? The specific products and services differ by country, and they change within countries over time. In some countries, growth has been driven at least partially by primary commodity products: oil, gas, iron ore, metals, timber, and other similar products. In large part, the growth in demand for these products comes from other developing countries themselves, especially the large emerging economies such as China, India, Brazil, Indonesia, and Turkey, where the appetite for commodities is growing with their incomes. Prices for many commodities on global markets have soared. Mozambique is exporting aluminum; Ghana, oil; Peru, copper; the Philippines, nickel; and Mongolia, coal and iron ore. Almost all developing countries export some kind of mineral or agricultural commodity, and many are highly dependent on these products.

Some people worry that the recent surge in growth in developing countries is just a commodity boom, and nothing more. If commodities were the full story, it would suggest that the growth turnaround is

temporary and shallow, and unlikely to last or bring about more fundamental development progress over time. It also could be risky, in that it
could lead to macroeconomic instability when prices fall or could create
other long-term damage associated with the "resource curse."

The idea that the turnaround is just a commodity boom is at best
incomplete and is too simplistic. Yes, the demand for commodities has
grown and prices have increased since 2002, which has helped but-
tress the economic turnaround in many countries, but it can't be the
full story. The turnaround in developing countries started in 1995, long
before the current commodity boom started. In fact, in the late 1990s,
global commodity prices were *falling*, not rising. Nonenergy commodity
prices fell 30 percent between 1995 and 2001. Moreover, while export
prices for many countries have been rising since 2002, so have import
prices. The sharp rise in global food prices in 2008 may have helped
some food exporters, but it hurt many people who rely on imported
food products.

From a broad economic perspective, one way to measure the impact
of world prices is the ratio of export to import prices, known as the
"net barter terms of trade." Figure 3.4 shows the terms-of-trade index
for developing countries, alongside an index of GDP per capita levels.
The terms of trade fell steadily from the 1980s until 2002, indicating
that export prices were falling relative to import prices. This pattern
continued throughout the late 1990s, even as economic growth began to
accelerate. Between 1995 and 2002, the terms-of-trade index fell by 10
percent, and yet average GDP per capita rose almost 20 percent. At the
very same time that the economic turnaround began—and for several
years thereafter—commodity prices were working *against* developing
countries. But their economies started to grow nonetheless.

The terms-of-trade ratio has been rising since 2002, meaning export
prices have been rising faster than import prices, which has helped support the recovery. On average, across all developing countries, the index
is still below its level of the early 1980s. So while the recent commodity
boom has helped, it has just made up for the fall in prices that took place
in the 1980s and 1990s. There is much more than a commodity boom
at work.

FIGURE 3.4: COMMODITY PRICES AND GDP PER CAPITA GROWTH

The Net Barter Terms of Trade Fell in the Late 1990s, While Growth Accelerated

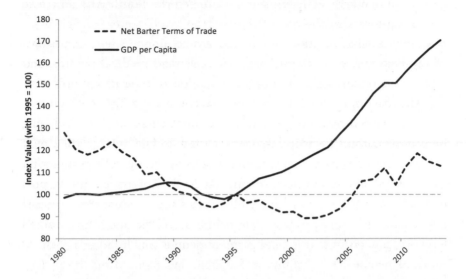

Source: World Bank, World Development Indicators. The figures in the graph are indexed values, with the original commodity prices and GDP per capita figures recalculated to equal 100 in the base year of 1995 for all countries.

Indeed, a wide range of businesses are growing rapidly. In many countries, services are the fastest-growing part of the economy, reflecting rapid growth in cell phone services, hotels, restaurants, construction, call centers, financial services, and other activities. Across all developing countries, output in services has been increasing by more than 5 percent per year since 1995, so that the total value of services (in real terms after accounting for inflation) has increased 150 percent. In some countries, there is a particularly important shift toward more modern services such as software development, technical services (engineering and architecture), outsourced business processes (from insurance claims to transcribing medical records), and call centers, all of which create jobs and increase skills over time. Advances in technology and much deeper global connectivity have allowed developing countries to provide services to other countries as never before: developing countries accounted for 14 percent of global service exports in 1990; two decades later, the share had jumped to 21 percent. Indian software companies are the most famous example, but they are not alone. Sri Lankan engineers are working with firms around the world, South African banks are spreading across the rest of the continent, call centers in Belize are answering billing questions for American cell phone users, companies in the Philippines are transcribing insurance and medical records, and Kenyan accounting firms are providing services to their neighbors.

Manufacturing and industry have expanded just as fast, with growth exceeding 5 percent per year. More and more countries are producing light manufactures for world markets, and processing more of their own raw materials for local and international consumption. Depending on the country, production has expanded in textiles, shoes, garments, processed foods, furniture, machinery, electronics, toys, costume jewelry, and a wide range of other products. Vietnam has become one of the world's largest producers of textiles and garments, employing hundreds of thousands of people. The Dominican Republic has focused on the nearby US market and produces a wide range of electronics, clothing, shoes, and leather goods. The blue jeans I am wearing as I write were made in Bangladesh, and my Nikes were made in Indonesia. Albania now produces underwear for Europe. In Ethiopia, fifty-eight new textile factories opened up in just three months in the middle of 2013.[10]

In many countries, agriculture is also growing. Agricultural production has grown more slowly than other sectors, which is the typical pattern as economies begin to expand, but the performance has hardly been shabby. Across all developing countries, agricultural production has increased about 3 percent per year, meaning a 75 percent increase in production since 1995. Food production alone is 50 percent larger than it was in the mid-1990s.

Peru's agricultural sector used to be a disaster: the military expropriated land from big estates in the 1970s and created state-run cooperatives, many of which failed. Heavy price controls aimed at pleasing urban consumers kept prices low and hurt farmers. The decollectivization of agriculture that began in the 1980s and the easing of price controls created much stronger incentives for farmers, and production began to grow. Production has spread to areas where land was previously unusable: in the 1980s, the Villacurí plain outside Ica was a barren desert, but by 2005, it was home to six thousand hectares of export crops. Much of the production has been in vegetables and fruits for export: asparagus, artichokes, olives, mangoes, quinoa, avocadoes, and grapes.[11] Paprika exports went from $6 million in 2000 to $100 million in 2012. In the twenty years between 1973 and 1992, Peru's agricultural production grew by a paltry 24 percent; in the twenty years since, it has increased 170 percent, with higher incomes accruing to many Peruvian farmers.

Some of this renewed growth around the world comes from large international conglomerates, but a lot of it comes from millions of hardworking and resilient local entrepreneurs such as Lesotho's Masetumo Lebitsa. When the European women who had started Lesotho's mohair-weaving industry left in the early 1990s because of the political turmoil surrounding the end of apartheid in neighboring South Africa, the local weavers had to fend for themselves. With little education and less business management training, these women faced a myriad of challenges trying to operate successful businesses. Many failed. Lebitsa organized the women that remained in a small company called Matela Weavers, formed an association, and changed the name to Maseru Tapestries and Mats. She signed up for free artisan training programs financed by aid programs to develop her business skills. She interviewed her clients to get a better idea of what they wanted and needed—her own marketing survey, as it were—and she kept at it. Despite a number of initial difficult years, Lebitsa focused on succeeding on her own merits, noting, "I want to have my business run like a real business. I don't want to continue to take handouts." Lebitsa has built Maseru Tapestries and Mats into a thriving business, taking orders from visitors, diplomats, and even the king. Her business has gone international, and her weavings are now sold in southern Africa, Europe, and the United States.[12]

MORE JOBS, HIGHER WAGES

All this economic growth is creating jobs—hundreds of millions of them. According to the United Nations' International Labour Organization, there were 700 million more economically active people working in developing countries in 2010 than there were in 1994, an increase of more than one-third in just sixteen years.* Men and women have found new economic opportunities in office positions in Costa Rica, financial markets in Johannesburg, fruit markets in Tanzania, shipping ports in Rio de Janeiro, and soccer ball factories in Pakistan.

Brazil is a good example. Economic growth was fairly modest between 1999 and 2003, during which time about 2.4 million formal sector jobs were created. As economic growth accelerated, so did job creation: between 2003 and 2007, the number of new jobs added doubled to 5.1 million, and between 2007 and 2011, job creation soared to 8.7 million.[13] Brazil's growth has slowed somewhat since then, but there are millions more jobs today than there were fifteen years ago.

To be sure, many of these jobs are low paying and difficult, especially by rich-world standards. Making shoes, working on the docks, and digging ditches on construction sites is hard work, especially where working conditions are subpar. However, difficult jobs are better than no jobs, and they are allowing more and more people to escape abject poverty and provide for their families. In too many countries for too many years, there were no jobs at all. While working on the factory floor is often referred to as sweatshop labor, it is often better than the granddaddy of all sweatshops: working in the fields as an agricultural day laborer.

When I lived in Indonesia in the early 1990s, I arrived with a somewhat romanticized view of the beauty of people working in rice paddies, together with reservations about the rapidly growing factory jobs. The longer I was there, the more I recognized how incredibly difficult it is to work in the rice fields. It's a backbreaking grind, with people eking out the barest of livings by bending over for hours in the hot sun to terrace the fields, plant the seeds, pull the weeds, transplant the seedlings, chase the pests, and harvest the grain. Standing in the pools of water brings leeches and the constant risk of malaria, encephalitis, and other

---

*"Economically active" is a broad concept used by the International Labour Organization to measure the number of people who supply labor for the production of goods and services, and counts formal sector "jobs" as well as seasonal labor (as in agriculture) and informal activities such as selling wares in marketplaces.

diseases. And, of course, it is hot, all the time. So, it was not too much of a surprise that when factory jobs opened offering wages of $2 a day, hundreds of people lined up just to get a shot at applying.

Critically, many factory jobs go to young women, providing them with a source of independent income. In Bangladesh, employment in the garment industry has mushroomed from forty thousand people in 1983 to more than 4 million today, and 80 percent of the employees are women. Economists Rachel Heath of the University of Washington and Mushfiq Mobarak of Yale University estimate that around 15 percent of Bangladeshi women between the ages of sixteen and thirty are employed in the garment industry. They find compelling evidence that women's employment in the garment industry has had a significant positive effect on reducing fertility rates, delaying marriage, and increasing girls' educational attainment.[14]

Although some fear that global integration creates a "race to the bottom" with falling wages, the increase in investment and economic activity more typically has led to *rising* wages—fairly significant rises. The wage increases are largest in "tradable" sectors: firms that have integrated into world markets by exporting or competing with imports. According to the World Bank, wages in traded goods and services for both unskilled workers (such as sewing machine operators) and skilled workers (chemical engineers) have risen by 60 percent in real terms since the mid-1990s. Wages for workers in nontraded activities (such as construction) have also risen, but not as much. Not only are there more jobs, but also over time those jobs are paying better, slowly but surely. The World Bank makes a direct connection between the massive reduction in extreme poverty and job creation: it concludes that the reduction in global poverty "is the result of multiple factors, but the creation of millions of new, more productive jobs, mostly in Asia but also in other parts of the developing world, has been the main driving force."[15]

There is no doubt that many of these jobs are difficult, and that the pay, while higher than in the past, is still low. Throughout history, we have learned that growing prosperity is far from immediate and takes decades of steady, hard work from one generation to the next, especially when countries start with low levels of skills and education. Today's poorest countries are the last to begin to benefit from the great changes that began in earnest with the industrial revolution, but finally life is slowly getting better.

In today's advanced economies, most of our ancestors worked in tough jobs just a generation or two ago. My grandfather John Radelet never attended high school. He started as a farm boy, then learned his trade as a carpenter and a logger in the deep woods north of Green Bay, Wisconsin. When he was a young man, during the winters, he and his friends would skate across the frozen Green Bay, make winter camp on the north side, and cut logs for the local sawmills, to be shipped by way of the Great Lakes. It had all the elements of sweatshop labor, except that as soon as he would begin to sweat, the sweat would freeze. My grandmother, who also never made it to high school, was a laundry woman for a hospital in Green Bay, where she did her share of sweating.

As difficult as they were, the jobs my grandparents had and the incomes they earned were far better than anyone in my family who preceded them could have imagined. They eventually owned a fine home overlooking a small park in Green Bay, complete with in-home plumbing, heating, electricity, refrigerator, and a 1928 Buick in the driveway—firsts in my family's history. All of it would have seemed impossible just a generation or two before. They worked hard for their whole lives, and while they enjoyed some of the benefits, I have reaped even more from their efforts. Across the United States, Western Europe, and Japan, the vast majority of families have shifted across the generations from farming and hauling logs to manufacturing, architecture, engineering, management, law, and business. We have better health, cleaner water, better food, and more education.

And so it is with the process of development and poverty reduction around the world. It tends to be an intergenerational process rather than an overnight story. The launderer becomes the seamstress, then the tailor, then the designer. The sweeper joins the assembly line, then becomes the shift leader, then the manager. The logger becomes the carpenter, then the skilled cabinetmaker. Their children gain their collective skills and wisdom and take them to the next level.

BUT IS IT SUSTAINABLE?

The news is not all good. The surge in economic growth has been accompanied in many countries by losses in natural resources and growing environmental degradation, including air and water pollution, reductions in soil quality, biodiversity loss, and increased greenhouse gas emissions that contribute to climate change. Production of timber comes at a cost of clearing forests; overfishing can lead to depletion and species loss; industrial production generates waste that can be dumped into groundwater supplies; and increased economic activity brings greater automobile, factory, and power plant emissions. These developments are problematic in and of themselves because of the basic importance that people, including citizens of developing countries, put on nature and natural resources. Duke University economist Jeffrey Vincent and his colleagues have shown that public demand for conservation grows in tropical developing countries as they reach upper-middle-income status. At least as important, as Cambridge University's Partha Dasgupta has pointed out for many years, environmental degradation raises important questions about the sustainability of development progress and its links to poverty and destitution.[16]

Standard figures on economic growth are based on gross domestic product. GDP is a powerful measure: it provides an aggregate calculation of the quantity and value of a wide variety of goods and services that are produced, and simultaneously gives an estimate of overall income. However, it is far from perfect. One of its shortcomings is in its first word: *gross*. GDP measures the total value of production but does not net out the costs of the depreciation of capital (for example, machinery and buildings). That adjustment is made easily through the less widely quoted net national product. More worrisome, GDP (and NNP) ignores the costs of the depreciation (or destruction) of natural capital such as forests, water and air supplies, biodiversity, and natural resources. If GDP is expanding because loggers are clear-cutting forests with no replanting, that growth is unsustainable. In such cases, GDP growth overstates the improvement in the country's welfare, since it doesn't count the loss of the trees.

Perhaps the most visible example of this problem is the massive increase in air pollution in China's cities. When at its worst, as Beijing was in the early months of 2013, it is hard to see more than a few hundred yards, and people can smell, taste, and gag on it. China's rapid growth rates are extraordinarily impressive, but they overstate actual progress and welfare because they ignore this pollution and its real costs. You can't breathe GDP.

The biggest question is the extent to which these problems will undermine the sustainability of development progress in the future, which I will discuss in the last chapters of this book. But how do they affect our measures of progress over the last two decades?

Environmental economists think about sustainability in terms of whether a country's savings and accumulation of other forms of capital assets are sufficient to offset the depletion of natural resources and other natural capital (known as Hartwick's rule). If the increase in one type of capital asset is sufficient to offset losses in other capital, growth can be sustained. The World Bank has begun to research these issues in recent years, and has begun to measure total *wealth* (not just annual income) by incorporating measures of the value of the assets of "produced" capital (machinery and equipment), "natural" capital (land, protected areas, forest, minerals), and "intangible" capital (human, social, and institutional capital).[17] The World Bank's researchers find that depreciation of natural capital reduces the aggregate gains. After including changes in the value of natural capital, per capita wealth in the lowest-income countries increased 16 percent between 1995 and 2005 (the last year of the full data as of this writing). In lower-middle-income developing countries (including China), per capita wealth increased a substantial 49 percent. The improvement was not across all countries. In Nigeria, per capita wealth fell because of rapid depletion of petroleum deposits and other resources. In the majority of countries, per capita wealth grew, after adjusting for changes in natural resources and other types of capital assets.

More detailed studies on a smaller number of countries provide similar results. Nobel laureate Kenneth Arrow, Partha Dasgupta, and their coauthors provide an in-depth accounting of what they call "comprehensive" wealth and different forms of capital, including natural capital, in five countries: the United States, China, Brazil, India, and Venezuela.

They explore the extent to which different types of capital are changing and comprehensive wealth is increasing. They find that the stock of natural capital declined between 1995 and 2000 in all five countries studied. In China, for example, it fell by around 5 percent, and in India by about 1 percent. However, in four of the five (the United States, Brazil, China, and India), other forms of capital grew sufficiently so that comprehensive wealth increased, indicating sustainability. By contrast (and alarmingly), in Venezuela, the stock of natural capital fell by 12 percent in just five years and comprehensive wealth declined.[18]

After accounting as best we can for changes in natural assets, we find that developing countries have registered significant increases in overall welfare and wealth in recent years. But not all countries have done so. The big concern, of course, is whether this pattern of increasing wealth can continue in the future, especially with growing climate change, biodiversity loss, and other environmental concerns. Continued progress with less environmental degradation won't happen automatically: it will require strong leadership that focuses more on natural assets, investments in new technologies, changes in behavior, and wise policy choices.

HAS THE SURGE IN GROWTH HELPED THE POOR?

When I give talks on economic growth, I am almost always challenged by someone in the audience who will say something like the following: "I understand that there has been a lot of growth, but isn't it true that all of this new wealth is just accruing to the richest people, with the poor getting next to nothing?" There is often a follow-up example: "I was recently in Bangkok, and I saw gleaming skyscrapers, new cars, and lots of fancy restaurants, but also lots of poor people in urban slums. The rich are doing fine, but the poor seem to have been left out."

It's a good question. There's a lot of skepticism that economic growth helps the poor, and it is partially correct. It is true that there are lots of newly rich people in developing countries, some of them extremely rich. It is also true that there are still *many* poor people, some of whom have not gained much from the recent surge.

But that picture is incomplete. In most countries where economic growth accelerates, millions of poor people are finding new economic opportunities and seeing their incomes grow. Many are still poor, even as their incomes grow from $1 a day to $2 a day to $3 a day. But they are much *less* poor than they once were. Economists have produced reams of research on the relationship between economic growth and poverty, and the results are clear: while growth is not the only driver of poverty reduction, there is no force more powerful for reducing extreme poverty than sustained economic growth.

Martin Ravallion, now of Georgetown University, has written a great deal on the relationship between growth and poverty, much of it while he was at the World Bank. Time and again, he and others have shown that the faster the economic growth, the faster the poverty reduction. The precise size of the relationship differs by the country, the level of income inequality, the extent of dependence on commodities, and the structure of the economy. This dynamic should make sense: the worse the initial level of income distribution, the weaker the impact of growth on poverty reduction. As a general matter across developing countries over the past several decades, the relationship between growth and poverty reduction is strong.

Other researchers have taken a different approach. Instead of examining changes in the poverty rate, they look at changes in the income levels of the poorest people, and, more specifically, at the relationship between the growth rate for incomes of all people in a country and the growth rate of the incomes of the poor. Once again the research leads to the same basic conclusion: on average, each 1 percentage point increase in overall economic growth is matched by a 1 percentage point increase in the growth rate of the incomes of the poor.[19]

It's important to emphasize that this relationship is not automatic. It depends a lot on the policies and strategies that countries pursue. Growth tends to help the poor most when economic activity is based in areas that provide the greatest job opportunities for unskilled workers, such as agriculture, manufacturing of simple consumer goods, and basic services. It is weakest where income is already highly unequal, or when growth is concentrated in natural resources or activities that use fewer low-skilled workers. But the cases in which the poor do not benefit from growth are the exception, not the rule. In most instances, as one well-known research paper by World Bank economists David Dollar and Aart Kraay was entitled, growth is good for the poor.[20]

INCOME INEQUALITY: KEEPING UP WITH THE JONESES, THE CHANGS, THE GARCIAS, AND THE SISAYS

We have seen that *average* incomes are rising in the majority of developing countries. How widely shared are the benefits from growth? The massive decline in extreme poverty that we saw in chapter 2 gives us a big hint that the benefits from growth are not accruing just to the rich, but this is not the full story. Is income inequality getting worse, better, or remaining about the same?

This seemingly straightforward question is tricky to answer because there are several different ways to think about and measure inequality. Income inequality is a *relative* concept, comparing one person's (or a group of people's) income with someone else's, so the answer depends on which people or groups of people you compare. Are we comparing the incomes of rich and poor individuals, or rich and poor countries? If individuals, are we looking within one country, or around the world? If countries, do we weigh them all the same or count large countries more than small ones? Because of these variables, it is not unusual to hear contrasting claims about income inequality. One person claims it is getting better, while another claims it is getting worse, but the difference comes down to how he or she defines inequality. In the context of development, the two most common notions of inequality are *within* countries and *across* countries. Economist Branko Milanovic explores these and other ideas about inequality in developing countries in his terrific book *The Haves and the Have-Nots: A Brief and Idiosyncratic History of Global Inequality.*[21]

Inequality Within Countries

Most people have a strong presumption that inequality within countries worsens as economic growth proceeds, and—possibly—gets better at higher income levels. Much of the early research on development, especially the work of Simon Kuznets and Sir Arthur Lewis in the 1950s, suggested that would be the case. Stylistically, everyone starts out poor but equal; then some people begin to earn higher incomes, creating a widening income gap; and then over time others catch up and partially close the gap. But extensive research shows that, over the past several decades, this pattern has not held. It is true that within some countries, inequality has gotten worse—such as in China—but inequality has improved in others—such as in Brazil. For the majority of developing countries, income inequality hasn't changed much at all, even alongside the acceleration in growth.

There are around seventy-five developing countries for which decent data on income distribution are available over several decades (measured by the Gini coefficient, a widely used index of inequality that measures the extent to which income distribution deviates from perfect equality). In about half, inequality hasn't changed much either way. In slightly more than one-quarter, inequality has improved somewhat. In slightly less than one-quarter, inequality has worsened.

In China, inequality has deteriorated steadily, to a large extent along geographical lines. The coastal cities are booming, not just for the rich but also for low-skilled workers who are able to get service or manufacturing jobs in one of the thousands of factories making shoes, shirts, electronics, and other products. But in the rural areas where most of the poor live, income growth has been slower (although still fast by most standards), so the gaps across income groups and across the country have widened. Of course, in China, the incomes of the poor are growing rapidly, so from an absolute sense, they are far better off. In some other countries, however, economic growth has been slow *and* inequality has worsened. In Yemen, there has been very little income growth for the poor, the number of people living in extreme poverty has doubled, and the gap between rich and poor has grown.

In other countries, inequality has improved. In Brazil, where inequality was among the highest in the world two decades ago, both poverty and income inequality began to decline in the mid-1990s, even though overall economic growth did not accelerate until the following decade. Between

1995 and 2009, the average income of the poorest 20 percent of the population increased a huge 127 percent, while the incomes of the richest 20 percent increased 54 percent. As a result, the ratio between the average incomes of the top 20 percent and the bottom 20 percent declined by one-third.[22] Brazil's economic growth has created millions of new jobs over the last decade, many for the poor, but it is more than growth: Brazil invested in education and health, instituted strong new minimum wage laws (which have more than tripled the basic wage in real terms since the mid-1990s), reduced substantially its historically high rate of inflation (which had hurt the poor), and strengthened its social security system to protect the elderly. Perhaps most famously, it introduced its innovative Programa Bolsa Família (Family Benefit Program), which provides cash grants to poor families on the condition that children go to school and get vaccinated. The program has helped boost consumption levels for thousands of poor around the country. Ecuador and El Salvador have also seen moderate improvements in measures of inequality.

The most dominant pattern in recent decades, however, has been little or no change in inequality. In Mozambique, Morocco, Bangladesh, the Philippines, Senegal, Uganda, and Vietnam, among many others, income distribution has changed little over the last two decades, even alongside moderate or rapid rates of growth.

There is more debate than firm evidence on exactly why inequality gets worse in some countries, gets better in others, and doesn't change much in most. But it seems to depend on the characteristics and history of individual countries that are hard to generalize, alongside policy choices. Incomes tend to become more concentrated during conflict or major macroeconomic shocks, since the poor are less able to protect themselves from catastrophic events. Where economic growth is based on exploitation of a few natural resources (like oil), incomes tend to become more concentrated in the hands of a lucky (or politically well-connected) few. By contrast, where growth is based on agriculture and job opportunities for low-skilled workers (in manufacturing or services), the gains tend to be more broad based and equitable. In countries where ownership of land or other important economic assets is more concentrated, growth often perpetuates this pattern. The high levels of inequality in Latin

America are due in part to landholding patterns that date back centuries. South Africa's history of apartheid left a legacy of inequitable access to land and other assets that continues today. South Korea's massive land redistribution program following World War II laid the foundation for today's more equitable distribution of income. It isn't just history: Brazil illustrates that equitable growth typically doesn't just happen from the beneficence of the market. It requires a growth-and-development strategy focused on creating economic opportunities for the majority of people (including the poor), coupled with strategic investments in health, education, and infrastructure, and well-designed safety nets.

That the dominant trend across developing countries has been little change in inequality will come as a surprise to those who have been following the big debates about growing income inequality in rich countries. Thomas Piketty's blockbuster *Capital in the Twenty-First Century* sparked widespread debate on the nature of economic growth and income distribution in the world's richest countries, especially the United States, France, and the United Kingdom. The debates start with the fact—and it is a well-documented fact—that income inequality improved between the end of World War II and the late 1970s but has worsened in many rich countries since then. In the United States, median household income has barely increased since the late 1970s, while the incomes of the richest 10 percent have risen by one-third. The share of total US income received by the top 1 percent has more than doubled from 9 percent in 1976 to 20 percent in 2011. Piketty believes that this recent trend is not an unfortunate historical exception but the natural tendency in advanced capitalist countries. He argues that in wealthier countries, the rate of return on capital (i.e., income earned on investment) will outpace the overall rate of economic growth, so that income growth will continue to accrue to the rich—that is, unless strong countermeasures are introduced, such as much higher marginal income tax rates.

As important as Piketty's ideas are, they focus on the most advanced capitalist countries and have less relevance for today's developing countries. He says little about middle-income countries, and nothing at all about the world's poorest countries. As we have seen, in the majority of developing countries, the incomes of the poor and the middle class are growing, which differs significantly from the pattern of stagnation experienced by the middle class in wealthier countries that drives his research. Piketty's insights have less to say about countries in which the dominant economic issues continue to be increasing agricultural productivity, shifting workers over time to manufacturing and services, managing natural resources, and building effective economic and political institutions.

The overall tendency for income inequality in developing countries over the last two decades has been no clear tendency at all. In some developing countries, inequality is getting worse, but in many others it is getting better. In most, there has been little change, even alongside rapid economic growth and poverty reduction.

Inequality Across Countries

Many people have in mind a different concept when they discuss global inequality: the differences *across* rather than *within* countries, and the gaps in average incomes between rich and poor nations. During the most heated debates about globalization in the late 1990s and early 2000s, critics claimed that the gap between the richest and poorest countries was ever widening.

That gap *was* growing, at least until recently. Before the industrial revolution, the differences in average incomes across countries were much smaller than today. When growth took off in Europe and North America in the nineteenth century and most of the twentieth century but lagged elsewhere, the gap between the richest and poorest countries grew very wide, very quickly. Over these two centuries, the world went from being much poorer but much more equal to much richer but much more unequal.

However, that pattern has begun to change. Since so many poor countries have been growing so fast for the last two decades, the income gap between rich countries and most poor countries has been *shrinking*. How much it has been shrinking and when it started depend on a debated question: In measuring intercountry inequality, should all countries count the same, or should large countries count more? In the first system, China and India count the same as Burundi and Belize; in the second, China and India count for a lot, and Burundi and Belize don't count much. It matters (or at least it used to) which you choose.

Figure 3.5, constructed by economist Branko Milanovic, depicts both stories.[23] The bottom line shows intercountry inequality based on unweighted averages (every country counts the same), and the top line represents the weighted average (proportional to population size). Each measures inequality using the Gini coefficient in which 0 means perfect equality and 1 means perfect inequality. The two lines show very different patterns—at least until around 2000.

FIGURE 3.5: GLOBAL INEQUALITY—GETTING BETTER

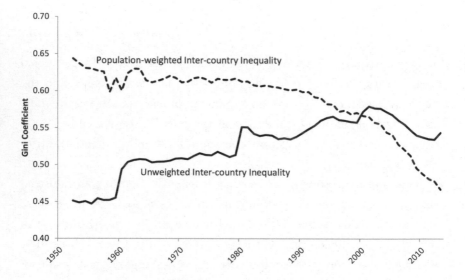

Source: Branko Milanovic, "Global Income Inequality by the Numbers: In History and Now—An Overview," policy research working paper 6259, World Bank, Development Research Group, Poverty and Inequality Team, Washington, DC, November, 2012.

In the unweighted measure, inequality did not change much from 1960 until around 1980. Then it *worsened* until the mid-1990s. Since there was essentially no economic growth, on average, in developing countries for twenty years between the mid-1970s and mid-1990s, it makes sense that the gap between rich and poor countries would widen, and so it did. A lot.

Starting in the mid-1990s, as with so much in developing countries, the pattern began to change. Rising inequality slowed, and beginning around 2000, it began to improve: the poorest countries began to grow faster, on average, than the richest countries and close the income gap.

The second line—the population-weighted average—differs significantly in the earlier years. Between 1960 and 1990, this measure of inequality changed little, even during the 1980s, when so few developing countries were growing. That's because several of the countries that *were* growing fast were enormous, including China, Indonesia, and South Korea. Starting in 1990, as growth accelerated in both China and India, and as dozens of other developing countries joined the growth club, inequality began to improve, quickly.

The huge differences between the two lines during the 1980s and early 1990s led to what Milanovic called "the mother of all inequality disputes."[24] Just when debates were taking off around the effects of globalization, one measure showed global inequality worsening, while the other showed it improving. There was a big fight about which version was right, driven less by the merits of weighted and unweighted averages, and mostly by what people wanted to believe about globalization.

While many people still make the claim that inequality across countries is worsening, it is no longer true, no matter how you measure it. A simple statistic makes the point: in 1994 the average income in the world's 20 richest countries was more than eight times larger than the average in 109 developing countries; by 2011, the ratio had closed to around six. That's still a large gap, but it's also a big drop in less than two decades. And those are unweighted averages. If we counted China and India by their population size, the gap would be shrinking much faster.

There is a long way to go, to be sure, and not every country—nor every person in developing countries—is catching up. But across the majority of developing countries, incomes have risen substantially since the mid-1990s. For the first time since the industrial revolution, the income gaps between the wealthiest countries and the majority of the poorest countries are beginning to close.

FOUR

MORE CHILDREN NOW LIVE—AND LIVE BETTER

Ekwefi had suffered a good deal in her life. She had borne ten children and nine of them had died in infancy, usually before the age of three. As she buried one child after another her sorrow gave way to despair and then to grim resignation. The birth of her children, which should be a woman's crowning glory, became for Ekwefi mere physical agony devoid of promise. The naming ceremony after seven market weeks became an empty ritual. Her deepening despair found expression in the names she gave her children. One of them was a pathetic cry, Onwumbiko—"Death, I implore you." But Death took no notice; Onwumbiko died in his fifteenth month. The next child was a girl, Ozoemena—"May it not happen again." She died in her eleventh month, and two others after that. Ekwefi then became defiant and called her next child Onwuma—"Death may please himself." And he did.

—*Chinua Achebe*, Things Fall Apart[1]

IN 1960 MORE THAN 22 PERCENT OF ALL CHILDREN BORN IN DEVELOPING COUNTRIES died before their fifth birthdays. Imagine, or at least try: more than one out of five children, dead before age five. For the poorest people, of course, the death toll was even higher: one of three in some countries, and even one of two in some poor villages or regions. Some newborns never had a chance, passing away within hours or days of birth. Others made it for a year or two until being struck down by malaria, pneumonia, diarrhea, or malnutrition. Those who lived faced an enormous disease burden, mostly from diseases that we can control or cure. Few children had a chance to go to school or get a decent education, especially girls. The vast majority of people did not have access to clean water and basic sanitation.

But that was then. Over the last several decades, there have been dramatic reductions in infant death, huge gains in fighting a range of killer diseases, big improvements in access to clean water and sanitation, and sizable increases in primary and secondary school enrollments. As with other dimensions of development, there is still far to go, and not everyone has been reached. But the facts are clear: *there has been much greater progress in health and access to education across the world's poorest countries over the last several decades than ever before.*

The rate of childhood death has been falling *fast*. Between 1960 and 2012, the share of children dying before their fifth birthday fell from 22 percent to 5 percent—a decline of three-quarters in just five decades (figure 4.1). Out of every four children that died before their fifth birthday just a few decades ago, three now live.

These changes translate to *millions* of saved lives. In 1990, 12.7 million children died before their fifth birthday from preventable causes; by 2013, the number was down to 6.3 million, and it continues to drop fast.[2] *More than 6 million more children a year are living today who would have died senselessly just two decades ago.* That's per year: since 1990, more than 60 million children around the world have lived to adulthood who previously would have died far too young.

Sometimes people worry that the reduction in child death just means bigger populations and more adults living in deeper misery. However, as we will see later in the chapter, this view is incorrect. Reducing child mortality is one of the most important ways to reduce fertility rates and, over time, slow population growth. As child death declines, mothers have fewer children. As fertility rates decline, the children they do have tend to lead healthier and better-educated lives. The reduction in child death is not just good for the individuals involved but is also enormously important for the larger process of development and improved well-being. When combined with the dramatic changes in poverty reduction, income growth, access to education, and reduction in violence (which we will see in the next chapter), not only are more children living, but they are living much better.

FIGURE 4.1: MORE CHILDREN LIVE TO AGE FIVE

Percentage of Children Dying Before Age Five (All Developing Countries)

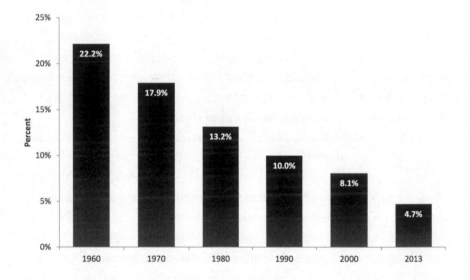

Source: World Bank, World Development Indicators.

The gains in health go well beyond children. Far more mothers are surviving childbirth. In 1990, out of every 100,000 live births around the world, 420 mothers died in childbirth. (In the United States, the figure is around 20.) Just two decades later, in 2011, that number was down to 238—almost cut in half. The number of maternal deaths worldwide has fallen by more than 250,000 per year since 1990, which means that several million fewer mothers have died in childbirth. There are still too many maternal deaths, but developing countries are on the right path.

There's more. A wide range of diseases are doing less damage:

- Malaria mortality declined 47 percent between 2000 and 2013, saving 4.3 million lives, most of them children under five years old.
- AIDS-related deaths fell from 2.4 million in 2005 to 1.5 million in 2013, a decline of 35 percent *in just eight years.*
- Tuberculosis deaths fell 33 percent between 2000 and 2013, saving more than 4 million lives.
- Diarrhea killed 5 million children a year in the early 1990s, but by 2013 the number was down to 760,000.[3]

The improvements in health among the global poor in the last few decades are so large and widespread that they rank among the greatest achievements in human history. Rarely has the basic well-being of so many people around the world improved so substantially, so quickly. Yet few people are even aware that it is happening.

MALIA AND ROSA

My wife, Carrie, and I saw the beginnings of these changes firsthand when we were Peace Corps volunteers in what was then Western Samoa in the 1980s. One of our friends was a wonderful woman named Malia, who along with her husband, Sione, had, at the time this story begins, eight children.[4] They all lived in a small hut, no more than forty feet long and twenty feet wide, in the traditional Samoan style with a thatched roof supported by about a dozen wooden beams made from the trunks of coconut trees, and no walls. They were poor, living off the meager income Sione earned from selling taro and other crops grown in their plot of farmland, several miles up the slopes of the inland mountain range. They didn't have much in terms of material goods, but Malia had a bright outlook, abundant energy, and plenty of courage.

One day Carrie went to visit Malia and found her in tears. Child number nine was on the way, and Malia couldn't bear the thought. Sione had not allowed any birth control, and Malia was beside herself with worry. She sensed that, at age thirty-two, with eight children already, this next birth was going to be risky, and she was right.

Carrie did some asking around and learned that a new clinic had opened in a nearby village, and it had a midwife on staff. She and Malia went for a visit. Within minutes, the midwife recognized that Malia's was a high-risk pregnancy and recommended that she start taking iron folate tablets, come in for monthly checkups, and, most important, deliver the baby in the clinic, not at home. Malia said thanks, but this was not going to fly—Sione might agree to the tablets and the checkups, but not to the birth in the clinic. Tradition was tradition: Samoans began life on the floor of the family home, not in some sterile clinic in another village. She saw little chance that he would agree to break custom and allow the child to be born anywhere but at home.

In some countries, the big issue for safe births is the lack of a nearby clinic, the absence of a road to get there, or the dearth of trained health care workers. Many women die just because they have no way to get to a clinic. Sometimes the issue is prejudice and bigotry, where workers or patients scorn lower-caste women when they arrive at health facilities. In others, the problem is just plain poverty: the family doesn't have the money to pay for the visit. In Malia's case, the constraint was cultural values and traditions. Culture dictated that women have lots of children, and they have them on the floor at home, and that's the way it is.

The wise Samoan midwife had worked with traditional husbands before, and she knew what to do. She proceeded to take the time to visit Malia in her home, with Sione sitting nearby, for prenatal consultations. Over time she gained Sione's trust, and pointed to the examples of a few local courageous path breakers who had chosen the clinic over the floor. Sione shifted his views.

When the big day came, they piled Malia into the back of a neighbor's dilapidated pickup truck and got her to the clinic on time. Beautiful baby Rosa arrived a few hours later.

Then the trouble began. Ten minutes after the birth, Malia suddenly began hemorrhaging. She was slipping fast. It could have been a disaster, but she was in a clinic, which had a trained birth attendant and the right equipment and supplies. She lived. At home, she would have died.

Small things. A new clinic in a nearby village. A midwife on staff, skilled not only in delivering babies but also in working with recalcitrant husbands. A husband who, gradually, was willing to modify his view about what he thought was right. A healthy baby, still thriving today as an adult (and now a mother herself). And a courageous—and determined—mother (also still alive today, with no additional children) able to bring her baby home and care for all nine of her brood.

LONGER LIVES, FEWER BIRTHS

Malia's story has been repeated in various forms millions of times in recent decades, increasingly so as technology spreads, knowledge grows, clinics are built, health workers are trained, and attitudes change. Millions of lives blossom and thrive in a world where today there is much less extreme poverty.

The roots of the recent gains in health in developing countries stretch back more than two centuries to the improvements in health in Western Europe that began with the Enlightenment and the industrial revolution.[5] The combination of increased incomes, improved nutrition, better living conditions, education, and public health interventions for clean water and improved sanitation led to rapid gains in mortality and morbidity. One of the most important breakthroughs was the discovery in 1855 by the London physician John Snow, known now as the father of modern epidemiology, that deadly cholera was being spread by contaminated drinking water.[6] Snow's work, alongside that of several others, led to the development of modern germ theory. This knowledge and the public health interventions it spurred were central to the reductions in child death and improvements in health in Western Europe. The development of vaccines, antibiotics, and other medicines further accelerated progress. Life expectancy in England jumped from around forty years in 1850 to seventy years a century later.[7]

Initially, these gains were far from global. They were centered almost exclusively in Western Europe, North America, and a few other places such as Australia and New Zealand. Few people in the rest of the world saw much improvement. A huge health gap emerged, mirroring the huge gaps in wealth, education, and other aspects of human welfare that arose in the nineteenth and twentieth centuries. The rich countries saw enormous gains, while poor countries were left behind.

This dynamic began to change in the middle of the twentieth century. Following the end of World War II and the European colonial period, knowledge about good health practices, alongside critical medicines and vaccines, began to spread to developing countries. Child deaths began to fall, disease morbidity began to decline, and life expectancy began to increase, even in most of the world's poorest countries.

The combination of the dramatic declines in infant mortality, reductions in maternal mortality, and fewer deaths from malaria, tuberculosis, measles, and other diseases is translating into much longer and healthier lives. Whereas in 1960 the typical person born in a developing country could expect to live around fifty years, today their grandchildren will live sixty-five years, as shown in figure 4.2. People born today in developing countries can expect to live one-third longer, on average, than their grandparents just two generations ago. In many developing countries, they can expect to live even longer. Life expectancy at birth in Chile is now a hardy seventy-six years; Vietnam has reached seventy-three years; and Algeria and Jordan, seventy-two years.

The increases in life expectancy come from *both* the reduction in child mortality and the progress in fighting diseases that affect older adolescents and adults. Without question, the most dangerous years of life are the first ones. The most dangerous day of any life is the first day. If a child lives to age five, his or her chances of living a long and healthy life improve considerably. Life expectancy for someone who reaches age five in developing countries is now a total of around sixty-nine years, up from sixty-one years in 1960.[8] Together, the figures on life expectancy at birth and contingent on reaching age five show that more than half the gains in life expectancy at birth are because of the declines in child mortality, and the remainder from reductions in disease and other gains in health that have been achieved for people at older ages.

FIGURE 4.2: PEOPLE ARE LIVING LONGER

Life Expectancy in Developing Countries

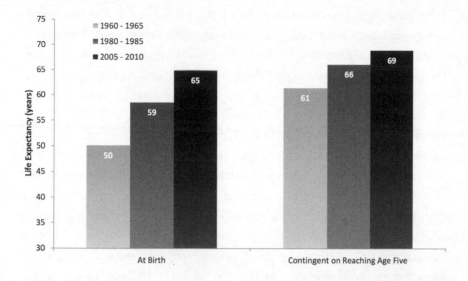

Source: "Life Expectancy at Exact Age," in *World Population Prospects: The 2012 Revision*, United Nations.

In part, longer and healthier lives are due to big advances in basic nutrition and reductions in hunger. The Food and Agriculture Organization of the United Nations reported that 200 million fewer people were living in chronic hunger in 2013 compared with 1991, a 20 percent reduction in two decades. *The share of people living in chronic hunger fell from nearly 24 percent to 14 percent*—still too high, but a significant reduction in just twenty years. Importantly, the share of people living in hunger fell in every region of the world. At the same time, the shares of both stunted and underweight children have also fallen.[9]

Food production grew rapidly in the 1960s and 1970s as a result of the Green Revolution: the introduction of new seeds and fertilizer technologies that increased rice, wheat, and other grain yields dramatically, especially in Asia. Food production grew more slowly during the 1980s, but since the early 1990s, the pace has accelerated again. Over the last two decades, annual food production has increased by more than 50 percent.

Part of the improvement in nutrition comes from the increase in average incomes; as incomes have grown, people have been able to buy more and better food. At least as important has been increased knowledge about good nutrition, related to the education of girls (as future mothers), which has translated into better diets and increased attention to the basic nutrition of infants and small children. It is not just nutrition: the share of people with access to clean water has increased from 70 percent to over 80 percent, and the share with access to improved sanitation facilities has increased from 50 percent to 60 percent.

There is still a long way to go. Upward of 50 percent of remaining preventable child deaths—3 million children a year—are due to malnutrition.[10] As many as half of all adolescent girls in some countries are stunted, increasing risks of complications in pregnancy and poor fetal growth. However, nutrition levels are rising steadily around the world, adding to the gains in health.

As people are healthier and living longer, fertility and population growth rates are beginning to fall. In the early 1960s, women in developing countries gave birth, on average, 6 times, and, of course, for some women it was many more. But fertility rates have been dropping steadily. By the mid-1980s, the average was down to 5; in 1997 it was 4; and by 2010, it had reached 3.25 births per woman. This rate is still well above the so-called replacement rate: the fertility rate at which adults essentially replace themselves with their children (which varies from 2.1 in industrialized countries to 3 or higher in some developing countries because of differences in mortality rates among women of child-bearing age[11]). The good news is that for hundreds of millions of women in developing countries, the fertility rate is almost half of what it was for their grandparents.

In turn, these changes are beginning to affect population growth rates. At first, as people lived longer and health improved, population growth rates soared. From 1960 until around 1987, population growth in developing countries averaged 2.4 percent per year—a rate at which populations double every thirty years. Starting in the early 1990s, population growth rates began to fall in many countries around the world, so that since 2003, the rate has averaged around 1.6 percent per year. The change coincides with the economic and political turnaround ignited by the end of the Cold War, the wave of new technologies, and deeper global integration. As fertility rates continue to drop in the future, world population growth will continue to slow. Partly because of the improvements in health in the world's poorest countries, global population is now expected to peak sometime around the end of this century, and then to decline.

The progress toward better health and longer life has hardly been smooth or automatic. Sometimes individual countries or regions within countries have slipped backward because of conflict, political upheaval, the emergence of new diseases, or mismanagement. One of the most infamous examples of a big step backward was China's Great Leap Forward. Mao Tse-tung's misguided attempt to force rapid industrialization and extract food supplies from the countryside led to widespread famine and the deaths of more than 40 million people from starvation. The wars in Korea in the 1950s, across Central America in the 1980s, and in the Democratic Republic of the Congo over the past two decades all undermined health, not to mention development more broadly.

Two other major disruptions occurred in the 1990s. First, the dissolution of the Soviet Union created economic and social upheavals that undermined health systems in many countries for several years, and progress on health receded before beginning to recover a decade later. Second, the HIV/AIDS pandemic exploded around the world in the 1980s, wreaking havoc in many countries, with extraordinary devastation across central, eastern, and southern Africa.

Largely because of these latter two forces, during the 1990s, life expectancy across all developing countries increased by only about one year, on average, and in several countries, it fell sharply. In Russia, life expectancy fell from sixty-nine years in 1989 to sixty-five years in 2005. Tragically, in Botswana, otherwise a burgeoning success story, life expectancy fell from sixty-four years in 1990 to forty-nine years in 2002 as a result of the HIV/AIDS pandemic.

Fortunately, health indicators have again begun to improve both in the countries of the former Soviet Union and for most countries affected by HIV/AIDS. Life expectancy is on the rise, and although it has not yet returned to its peak levels in the countries hit by HIV/AIDS, it is grow-ing. As a result, the pace of improvements for developing countries as a whole has accelerated. After rising by just one year during the 1990s, average life expectancy in developing countries increased by three years during the first decade of the 2000s.

The threats from major diseases are hardly over, as we have been reminded in recent years by the outbreak of severe acute respiratory syndrome (SARS) in China in 2002, the global eruption of the H1N1 influenza virus (swine flu) in 2009, and the Ebola pandemic that swept through West Africa in 2014. The last, in particular, was a huge setback in three extremely poor countries (Liberia, Sierra Leone, and Guinea) that had been making major gains since the end of civil wars a decade earlier. The speed and intensity of the outbreak and the slow interna-tional reaction exposed major weaknesses in the global capacity to re-spond to new disease outbreaks. Despite these challenges and setbacks, there is no question that the advancements in health in the world's poor-est countries have been nothing short of astonishing.

BETTER HEALTH GOES GLOBAL

One of the most striking characteristics of the gains in global health is how widespread they have been. More than any other development change, the advances in health are reaching nearly every corner of the world. With the changes in income and poverty, several countries are still left behind with little noticeable progress. That is not the case for health. In Myanmar under military rule, the under-five-year mortality rate has been cut in half since 1980, and life expectancy has increased from fifty-five to sixty-five years. In Zimbabwe, the child mortality rate has fallen by one-third in the last decade, and life expectancy— after falling to just forty-three years in the early years of the AIDS pandemic—has rebounded to fifty-one years. In Haiti, child mortality has fallen 60 percent since 1980, maternal mortality has been cut by more than half, and life expectancy has increased from fifty to sixty-two years.

Some of the biggest gains have been in the Middle East and North

Africa, where life expectancy has increased thirteen years, maternal mortality is down by two-thirds, and child mortality has declined a remarkable 80 percent. Every region of the world has seen big gains. In sub-Saharan Africa, the region with the least development progress, life expectancy has increased eight years, on average, since 1980—despite the impact of HIV/AIDS. Maternal mortality is down 40 percent, and child mortality has been cut in half.

Here is the extraordinary bottom line: since 1980, the rate of child death has declined in every single developing country in the world where data are available. *There are no exceptions*.

The long fight has not been won yet. Millions of people—especially in remote rural and mountainous areas—have not been reached by the global advances in health. Poor women and minorities are often excluded from health care services, and violence against women is a major public health threat. Six million children still die from preventable diseases every year: every minute of every day, ten more children slip away because they drank contaminated water, or they weren't immunized, or there was not enough food, or they didn't have a bed net, or they couldn't get antibiotics to fight pneumonia. Death is still all too common in the world's poorest countries.

IS THE DECLINE IN CHILD MORTALITY REALLY SUCH A GOOD THING?

Sadly, and shockingly, some people wonder (usually quietly to themselves, but sometimes out loud) if keeping these poor people alive is such a good thing. The argument goes that it only condemns them to lives of misery and poverty, and just adds to global population growth. A recent online commentary in the *Washington Post* following an interview with Bill Gates on his foundation's efforts to improve child health was revealing.[12] One commenter wrote:

"Gates might be doing what he believes is helpful to mankind. But his efforts are as hurtful as helpful. Why 'save' millions of infants and children in, say, Bangladesh or Nigeria, when they, in their unschooled ignorance will undoubtedly grow up and beget families of eight or ten

additional kids that can't be adequately supported physically, education-
ally economically [*sic*]?"

These reactions are sobering. They reflect a more widely held misunderstanding that saving the lives of the underclass may not be helpful
because doing so will add to population pressures and deepen poverty.
But this view is incorrect: saving children's lives does not lead to faster
population growth. In fact, over time it does the opposite: saving children's lives contributes to *slower* population growth.

At first, this pattern seems counterintuitive, but it makes perfect
sense. When lots of children die, parents tend to have more children to
compensate. They tend to overcompensate because they want to ensure that enough of their children survive to adulthood to take care of
them when they grow older. When child death rates are high, parents
face great uncertainty about how many will survive, so they have extra
children, and population growth soars. The full story of the relationship
between infant mortality and fertility is complex, and is influenced by
culture, economic opportunities, family planning options, war, and other
factors. But there is a clear relationship: where infant death rates are
high, fertility and population growth rates also tend to be high. Mali,
Chad, and Congo each has among the highest child mortality rates in
the world, with more than 16 percent of children dying before age five.
All three have some of the highest population growth rates, exceeding
2.6 percent per year.

As more children begin to survive to adulthood and the risks of child
death decline, parents begin to expect that their children will live to
adulthood, and so they have fewer children. In El Salvador, Mauritius,
and Thailand, less than 1.5 percent of children die before age five, and
population growth in all three is around 0.5 percent per year or less.
Even after controlling for other factors that influence fertility, it's clear
that saving children's lives leads to lower population growth.

To see how these changes interact over time, let's focus on Indonesia, where my wife and I lived for four years, and where she has worked
extensively on maternal and child health. As you can see in figure 4.3,
child mortality declined in the 1960s. Beginning in 1968, fertility rates
started to fall, aided by government investments in family planning and

education. Then, after continuing to rise initially, population growth began to decline rapidly after 1970. Between 1970 and 2012, Indonesia's fertility rates dropped from 5.5 to 2.4 births per woman, and its population growth rate fell from 2.6 percent to just 1.2 percent. The reduction in child mortality was not the whole story behind the drop in population growth, but it was an important part of it.

FIGURE 4.3: AS MORE CHILDREN LIVE, POPULATION GROWTH SLOWS

Child Mortality, Fertility, and Population Growth in Indonesia

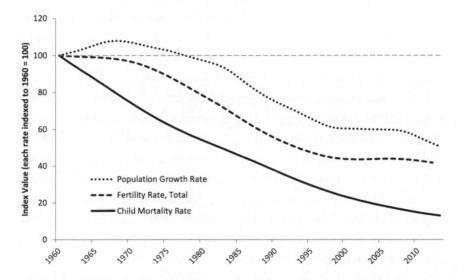

Source: Author's calculations, based on data from the World Bank's World Development Indicators. The figures in the graph are indexed values, with the original population growth, fertility, and child mortality figures recalculated to equal 100 in the base year of 1960 for all countries.

MORE CHILDREN IN SCHOOL THAN EVER BEFORE—ESPECIALLY GIRLS

One of the most important forces behind long-term development is education and skills development. There are many reasons why Europe and North America began to develop rapidly in the nineteenth century, but education was central to this process. Economist Richard Easterlin made this point thirty years ago in an article titled modestly "Why Isn't the Whole World Developed?":

"The worldwide spread of modern economic growth has depended chiefly on the diffusion of a body of knowledge concerning new production techniques. The acquisition and application of this knowledge by different countries has been governed largely by whether their populations have acquired traits and motivations associated with formal schooling."[13]

In developing countries, education plays a similarly important role, alongside other public investments. The Commission on Growth and Development—a group of highly regarded policy makers, business leaders, and academics, chaired by Nobel laureate Michael Spence—examined an array of factors behind the most rapidly growing developing countries in the world over the last few decades and argued:

"No country has sustained rapid economic growth without also keeping up impressive rates of public investment in infrastructure, education, and health. Perhaps the best protections a government can provide are education, which makes it easier to pick up new skills, and a strong rate of job creation, which makes it easy to find new employment."[14]

Educating girls is especially important, in part because girls and women have been marginalized and discriminated against in so many countries for so long. As a result, the potential for big impact from an underutilized resource is huge. The returns on the first few years of education are particularly large, and too many girls have not even had the chance to begin primary school, much less complete it. The impacts from investing in girls' education go further: ample evidence shows that the health and schooling of children are related to the mother's education, so educating a girl has a multiplier effect across generations. More educated women tend to be healthier themselves, provide better health care and education to their children, earn more income, and have fewer children. Educating girls is at the core of improving individual, family, and societal well-being, and is a powerful lever to lift their families out of poverty.

Until a few decades ago, developing countries had made little progress in the education of either boys or girls. Colonial governments made little effort to build schools and provide teachers or even the most basic resources. At the time of the great independence movements, the majority of people in developing countries were illiterate, and few had the chance to go to school. It takes a long time for countries to catch up in terms of educational progress.

Fortunately, that has begun to change—slowly, steadily, but surely. In the 1960s, only about 33 percent of adults in developing countries were literate. By the late 1980s, the figure had doubled to around 67 percent. Today it exceeds 80 percent. Literacy rates for women still lag behind, but they are improving even faster, from just 58 percent in the late 1980s to nearly 75 percent today.[15]

Tens of millions more children around the world are in school. In the late 1980s, only about 72 percent of primary-school-age children were enrolled in school, but by 2010, it was over 87 percent. The number of out-of-school primary-age children fell from 106 million in 1999 to 68 million in 2008, a drop of more than one-third in just a decade.[16] Think of it: 40 million more children are in primary school today than were just fifteen years ago.

Also, far more of them are completing school. In the 1980s, just 50 percent of girls completed primary school, but today 80 percent are doing so. Girls' secondary school completion rates have nearly doubled from 30 percent in the early 1980s to 60 percent today. Girls are still behind, but they are catching up. The ratio of girls to boys in primary and secondary schools in developing countries was just 84 percent in 1991, but today it has reached 96 percent. In Bangladesh, girls' secondary school enrollment has risen from just over 1 million in 1991 to more than 6 million today. In the twenty most underprivileged provinces in Burkina Faso, the share of girls enrolled in school jumped from 36 percent in 2000 to 55 percent in 2006—a huge increase in just six years.[17]

Harvard economist Robert Barro and Korea University's Jong-Wha Lee have calculated that in 1970, adults in developing countries had completed, on average, just 3.4 years of education. By 2010, that figure had doubled to just over 7 years (figure 4.4). Perhaps the best news is that there have been big advancements among women, for whom the average number of years of schooling has jumped from 2.7 years in 1970 to 6.5 years today.[18]

FIGURE 4.4: MORE PEOPLE WITH MORE EDUCATION

Average Years of Schooling Completed Among Adults in Developing Countries

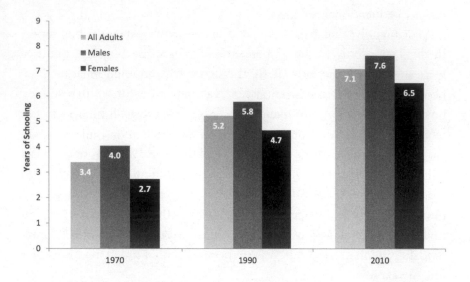

Source: Robert Barro and Jong-Wha Lee, "A New Data Set of Educational Attainment in the World, 1950–2010," working paper 15902, National Bureau of Economic Research, Cambridge, MA, April 2010.

Evidence suggests that investment in education pays off. MIT economist Esther Duflo examined Indonesia's efforts to expand the number of both schools and teachers. She found that the program led to substantial increases in school enrollments and, subsequently, to higher wages after these students left school. Abundant research with larger studies looking across countries over time has found high rates of return on investments in education. Not surprisingly, the returns are highest where there is very little education to begin with, especially the first years of school. Investing in girls' education is particularly important. In 1992 Lawrence Summers, then the chief economist of the World Bank, argued that "when one takes into account all of its benefits, educating girls quite possibly yields a higher rate of return than any other investment available in the developing world." He concluded that giving one hundred girls just one extra year of education would lead to the prevention of

sixty infant deaths and three maternal deaths, and would bring about fertility declines that would avert five hundred births.[19]

However, while there have been big advancements in increasing access to education, there has been much less progress around the *quality* of education. Student skill levels have not improved in step with the advancements in years of schooling. Economist Lant Pritchett, in his book *The Rebirth of Education: Schooling Ain't Learning*, describes the lags in the quality of education in developing countries.[20] Teachers do not always show up, and many are not particularly well qualified. Systems tend to focus on rote memorization rather than on building skills, and test scores show little improvement. Too many children start school only to drop out before finishing, in part because of quality issues. Test scores and other measures of achievement continue to lag. Nevertheless, the global progress over the last two decades is a big start, and, ever so slowly, more children are beginning to get an education.

VIRTUOUS CIRCLES: HEALTH, EDUCATION, AND INCOME

It's not just coincidence that both health and education have improved in the last several decades, and that the two have done so alongside the surge in economic growth. The three are deeply interrelated (although other forces have also been at play, as I discuss below). Advances in education and knowledge help improve health, better health helps improve learning ability, and both together contribute to economic growth. At the same time, increases in income can lead to advances in health and education. Over the last several decades, the improvements in health, education, and income have all supported one another in a positive self-reinforcing cycle, as they have in the West for nearly two centuries.

It's easy to see how better education can lead to better health. Princeton's Angus Deaton argues that "improvements in education may be the single most important cause of better health in lower-income countries today."[21] Education of girls and women is especially important, given their roles as mothers and primary caregivers for their families. Through both school and community education programs, basic

knowledge about good health and hygiene has spread rapidly in recent decades: clean water, properly prepared foods (washing raw vegetables), improved sanitation, and the basic understanding of the transmission of germs and disease.

In turn, better health helps improve educational outcomes. When children are healthy and have adequate nutrition, they are more likely both to attend school and to learn more while they are there. Growing evidence shows that healthier children—as evidenced by greater height and weight—tend to have better learning outcomes. Equally powerful are broader efforts to improve adult health and longevity: the longer people live, the stronger the incentives to invest in education and spend more time in school.

Both health and education build across generations: the healthier and more educated the parents, especially the mother, the healthier and better educated their children. That has certainly been the case across the United States and Western Europe: in three generations, we have shifted from high school being a rarity to a college education being the norm, with each generation becoming healthier along the way.

There are also important interrelationships between income and both health and education. As incomes rise, individuals and families can more easily buy medicines, eat better food, live in higher-quality housing, and pay for visits to the local clinic or doctor's office. They also are more able to pay for school fees, books and supplies, and uniforms. Importantly, as incomes rise, parents are more likely to allow children to go to school instead of making them stay at home to work.

One of my Georgetown graduate students, Brendon Thomas, saw this relationship up close when he was a Peace Corps volunteer teaching at a university in northwest China. His best student, a young woman named Wang Huan, came from the neighboring county of Ning Xiang. Her family had lived there for centuries, scratching out a minimal existence through farming on the dry, wind-blown soil of the Loess Plateau. Not long after Huan was born, with the Chinese economy beginning to boom along the coastal areas, her parents decided to take a huge risk and leave their ancestral home in search of higher wages and greater economic opportunities in the special economic zone of Shenzhen. They

had to leave Huan behind with her grandparents, which was a major sacrifice for everyone. Fortunately, her parents were successful in getting good jobs and earning some money, so they could send her to a better primary school and to the only college in the region. Huan excelled as a student at Longdong College. She was one of the few students to pass a rigorous postgraduate entrance examination, and was admitted to Xi'an International Studies University to study linguistics. Huan hopes one day to return to Ning Xiang after her graduation to help build the rural education system. Huan's parents took a major chance, but it paid off. It's one small example of how China's economic growth is helping to contribute to even stronger education in the future.

This process works not just for individual families but also at a broader level: richer *societies* are more able to build clinics and schools, send more of their children to better schools, and provide the doctors, nurses, midwifes, teachers, and other resources to operate them well. As economies grow, tax revenues grow, and governments can invest more in building strong health and education systems. That's one reason why people in rich countries live longer and healthier lives than those in poor countries: higher incomes typically mean more effective health systems.

At the same time, improved health and education contribute to higher income. Healthier individuals tend to work harder and longer, miss less work, spend less of their money on medicines, and devote less time to caring for sick family members. Public health programs can also create new economic opportunities. Fertile lands open up when disease vectors are controlled, such as the opening of the fertile Terai in northern India when malaria came under control, creating new opportunities for farmers to increase their incomes. The Global Health 2035 Commission—a distinguished group of health and economics experts assembled by the British medical journal *Lancet*—concluded that reductions in mortality account for about 11 percent of recent economic growth in low-income and middle-income countries.[22]

So income matters for improving health and education, and vice versa. But it would be a mistake to think that the improvements in health and education are only about income. They are not.

Let's look more closely at the relationship between income and health, and more specifically the statistical relationship between life expectancy and income and how it has changed over the last few decades. Figure 4.5 shows the so-called Preston curves—named for the pioneering work on this topic by the demographer Samuel Preston—for 1980 and 2012.

The relationship is positive: higher incomes correlate strongly with longer life expectancy, and vice versa. Note that the relationship diminishes in magnitude: the curve is steep at lower levels of income and becomes flatter as incomes rise. The biggest improvements in health occur when incomes are low and rising. That's because at low incomes, the majority of deaths are due to so-called diseases of poverty. Infant deaths, diarrhea, measles, malaria, and infectious diseases are largely preventable, but they devastate the poor. It is not unusual in poor countries for half of all deaths to be children under five years old. But as countries get richer, child death becomes much less common and most deaths occur from chronic diseases affecting primarily older people. Hence, as incomes continue to grow beyond this point, life expectancy continues to rise, but at a slower pace, and disease burdens shift from infectious diseases toward noncommunicable diseases and injuries.

Look what happened to this relationship between 1980 and 2012: the entire relationship shifted up by about five years. *At every level of income—from poor to rich—people are living far longer, on average.* Let's look where income equals $1,000 per person per year (the vertical line on the left). Whereas in 1980 someone with an income of $1,000 might have expected to live around fifty-two years, by 2012, people with *the same income* lived more than fifty-seven years, or about five and a half years longer. For those with incomes of $10,000, life expectancy jumped from sixty-seven years to nearly seventy-two years, an increase of about five years. (At higher levels of income, the upward shift is smaller, reflecting the shift to noncommunicable diseases.[23]) Across the whole range, people with the same incomes are living much longer today than they were just three decades ago. The gains in health over the last few decades far surpass what would be expected from the gains in income alone.

Two other pieces of evidence make it clear that more than incomes are at work in improving health (and a similar story holds for education, although to a lesser extent), as economist Charles Kenny points out in his book *Getting Better: Why Global Development Is Succeeding—and How We Can Improve the World Even More*. First, the gains in health began long *before* economic growth accelerated in the mid-1990s. Even when incomes were stagnating in the 1970s and 1980s, health was improving. Recall that between the late 1970s and the mid-1990s, the average rate of economic growth per person across all developing countries was essentially zero, yet child mortality fell by an average of 35 percent and life expectancy grew by five years. Second, as we saw, in many countries, the gains in health are outpacing the gains in incomes and are reaching countries where growth has not yet accelerated. In countries such as Myanmar, Chad, and Haiti, even when income has stagnated, health has improved.

FIGURE 4.5: LIFE EXPECTANCY HAS INCREASED AT EVERY LEVEL OF INCOME

Income Levels and Life Expectancy, 1980 and 2012

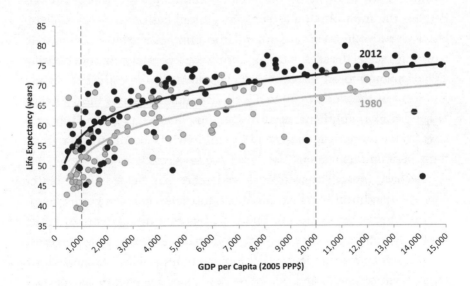

Source: Author's calculations, based on data from the World Bank's World Development Indicators.

TECHNOLOGY, LOCAL LEADERSHIP, AND GLOBAL INITIATIVES

In the chapters that follow, I will discuss in more detail some of the forces behind the gains in health and education, as they parallel the forces behind the gains in income, reductions in poverty, and shift toward democracy. Three are worth highlighting here.

First, technology has been central to the improvements in global health, including both the development of new technologies and the dissemination of older technologies long taken for granted in the West. Basic medicines such as antibiotics are much more widely available, alongside new drugs to treat malaria, insecticide-treated bed nets to ward off mosquitoes, vitamin-enriched foods, antiretroviral drugs to suppress the progression of HIV/AIDS, and other new technologies. The development of oral rehydration therapy (ORT)—a simple salt, sugar, and water solution that prevents childhood death from dehydration and diarrhea—has been one of the most important medical advances of the last century. Diarrhea killed 5 million children every year just two decades ago. Today that number is down to 760,000,[24] and a big reason for the decline is ORT. Perhaps the most important technology of all has been vaccines. There has been a revolution in vaccines and immunization coverage around the world in recent decades, brought about by a combination of scientific advancement and organizational management. In the early 1970s, only 5 percent of the world's children were immunized against the six major target diseases: diphtheria, pertussis, tetanus, measles, polio, and tuberculosis. Today more than 80 percent of children around the world receive these basic immunizations. Vaccines have saved millions of lives.[25]

Second, much stronger local leadership has helped build better education and health systems. In most countries, colonial governments did little to deliver services or build local governance systems, so in the 1960s and 1970s, most developing countries were starting with almost nothing. Over time, leaders in developing countries have recognized the importance of health and education, and have begun to make investments to strengthen them. Public health and education systems in most developing countries are still rudimentary, and too often there are not enough facilities, supplies, and trained educators and health workers. However, as we saw earlier with the story of Malia and the newly arrived local midwife, access to health care is getting better. Most developing countries have more doctors, nurses, and teachers. While there are not as many skilled workers as are needed, and enormous shortcomings remain, the health and education systems in which they work are improving. For example, between 2003 and 2010, Indonesia increased the number of nurses, midwifes, and physicians per person by more than 50 percent, and the number of trained skilled workers attending births jumped by a quarter.

Third, these country-level improvements have gone hand in hand with global initiatives and foreign aid programs aimed at fighting diseases and spurring education. More than any time in history, fighting disease has gone global. The rapid increase in the availability of vaccines required a *combination* of the right technologies, focused global campaigns, robust foreign assistance, and strong local leadership and local funding. Global campaigns often led by the World Health Organization (working with local leaders, and funded jointly with foreign and local funds) eradicated smallpox and have led to significant advances in fighting guinea worm, polio, tuberculosis, malaria, HIV/AIDS, and a wide variety of other diseases. The Global Fund to Fight AIDS, Tuberculosis and Malaria has had a major impact in combatting those three diseases. Much of the progress in vaccines has been supported by major funders like the US Agency for International Development (USAID), the Bill & Melinda Gates Foundation, and the Global Alliance for Vaccines and Immunizations (GAVI). The Millennium Development Goals (MDGs) played a critical role in helping focus attention (and resources) on specific goals to reduce child mortality, improve maternal health, combat HIV/AIDS and malaria, and achieve universal primary education.

The last several decades have brought about a revolution in health among the global poor, alongside the beginnings of major advances in education. People around the planet, even in the world's poorest countries, are living longer and facing fewer killer diseases. More mothers and children are living, fertility rates are dropping, population growth is slowing, and more children are getting a chance to go to school, especially girls. As with the reductions in poverty and the increases in income, not everyone is benefiting from the gains in health and education. Many people still face a range of disease and the risks of childhood or maternal death, and too few are getting a good education, especially the rural poor. The global problem is hardly solved. But the numbers are shrinking. Compared with the late 1990s, today 40 million fewer primary-age children are out of school. Far fewer children are dying young. More than 6 million fewer children die every year than did twenty-five years ago.

That means the day you are reading this page, seventeen thousand fewer children will die than would have been the case in 1990. Most will live longer, healthier, and better-educated lives.

FIVE

DICTATORS OUT, DEMOCRACY IN

Democracy is the worst form of government, except for all those
other forms that have been tried from time to time.
—*Winston Churchill, November 11, 1947*

IN 1904 THE AMERICAN NOVELIST O. HENRY (WILLIAM SYDNEY PORTER) PUBLISHED HIS
classic book *Cabbages and Kings*, which depicts a series of adventures
and misadventures in the rather hapless and dysfunctional Republic of
Anchuria. Henry's Anchuria is a thinly disguised portrayal of Honduras
at the turn of the last century, where he was living on the lam from
American law enforcement. Henry described Anchuria as a "small, maritime banana republic"—and thus introduced the world to the most famous and familiar put-down for developing countries.[1]

Henry's depiction of a banana republic seemed more than a little
prescient just a few years later, in 1911, when a real-life mercenary army
financed by the Cuyamel Fruit Company, a forerunner to the United
Fruit Company, launched a coup d'état against the president of Honduras and installed its own man, with the US government "helping" to

choose the successor. That's right: a coup launched by the mercenary army of a *fruit* company. One that wanted to corner the trade in, well, bananas. If it weren't so tragic for the people involved, the whole thing might have been comical.

Sixty years later, things didn't seem all that much different, at least in a lot of developing countries. During the 1970s and 1980s, most poor countries were run by dictators of one sort or another. Many were incompetent. Others were ruthless tyrants who would stop at little for power or wealth, or both. Coups and countercoups were common, violence a regular occurrence, assassinations a policy tool, and human rights abuses widespread. Democracy was rare. In 1975 just 12 out of 109 developing countries were democracies: India, Botswana, Costa Rica, Mauritius, and a handful of other mostly small countries. The banana republic image of incompetence and failure deepened and endured.

However, the moniker no longer fits, at least for most countries. Since the 1980s, an enormous transformation toward democracy and improved governance has been under way. As of 2012, 56 out of 109 developing countries are democracies, *four times* as many as in the early 1970s. Today, for the first time ever, around half of the world's poor countries are democracies. By "democracies" I do not mean countries that just declare themselves democracies but hold sham elections. These countries meet basic international standards for supporting fundamental rights and freedoms, hold legitimate free and fair elections, and institute checks on power. Yes, many of these new democracies are fragile and flawed, and they wrestle with corruption, the rule of law, and basic rights. In some countries, progress toward democracy and good governance has stalled, and a few have moved backward.

Yet there is no question that there has been an unprecedented improvement in the quality of leadership and governance across the majority of developing countries during the past two decades: greater accountability, fewer dictators, less war and political conflict, fairer elections, and more effective institutions. And like just about everything else, it all really changed in the late 1980s and early 1990s.

THE RISE OF DEVELOPMENT DICTATORS[2]

Fifty years ago, as the great wave of independence movements swept around the world, there was enormous hope for democracy and for competent, accountable governments. Local citizens anticipated that the new governments, led by their own people, would reverse the dictatorial practices of the colonial rulers and bring prosperity and development. Many independence leaders pledged to protect political freedoms and civil liberties, and introduced constitutions that enshrined political pluralism. In some cases, the beginnings of competitive multiparty political systems began to emerge.

However, once the initial postindependence leaders were installed, many of them backtracked on their pledges and seized full control. Nascent pluralistic systems gave way to authoritarianism and military rule. Power became concentrated in strong executives, with weak judiciaries and easily co-opted legislatures. Authoritarian governments brooked little dissent. Most weren't even bothering with a façade of democracy, much less the deeper substance of accountability to their citizenry. They curtailed civil liberties and political freedoms, outlawed opposition parties, seized control of the press, weakened auditing and other public financial control mechanisms, and dismantled the few remaining institutions of restraint and checks on power.

By the mid-1980s, dictators were consolidating their power around the world. In sub-Saharan Africa, the era of the "big man" was at its zenith. General Ibrahim Babangida was in the midst of his reign as president of Nigeria, with the tyrannical rule of Sani Abacha not to begin for several more years. Samuel Doe's disastrous dictatorship in Liberia had several more years to run before it came to a bloody end, only to be replaced by fourteen years of civil war dominated by the even worse Charles Taylor. Mohammed Siad Barre was two decades into his oppressive rule in Somalia. In Indonesia, Suharto ruled with an iron fist and allowed no dissent. General Chun Doo-hwan was in full command of South Korea following his 1980 coup d'état, which had followed the assassination of another dictator, General Park Chung-hee, the previous year. El Salvador was reeling from the combination of intense civil war, the aftermath of the 1980 assassination of Arch-bishop Óscar Romero, and extensive violence and human rights abuses under President José Napoleón Duarte. Argentina's military dictators tried to divert attention from the country's economic collapse by in-vading the Falkland Islands, and ended up as laughingstocks. The list went on.

The politics of the Cold War bolstered the underlying forces be-hind dictatorial rule. Despots with the financial and military support of the United States or the Soviet Union could rule with impunity. The United States supported Mobutu Sese Seko of Zaire, Ferdinand Marcos of the Philippines, the Duvaliers in Haiti, the racist apartheid govern-ment of South Africa, and many others, while the Soviet Union backed the Marxist military junta known as the Derg in Ethiopia, Fidel Castro in Cuba, Kim Il Sung in North Korea, and a series of strongmen across Eastern Europe and Central Asia.

The Soviet Union had no interest in democracy or basic human rights, and in those years, the United States didn't focus much on these issues, either. Washington was far more interested in supporting its allies, no matter what their political persuasion, than building free democra-cies. At times the United States undermined democracy by supporting and in some cases initiating coups d'état, such as in Iran in 1953, Guate-mala in 1954, Congo in 1960, and Chile in 1973, among others. America also stood with those that started as democrats and turned into dicta-tors. Marcos—who originally became president through an election in 1965—declared martial law in 1972 and announced an indefinite exten-sion to his rule. The United States approved, since it needed allies in Southeast Asia in the early 1970s. The US attitude at the time is best captured by what Franklin Roosevelt purportedly said about Nicaraguan dictator Anastasio Somoza García: "He may be a son of a bitch, but he's our son of a bitch."

Perhaps most damaging, the United States and USSR fought violent and deadly puppet wars that engulfed developing countries in the Ko-rean peninsula, Vietnam, Mozambique, Namibia, Angola, El Salvador, Nicaragua, and beyond. Conflict raged, millions died, and institutions were destroyed. In these countries, development was impossible.

In most countries, authoritarian political systems went together with state-controlled economic systems. Buttressed by the powerful currents of global ideologies of the 1960s and 1970s, many governments introduced wide-ranging state controls over the economy, including manipulating exchange rates and interest rates, regulating a vast array of prices, running business empires extending from power companies to grocery stores, subsidizing favored private businesses, expanding the civil service, and introducing controls on imports and exports.

The political and economic systems were deeply intertwined. In the absence of competitive and accountable political systems, authoritarian governments didn't have to work to the benefit of the majority of citizens and could instead funnel economic benefits to their supporters: protected business cronies, the military, civil servants, and urban consumers. Farmers and others with little political clout were vulnerable. There were some exceptions—a few Asian strongmen delivered on economic growth and poverty reduction—but for the most part, political dictatorship and economic malaise went hand in hand.

So in the 1980s, as authoritarian governments tightened their political grip, economic performance plummeted precipitously. The global development crisis was in full swing.

THE WINDS OF CHANGE

Within developing countries, as the economic crisis deepened, authoritarian governments had fewer and fewer resources at their disposal to maintain power. The world economy stalled following the oil crises of the 1970s, and budget and trade deficits ballooned across developing countries, investment declined, and capital fled. As the deficits grew, governments borrowed more and more from abroad and printed more and more money at home, generating huge debts and stoking inflation.

Once Mexico defaulted on its debts in August 1982, everything began to unravel. Banks and other creditors would no longer lend to developing countries. Financing options disappeared. By the mid-1980s, many governments were running out of room to maneuver.

With no place left to borrow, they had no choice: they had to cut spending, reduce subsidies on food and fuel, limit health and education services, raise taxes, and devalue currencies. Many had to turn to the International Monetary Fund to obtain emergency funding and debt rescheduling in return for adopting stringent reform programs. These programs—always controversial because of the tough austerity measures and struggles over the role of states and markets that are at their core— came at a cost, both economic and political. Across most developing countries, the 1980s were a time of tough austerity, little growth, and no development progress. And growing anger.

Austerity meant big political trouble. The autocrats could no longer buy off their friends and supporters. Business cronies lost their subsidies and tariff protection. Civil servants and union workers saw their pay get cut or their jobs disappear. Urban consumers, including the military, watched electricity, food, and fuel prices rise, and had to pay steep black-market premiums for scarce foreign currency. Whereas in the past, dictators could respond to protests by raising civil service wages, cutting university tuitions, or increasing subsidies for food or electricity, they could do so no longer. Many of the groups that had supported authoritarian governments now turned on them. By the late 1980s, political protests were on the rise, often starting with university students and spreading to labor unions, civil servants, and other groups. Across sub-Saharan Africa alone, protests rose from fewer than twenty per year in the early 1980s, to more than fifty in 1990, to more than eighty in both 1991 and 1992, as they spread to more countries and occurred with greater frequency.[3]

Discontent was becoming widespread, and basic beliefs, ideas, and opinions were changing. Civic leaders, business owners, bankers, academics, religious clergy, and others began to recognize the failures of authoritarianism and to call for political and economic change. It was increasingly evident to everyone that, despite the claims of their leaders, the old systems were economically, intellectually, and politically bankrupt.

As discontent was growing in developing countries, the world began to change big-time. Mao's death and China's sharp turn in its economic direction marked the beginning of the retreat of Communism. Then came the collapse of the Soviet Union and the end of the Cold War. Many authoritarian governments lost their patrons, eliminating their funding and the last remnants of their international legitimacy. The dictators could no longer turn to their old friends to bail them out with impunity. Economically, Communism and strong forms of state control lost credibility. Politically, calls for more pluralistic and competitive governments in Eastern and Central Europe began to spread.

Polish labor leader Lech Wałesa's calls for change from the shipyards of Gdańsk echoed around the world. Protests against South Africa's apartheid regime inspired a generation. Cardinal Jaime Sin of the Philippines called on his flock to surround the police and military headquarters in Manila to protect military vice chief of staff Fidel Ramos, who had broken with President Marcos, prompting 1 million people to take to the streets. In Kenya, Presbyterian minister Timothy Njoya created an uproar with a 1990 New Year's Day sermon that criticized the corrupt government of Daniel Arap Moi and called on African governments to follow Eastern Europe and embrace democracy. Archbishop Desmond Tutu called for justice in South Africa and beyond.

Citizens in developing countries were not just angry. They were now emboldened. The push to democracy was on.

THE SPREAD OF DEMOCRACY

Changes began to unfurl around the world. Namibia gained its independence from South Africa and held its first elections for a new assembly the same day that the Berlin Wall fell. In February 1990—just twelve weeks later—South Africa released Nelson Mandela from jail. The apartheid government, propped up for so long by anticommunist fervor, followed its arch-nemesis the Soviet Union into the dustbin of history. Democracy spread across Africa: to Benin, Mali, Zambia, Lesotho, and Malawi. Czechoslovakia launched its Velvet Revolution against the ruling Communist Party just a week after the Wall fell, and just eleven days later, the government announced it would relinquish power and dismantle the single-party state. In 1990 Lech Wałesa became president of Poland. Between the spring of 1989 and the spring of 1991, almost every Communist or post-Communist country in Central and Eastern Europe held competitive legislative elections for the first time in decades. Chile and Nicaragua joined other countries across Latin America that had shifted to democracy earlier in the 1980s. Within a decade, democracy had displaced military rule as the normal form of government across Latin America. South Korea's generals stepped aside in favor of democracy. Student protests in Ulaanbaatar led to the overthrow of the Mongolian People's Republic and the ascent of democratic rule in 1990. In the Philippines, Ferdinand Marcos fled to Hawaii in 1986, and Cory Aquino became the first female president in Asia.

The change was profound, at global, national, and personal levels. People around the world could help select their own leader for the first time. Rev. Liborius Ndumbu of Namibia captured the mood after watching his countrymen vote for the first time:

"They feel like human beings. They have got rights; they are voting for the future of the country. It is very exciting for them. My dream has been fulfilled."[4]

Sierra Leone's 2002 elections following a decade of brutal war brought similar change:

"On Election Day in Sierra Leone," the *New York Times* reported, "the exhilaration was palpable at a camp for those with hacked-off limbs, the injuries that defined the horrors of that country's civil war. Among them was Lamine Jusu Jarka, whose hands were cut off in a rebel attack in 1999. Mr. Jarka voted by stamping his ballot sheet with an ink-stained toe. 'This morning, I am voting for the future,' he said."[5]

These historic changes in developing countries were part of a larger global transformation described famously as the third wave of democracy by the political scientist Samuel Huntington. By Huntington's reckoning, the first wave began in 1820 with the widening of suffrage to the majority of adult males in the United States and continued until 1926, encompassing a century during which twenty-nine countries became democracies. However, Benito Mussolini's ascension to power as Italy's Fascist premier in the 1920s marked the beginning of a two-decade reversal during which the number of democracies fell, ending with just twelve in 1942. Stop and consider that fact for a moment: less than seventy-five years ago, there were just twelve democracies in the entire world.

The second wave was ignited by the Allied triumph in World War II. By 1962, the number of democracies had grown to thirty-six. Once again there was a reversal, and the global total shrunk to thirty by the early 1970s. Huntington marks the beginning of the "third wave" in 1974 with the Carnation Revolution in Portugal, followed soon thereafter by transitions in Spain and Greece. By his counting, the number of democracies around the world reached sixty in 1990.[6]

FIGURE 5.1: DEMOCRACY ON THE RISE

Number of Developing-Country Democracies (Populations Greater Than 1 Million)

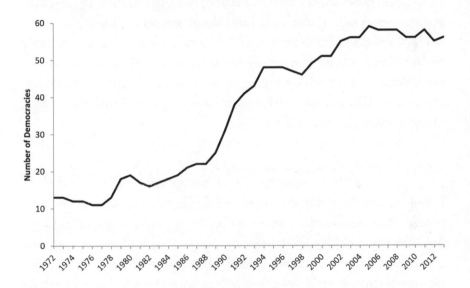

Source: Author's calculations, based on data from Freedom House and the Polity IV Project.

Huntington's numbers include all countries, rich and poor. Among developing countries, the numbers started small but have grown fast. Out of 109 developing countries with populations greater than 1 million, there were just twelve democracies in the mid-1970s, as shown in figure 5.1. The number began to rise slowly in the late 1970s, mainly because of changes in a handful of Latin American countries such as the Dominican Republic and Ecuador. In the mid-1980s, a few more joined the ranks, including El Salvador and the Philippines. The big surge came in the early 1990s—after Huntington's analysis was completed—when several dozen countries dumped dictatorship for democracy. By 1995, there were forty-eight developing-country democracies. While the pace of change has slowed, the number continued to grow in the early 2000s with transitions in Timor-Leste, Ghana, Indonesia, Liberia, Sierra Leone, and Nepal. Today there are fifty-six democracies among developing countries.

Of course, democracy is not universal. Not one of the countries of Central Asia is a democracy. In the Middle East and Africa, only Turkey, Tunisia, and Israel are democracies. About half the countries in Africa remain undemocratic. Cuba, Haiti, and Venezuela do not make the grade, nor do Cambodia, China, or Vietnam. The new democracies are far from perfect. Some countries have regressed to more authoritarian systems. But the fact that not all developing countries are democracies should not overshadow the dramatic change since the 1980s and the largest shift toward democracy in world history.

ARE THESE COUNTRIES REALLY DEMOCRACIES?

When I give talks about democracy in developing countries, I find that people often assume that I am including every country that calls itself a democracy and holds a perfunctory election. People often ask this kind of question: "How can you call Uganda [or Cambodia or Haiti] a democracy just because it had an election?" The answer: I don't. These countries are not democracies, even if they have held elections. Nor is Zimbabwe, just because Robert Mugabe called an election to provide a fig leaf of cover for his brutal rule. Nursultan Nazarbayev's 2011 reelection in Kazakhstan, in which he "persuaded" 96 percent of the population to vote for him, counts for nothing. It's not enough to hold an election and put up the façade of democracy.

There is no single universally accepted definition of democracy or standard way to determine which countries are democracies and which are not. I rely on two of the most widely used and respected data sources: Freedom House's *Freedom in the World* index and the Polity IV Project's data on *Political Regime Characteristics and Transitions.** The two indices capture different but complementary characteristics of democracy. Freedom House focuses on basic *rights*, and scores countries from 1 (the highest level of freedom) to 7 (the lowest level) on two separate indices of political rights and civil liberties. The Polity IV Project focuses on *institutions*, and measures the competitiveness and openness of elections, constraints on executive power, regulations on political expression, the duration of regime type, and other institutional measures of authority and governance. It measures countries on a scale from -10 (most autocratic) to +10 (most democratic). For our purposes, to be considered a democracy, a country must score *both* 4 or lower on its average Freedom House score *and* +1 or above its Polity IV score. Alternative indices of democracy generate similar numbers.[7]

Let me focus on four dimensions of democracy that stand out in the new democracies, and contrast them with other developing countries.

First, individual freedoms and rights are honored and enforced to a much greater degree. The new developing-country democracies are more likely to support basic freedoms of speech, the press, and assembly, alongside other basic civil liberties and political rights. The improvement in respect for basic rights and liberties in the new democracies is seen in the Freedom House numbers. The average score for the democracies dropped from around 5 in 1976 to 3.2 today— a big change of 30 percent. In some countries, the change has been even more dramatic. During General Augusto Pinochet's rule in the late 1970s, Chile registered a terrible score of 6 (of 7) on Freedom House's combined score for political rights and civil liberties, but today

*Freedom House is a U.S.-based nongovernmental organization that conducts research and advocacy on democracy, political freedom, and human rights. The Polity IV Project is a widely used source of data for political science research that contains information on the strength of democratic institutions for all independent states with population greater than five hundred thousand.

it registers a 1, making it one of the top countries honoring basic rights and freedoms. Following the end of Communism, Albania moved from 7 to 3, and Mongolia from 7 to 1.5. Opposition leaders can speak freely, there are more newspapers voicing a variety of opinions, and far fewer people are imprisoned for speaking their minds. Meanwhile, in the non-democracies, the Freedom House scores have changed little, remaining above 5.

These aren't just abstract numbers. People are enjoying much greater freedoms, as demonstrated by this sentiment following the 2002 elections in Mali:

> "Justice prevails a little more," said Sulamo Djiguiba, a wizened old man who was contemplating democracy on Election Day. "During the military regime, soldiers would just come and arrest us and make us work for the army or on their farms. Now that doesn't exist. We are free. We can go where we like." Ansema Djiguiba, twenty-five, agreed. "The mayor and his representatives come and we have the right to talk about our needs without fear," he said. "And now they have dug wells for us. Some villages have schools."[8]

Second, basic institutions of democracy are stronger and function more effectively. Elections, while not ensuring democracy, are more widespread and, in most countries, are fairer and more transparent. According to the Executive Index of Electoral Competitiveness (part of the Database of Political Institutions compiled by World Bank researchers[9]), in 1990 fifty-two developing countries had either unelected executives, or executives elected with no other candidate running. By 2012, that number had dropped to fourteen. Once elected, fewer executives declare themselves president for life. Today the norm has become that presidents leave when their term is up or when they lose to an opposition candidate. In sub-Saharan Africa, during the 1970s, presidents transferred power to their successor by *legal* means (through a lost election, voluntary resignation, end of term, or natural death) just 25 percent of the time. By the 2000s, it happened 80 percent of the time.[10]

These changes are reflected in the Polity IV Project's Index of *Political Regime Characteristics and Transitions*. The developing countries that are now democracies have moved from an average score of -4 in 1990 to +6 in 2012—a huge jump on its 21-point scale (-10 to 10)—reflecting the improvement in free and fair elections, constraints on the president's power, adherence to rules on transfer of authority, and other major changes. The institutions and rules on the limits of power have become much deeper and stronger, and citizens expect them to be upheld.

In the 1970s, Ferdinand Marcos of the Philippines had the power to declare martial law, suspend the constitution, and rule by fiat. By 1986, the opposition had gained sufficient strength so that when Marcos called a snap election and stuffed the ballot box to win, public outcry forced him from office. This outcome would have been unthinkable just a few years before. After Cory Aquino took office, disgruntled military officers attempted several coups, but they failed, in large part because the public, the rest of the military, and the courts would not go along. Fidel Ramos, who succeeded Aquino as president, attempted to change the constitution and get rid of term limits to keep himself in power, but the public pushed back, and the constitution held. The Philippines is hardly a perfect democracy, and, as with most young democracies (and some more mature ones), there are recurrent issues with flawed elections, corruption, and other problems. But the constitution has held, the courts are stronger, and the military's influence on political outcomes is weaker. The days of dictatorial rule are gone.

Third, the shift to democracy goes beyond the executive branch to include the legislative branch. Legislatures today are more diverse, with multiple parties and much greater competition, at least in emerging democracies. For the eighty-nine developing countries for which complete data are available, only forty-two had multiparty elected legislatures in 1990. By 2012, that number had doubled to eighty-one countries, as shown in figure 5.2. Only a handful of countries now have single-party or unelected legislatures.

FIGURE 5.2: THE RISE OF COMPETITIVE LEGISLATURES

Number of Countries with Multiparty or One-Party Legislatures

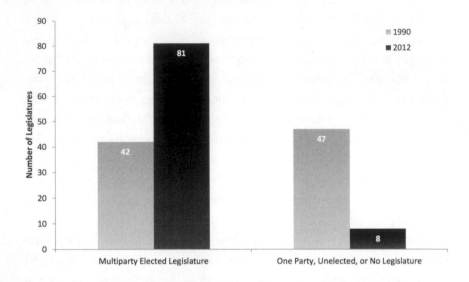

Sources: The Legislative Index of Political Competitiveness, from Philip E. Keefer, "The Database of Political Institutions" (updated January 2013), and Thorsten Beck, George Clarke, Alberto Groff, Philip Keefer, and Patrick Walsh, 2001, "New Tools in Comparative Political Economy: The Database of Political Institutions," 15, no. 1 (September 2001): *World Bank Economic Review* 165–76. The figure includes eighty-nine developing countries for which complete data are available.

Fourth, beyond political leadership, a wide range of citizen groups are much stronger and more active, including civil-society groups, nongovernmental organizations, "watchdog" groups, and other voices aimed at monitoring government actions and improving transparency and accountability. Stanford University political scientist Larry Diamond points out that growing accountability is coming from a combination of older civil-society organizations—student associations, trade unions, and religious bodies—alongside newer groups working for good governance and democracy such as think tanks, bar associations, human rights groups, women's groups, and election monitoring organizations. He describes the changes in Africa this way:

To a degree far beyond the early years of nationhood, the construction of democracy in Africa is a bottom-up phenomenon. Nongovernmental organizations are teaching people their rights and obligations as citizens, giving them the skills and confidence to demand accountability from their rulers, to expose and challenge corruption, to resolve conflicts peacefully, to promote accommodation among ethnic and religious groups, to monitor government budgets and spending, to promote community development, and to recruit and train new political leaders. Civic groups are also working at the national level to monitor elections, government budgets, and parliamentary deliberations; to expose waste, fraud, and abuses of power; and to lobby for legal reforms and institutional innovations to control corruption and improve the quality and transparency of governance.[11]

"But wait a minute," many people say. "Yes, things are better, but how can you call these countries real democracies? Their elections are flawed, there is still corruption, governments are hopelessly bureaucratic and ineffective, politicians and business leaders are far too cozy, and the courts don't always work very well." When I hear this, my first response is to say it's all true. My second is to ask if they are describing Washington, DC, or the capitals of developing countries.

It is true that the new democracies are far from perfect. The shift toward more democratic and accountable governments is a promising beginning but is far from complete. These democracies are fragile, but the history of more mature democracies shows that it takes many years to build the institutions, public attitudes, expectations, checks on power, and other systems required for democracy and accountability to become established. They must be monitored and strengthened. Democracy is a process: there are no shortcuts, and there are many setbacks along the way. Occasionally countries can evolve into strong democracies in a decade or two, especially when they have strong and gifted leaders, a unified society, and a favorable regional context. However, it often takes longer.

It is *hard* for groups of people—much less entire countries—to figure out how to govern themselves. Human societies are flawed. From our twenty-first-century perch, we forget that it took more than a century for democracy to solidify in Western Europe, and the process continues to unfold today. It took the United States 185 years to achieve universal suffrage, with numerous violent conflicts, a bloody civil war, disputed elections, massacres of American Indians, a divisive battle for basic civil rights, recurrent episodes of corruption, countless inside business deals, and human rights abuses along the way. The United States, for all its many strengths, today is far from an ideal democracy. The history of the world's oldest and strongest democracies teaches us that the democratic transition is neither fast nor easy, and that it does not progress in an orderly fashion.

That it can take many years to develop a strong democracy does not mean that today's dictators are off the hook. Nor does it mean that citizens calling for deeper change should back off. The excuses of long-ruling leaders that their societies are not ready for change—like the military leaders of Myanmar or Uganda's Yoweri Museveni—are unconvincing. When I lived in Indonesia in the early 1990s during Suharto's rule, I regularly heard from government officials that Indonesians were not ready for democracy. However, given the chance, in 1998, Indonesians dumped the dictator and moved toward democracy. The transition has not always been easy, but each leader since then has shown a strong commitment to democracy. The successful elections of 2014—just sixteen years after the fall of Suharto—solidified Indonesia as one of the strongest democracies in Southeast Asia.

Unfortunately, even when countries begin to move forward, there are no guarantees of ultimate success. If history is any guide, some of the new democracies will reverse course and return to autocratic rule. Other countries may oscillate for many years, at times moving more toward democratic rule only to lurch back toward more controlled systems, perhaps followed by some reopening, but never quite reaching full democracy or returning to autocratic rule. As political scientist and democracy expert Thomas Carothers has pointed out, democratization is rarely a linear process.[12] Samuel Huntington documented that democratic reversals followed both the first and second waves of global democratization, and so it is not surprising that there has been some backsliding in recent years.

Several developing countries once considered democracies have shifted back into nondemocratic rule, and there are growing concerns about democratic reversals or retreat. Armenia's fledgling democracy took a major step backward after the assassination of Prime Minister Vazgen Sargsyan and seven other officials in 1999, and with the deterioration of basic rights and liberties since 2003. Pakistan has at times flirted with democracy, but reversed course with the 1999 coup d'état in which General Pervez Musharraf overthrew Prime Minister Nawaz Sharif. The Gambia, one of Africa's three democracies in 1989, lurched back to dictatorship after a 1994 coup d'état. Venezuela slid backward as Hugo Chavez extended his rule into a fourth term and oversaw a steady deterioration in political rights and civil liberties. Russia's flirtations with democracy have gone in reverse. Nigeria moved toward democracy after the death of the notorious Sani Abacha in 1998, but flawed elections, corruption emanating from oil revenues, and weak enforcement of human rights have undermined its progress, and the transition remains incomplete (though the successful election in March 2015 may herald a new beginning). Zimbabwe's promising shift toward inclusive democracy in the 1980s following the end of Rhodesian rule came crashing down under the dictatorial regime of Robert Mugabe. Thailand swings back and forth, as the deep institutions needed for democracy have not taken hold. The military coup and imposition of martial law in May 2014 were a major step backward. The promise of democracy in Egypt that began with the dramatic ousting of Hosni Mubarak and the boisterous 2012 elections seems to have been destroyed by the 2013 coup d'état.

These setbacks are serious and have raised important questions about the future of democracy in developing countries. The sharp rise in the number of democracies in developing countries in the 1990s first slowed and then plateaued beginning around 2005. The global averages of Freedom House's scores on political rights and civil liberties have deteriorated in recent years (although most of the regression in scores is in nondemocracies). Surveys show that citizen attitudes toward democracy—strongly favorable in the 1990s—have softened in some countries. The growing ineffectiveness of democratic political systems in some of the most advanced countries—the United States, Japan, and several countries in Western Europe—has undermined the attraction of democracy for many, especially following the 2008 global financial crisis.

However, while some developing countries have gone backward, by far the more common experience for the new democracies has been to solidify the transition over time. Of the forty-eight developing countries that were democracies in 1995, forty-one were still democracies in 2013 (and thirty-three of those countries were democracies continuously throughout that period). *The developing countries that shifted toward democracy in the late 1980s and early 1990s are far more likely to have stuck with it and deepened democracy than to have reversed course.* While some countries have regressed, others have moved forward. The total number of developing-country democracies (out of my group of 109 countries) has remained at around fifty-five since 2002.

Indeed, several promising democracies that began to slip backward in recent years have regrouped and shifted again toward democracy. Senegal went off track in the last years of the administration of President Abdoulaye Wade, with a rapid rise in perceived corruption (particularly around his son) and his attempt to end term limits. But with the election of Macky Sall in 2012, governance has improved. Meanwhile, in neighboring Mali, a 2012 coup d'état undermined two decades of democratic advancement. Thanks to citizen outcry and military assistance from France, the country held presidential and parliamentary elections in 2013, taking a major step toward the restoration of democracy. Some observers feared that Indonesia was beginning to slide from democracy a few years ago, but the 2014 elections and transfer of power put it back on track.

Nevertheless, while the advance toward accountability and democracy is clear for the majority of developing countries, it is far from universal. Many countries have made little progress at all. Sudan, Equatorial Guinea, the Democratic Republic of the Congo, Azerbaijan, Belarus, Laos, and Turkmenistan remain as repressive as ever. Somalia has not had a functioning central government for two decades. Cambodia is far from the dark days of the killing fields under the Communist regime known as the Khmer Rouge in the late 1970s but is also far from being a functional democracy. Haiti has moved forward since the repressive days of the Duvaliers but continues to suffer from massive governance failures.

Most striking, there has been little democratic progress in oil-exporting countries. Algeria, Angola, Equatorial Guinea, Iran, Iraq,

Kazakhstan, Libya, Saudi Arabia, Sudan, Venezuela, and other major oil exporters have failed to transition to democracy. Oil creates intense incentives for elites to keep the spoils for themselves, and conflict erupts as different groups vie for control. It also provides the means by which dictators can buy off opponents. More hopeful, in several countries in which oil has declined in importance, such as Mexico and Indonesia, democracy has strengthened.

THE DECLINE IN CONFLICT AND VIOLENCE

Hand in hand with the spread of democracy have come reductions in war, conflict, and violence. Most people have a hard time believing this fact, since the daily news provides a stream of stories of war, conflict, and violence. But while violence has not ended, there is much less of it. *Much* less.

The Harvard psychologist Steven Pinker documented the decline in global violence during the latter part of the twentieth century and the early twenty-first century in *The Better Angels of Our Nature: Why Violence Has Declined*.[13] He shows, with abundant data and examples from around the world, that despite the pessimistic views to the contrary, we live in the most peaceful time in world history. To give just one example, battle deaths per conflict per year from interstate wars have fallen from sixty-five thousand in the 1950s, to fifty thousand in the 1970s, to twenty-five thousand in the 1980s, to around three thousand in the 2000s. He writes: "So believe it or not, from a global, historical, and quantitative perspective, the dream of the 1960s folk songs has come true: the world has (almost) put an end to war."[14]

Pinker's focus is global, including rich and poor countries alike. Most of the action is in rich countries, since that is where many of the most destructive wars were fought over the last several centuries. But it is clear that conflict has fallen in developing countries as well, especially in the years following the end of the Cold War.

The most dramatic change is in the reduction of civil war. Following the end of colonialism in the 1960s, the number of civil wars in developing countries rose as different factions vied for power. By the 1980s, civil

war was all too common, as economies stagnated, the prices of natural resources soared, and armed opposition groups fought to displace longtime
leaders. In the ten years from 1981 through 1990, there was an average of
nearly thirteen major civil wars going on in developing countries at any
one time—that is, about one of every eight developing countries (figure
5.3).[15] By the early 2000s, the number had fallen by more than half. In
the most recent ten years of data, from 2004 through 2013, the number
was down to around five per year. Civil war has far from disappeared, but
it occurs now in about one in twenty developing countries instead of one
in eight. And, not surprisingly, the number began to fall in 1992. As the
Cold War ended, democracy began to sweep across developing countries,
global trade expanded, and economies stabilized and began to grow.

FIGURE 5.3: CIVIL WARS ARE MUCH LESS COMMON

Number of Major Civil Wars in Developing Countries

Source: Uppsala Conflict Data Program, "UCDP/PRIO Armed Conflict Dataset, v.4-
2014, 1946–2013" (June 12, 2014), Uppsala University, Uppsala, Sweden.

Even more dramatic than the fall in the number of conflicts—and
more important—is the decline in the number of battle deaths from

conflict. To show this change, we need to draw from two data sources, one of which includes data from the 1980s but ends in 2008 (International Peace Research Institute, or PRIO), and another that begins in 1989 but continues through 2013 (Uppsala Conflict Data Program, or UCDP), as shown in figure 5.4.[16] In every year between 1981 and 1988, deaths from conflicts in developing countries (interstate and civil war) exceeded two hundred thousand people. Since then, the annual figure has never come close to that level. From 2002 through 2013, battle deaths have averaged well below fifty thousand per year. *Deaths from conflict in developing countries dropped by more than 75 percent in just two decades.* In countries that are now democracies (many of which were not democracies then), the decline was even greater, from more than fifty thousand per year in the mid-1980s to around five thousand in 2008.

FIGURE 5.4: FAR FEWER PEOPLE DIE IN WAR

Total Number of Battle Deaths in Developing Countries (All Types of Conflict)

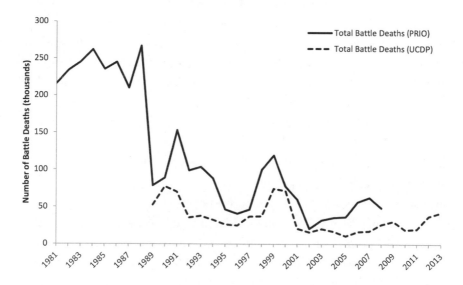

Sources: Peace Research Institute Oslo (PRIO) "PRIO Battle Deaths Dataset Version 3.0" (October 2009); and Uppsala Conflict Data Program "UCDP Battle-Related Deaths Dataset v.5-2014, 1989–2013," (June 12, 2014), Uppsala University, Uppsala, Sweden.

It is not just war. Other forms of political conflict have declined as well. In the ten years from 1970 through 1979, there were thirty-six successful coups in developing countries; in the ten years between 2000 and 2009, there were just seven. There were more than thirty political assassinations per year between the mid-1970s and mid-1990s, but in more recent years, the number is only half as large.[17]

I'm not saying war and violence have disappeared, just as infant death and extreme poverty have not vanished. Conflict continues in Afghanistan, Iraq, Pakistan, Somalia, Syria, and many other countries. Terrorism afflicts many countries, as it has in different forms throughout history. I have no intention of minimizing the horror that families go through every day when their country is at war or when they lose a loved one in battle. In some developing countries, although deaths from war have fallen, organized criminal violence and homicide have gone up, especially in Central America. Nevertheless, across most developing countries, war, violence, and death are much less common than they once were. We are not a world at peace, but we are closer than we once were.

The reduction in violence matters beyond the grisly direct human toll. It also matters for development. Oxford University economist Paul Collier has researched the economic and development costs of war. He shows that countries typically lose about 2.3 percentage points of economic growth each year they are at war. Thus, a seven-year war would leave a country around 15 percent poorer than it would have been.[18] It takes years of hard work and more than a little luck to recover. Once a country goes to war, the odds go up that it will return to war in a deep and destructive cycle. Collier and his associates show that once a war ends, there is about a 40 percent chance that the country will return to war within ten years.[19] Collier describes conflict as a development "trap" in his masterful work *The Bottom Billion: Why the Poorest Countries Are Failing and What Can Be Done About It*, pointing out how conflict undermines economic opportunities and good governance, which, in turn, reduces economic growth and income, which together increase the odds of greater conflict, and so on in a vicious cycle.

Conflict also undermines health and education. War shuts down clinics, hospitals, and schools, and disrupts supply chains for basic drugs and medicines. Disease spreads among refugees. The global effort to eradicate polio has been frustrated by its stubborn persistence in war zones in Afghanistan, Pakistan, Somalia, and Syria.

Conflict also deepens poverty. When conflict rages, economic growth stalls, education stops, public health deteriorates. People living in poverty suffer the most. The World Bank has found that in countries free of major violence, extreme poverty has fallen rapidly since the early 1980s (figure 5.5). Where there is moderate violence, extreme poverty falls some, but not nearly as much. In countries that have experienced major violence, there has been no change in extreme poverty rates, despite the historic declines in the rest of the world. The figure shows that after twenty-four years (1981 to 2005), poverty rates were 22 percentage points lower in the countries without major violence. Major violence costs a country about 1 percentage point of poverty reduction every year. Over a decade or two, it's devastating.

FIGURE 5.5: VIOLENCE AND POVERTY

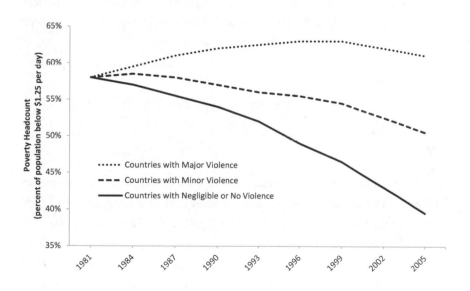

Source: *World Development Report 2011, Conflict, Security and Development* (Washington, DC: International Bank for Reconstruction and Development/World Bank, 2011), p. 60.

But it can be worse. Much worse. Consider the sad case of Liberia, as described by President Ellen Johnson Sirleaf:

> Riven by a tragic history of ethnic conflict, exclusionary politics, and authoritarian rule, Liberia plunged into violence in the 1980s and was nearly destroyed by a senseless civil war. An estimated 270,000 people were killed—about one in 12 Liberians—and hundreds of thousands more fled their homes. Families were uprooted, communities were destroyed, and infrastructure was left in ruins. Children spent more time at war than at school. The warlords used violence and intimidation to loot our national assets, smuggle diamonds, and traffic in arms and drugs. Anguish and misery were everywhere.[20]

The economy collapsed into ruins. GDP fell an unbelievable 80 percent, and poverty skyrocketed. Before the outbreak of the war in 1987, about 30 percent of Liberians lived in extreme poverty. Nine years later, it was 99 percent. In other words, essentially everyone left in Liberia in the midst of the war was living on the edge of subsistence. In the World Bank's database, since 1981, no other country has recorded a poverty rate approaching that of Liberia in the mid-1990s.

CAN POOR COUNTRIES REALLY BECOME DEMOCRACIES? HOW ABOUT ASIAN COUNTRIES? OR MUSLIM COUNTRIES?

Pessimism about the spread of democracy has a long history.[21] Since democracy's beginnings, people have claimed that it was suitable only for certain groups of people: Europeans, or Protestant Christians, or the rich. These claims usually came either out of a sense of pessimism about the possibilities of progress for the world, or from an arrogant belief about the superiority of the West. Out of German sociologist Max Weber's belief in the fundamental power of the Protestant work ethic came the argument that Catholic countries could never become capitalist or democratic, since their ultimate allegiance was to the Pope. Then, as more Catholic countries became democracies, the argument evolved that it was a Christian ethic and wouldn't work in non-Christian countries. Historian Arthur Schlesinger Jr. and others argued that democracy was ultimately a Western European idea and wouldn't work elsewhere. Others made a similar argument from a different starting point, suggesting that Confucian societies could never become democracies. Lee Kuan Yew, the long-serving prime minister of Singapore, claimed that "Asian values" and democracy couldn't mix. Many have claimed that democracy was possible only in middle-income and rich countries. Poor countries need not apply.

They've all been wrong.

Let's start with the idea that poor countries could not become democracies. Even the great Samuel Huntington was pessimistic on this front. When he wrote *The Third Wave: Democratization in the Late Twentieth Century* in 1991, only a handful of developing countries were democracies. He found the prospect of a rapid spread of democracy to developing countries to be unlikely. As he put it:

"Most wealthy countries are democratic, and most democratic countries—India is the most dramatic exception—are wealthy. In poor countries democratization is unlikely . . . The conclusion seems clear. Poverty is a principal—probably *the* principal—obstacle to democratic development."[22]

Huntington's comments partially reflected the idea of "authoritarian transition"—that is, that economic growth under an authoritarian leader would come first, and democracy later. His caution is understandable. After all, before the early 1990s, few of the world's poorest countries had become democracies, with the exception of India. Those that transitioned in the early 1980s were not the poorest countries, but middle-income countries such as El Salvador and the Philippines. American political scientist Seymour Martin Lipset argued, as part of "modernization theory," that democracy was much more likely to occur in countries that had achieved at least moderate levels of education and income, and that had formed a large middle class.[23] To become a democracy, a country had to develop economically, or so the story went. This idea was not just popular with academics but also provided convenient cover for authoritarian leaders making economic progress, who argued that democracy could wait: Park in South Korea, Suharto in Indonesia, Pinochet in Chile, and so on.

Yet when Mali became a democracy in 1992, it had an income per capita of just $300 (in constant price 2005 US dollars), making it one of the poorest countries in the world. Nepal's income was just $230 per person in 1990 when King Birendra Bir Bikram Shah Dev began a political transition. Timor-Leste launched its long-awaited independence in 1999 with an average income of $430, and Malawi made the jump in 1994 with an average income of barely $200. Today twenty-two democracies have average incomes below $1,000, the World Bank's cutoff that it uses to define "low-income countries," and fifteen of those have average incomes below $500.

Never before in history have so many low-income countries become democracies so quickly. Developing countries are in the midst of an enormous experiment in how societies govern themselves, based on the big idea that people do not have to have a certain level of education or income to make smart choices about their own leaders and hold them accountable. And it is happening right in front of our eyes.

What about Lee Kuan Yew's argument that democracy is incompatible with Asian values? India and Japan dented that argument long ago. More recently, South Korea, Taiwan, Mongolia, Nepal, Timor-Leste, the Philippines, and Indonesia have blown it away. Singapore is inching closer to becoming a democracy. That some Asian countries have not yet transitioned to democracy—such as China, to which I will return below—does not undermine the reality that so many other Asian countries have adopted democratic systems.

The argument about Asian values is reminiscent of the earlier debates about Confucianism and capitalism. Weber argued that countries with Confucian cultures could not achieve successful capitalistic development. Now that several such countries have become capitalist race engines, some scholars argue that it is precisely because of Confucian cultures that they are so successful. In discussing this rapid turnabout in views, Samuel Huntington asked, "In the longer run, will the thesis that Confucianism prevents democratic development be any more viable than the thesis that Confucianism prevents economic development?

Arguments that particular cultures are permanent obstacles to change should be viewed with a certain skepticism."[24]

The Nobel Prize–winning economist Amartya Sen—himself from Asia—never had any patience with Lee's Asian-values argument. As he saw it, "Any attempt to choke off participatory freedom on grounds of traditional values (such as religious fundamentalism, or political custom, or the so-called Asian values) simply misses the issue of legitimacy and the need for the people affected to participate in deciding what they want and what they have reason to accept."[25]

Even in China, there have been important changes. Mao Tse-tung was, in effect, the last of the emperors. He ruled with complete authority and, like his predecessors, ruled for life. China today is far from the days of imperial rule. Deng Xiaoping led China for only about fourteen years (1979 through about 1992, although his influence continued for many years thereafter), and while he was never officially head of state, he was indisputably China's paramount leader, and the first such leader to step down voluntarily from power rather than rule for life. He resigned the last of his formal positions—as chairman of the Central Military Commission of the Communist Party—on the morning of the same day that the Berlin Wall fell: November 9, 1989. Since Mao's death, the average tenure of the chairman of the Communist Party has been just seven years. In just a few decades, China has moved from de facto imperial rule to a form of term limits. At the same time, Chinese citizens have more freedoms than they once had, especially on the economic side, although personal freedoms remain highly restricted. To be sure, full power rests with the party, and there are few checks and balances. China is far from a democracy, but it has taken some important steps away from autocracy toward somewhat more accountable government. "Asian values" seems to be a rather elastic concept.

Similar arguments have been made about religion. The fallacy that Catholic countries could not become democracies was put to rest by the transformations in Portugal, Spain, Costa Rica, El Salvador, Brazil, Chile, the Philippines, and many other countries. Ah, but surely democracy is suitable only in Christian countries? Senegal, Indonesia, India, Nepal, Japan, Mali, Mongolia, Turkey, and many others invalidated that canard.

Today many argue that democracy is incompatible with Islam. Too many Westerners assume that the small but violent radical fringe of fundamentalist Islam represents Islam more broadly, which is false. While I claim no expertise on Islam, I lived for six years in two predominantly Muslim countries—The Gambia and Indonesia—and while some small elements of radical Islam existed, they were on the extremes and far from representative of the mainstream. It may be true, as former US ambassador to the United Nations Jeane Kirkpatrick argued, that radical Islamic fundamentalism is incompatible with democracy, but Western radical ideas of Communism, Fascism, Nazism, and radical forms of Christianity—such as those espoused by the Ku Klux Klan and many white supremacist groups—are also incompatible with democracy.

The argument that democracy won't work in Muslim countries writ large is hard to sustain following the historic democratic transitions in Indonesia, Turkey, Bangladesh, Senegal, Niger, and several other countries, as incomplete as those changes may be. In Tunisia, in early 2014, the National Constituent Assembly voted overwhelmingly to approve a new constitution that provides the foundation for a full restoration of democracy. Parliamentary elections were held in October 2014, and presidential elections—the first free and fair presidential elections since the country gained its independence in 1956—followed in November and December, with Beji Essebsi winning in a runoff.

The slightly more proscribed version is that democracy is not possible in Arab countries in the Middle East. Here the jury is still out. America's disastrous foray into Iraq, portrayed as an attempt to install democracy (among several other justifications), was in the end a major setback for global democracy. The invasion undermined the credibility of the United States and ultimately gave greater influence to decidedly nondemocratic regimes in the neighborhood—most importantly Iran. Egypt's nascent attempt at democracy with its 2012 elections was shattered by the poor design of political institutions, ineffective and divisive leadership, and the military coup in 2013, which sent a chilling message throughout the region that democracy isn't worth trying. However, the right lesson from Egypt is not that democracy failed, but that there was *not enough* democracy. The protestors in Cairo's Tahrir Square succeeded in getting rid of Hosni Mubarak, but not Mubarak's government apparatus or his military. Democracy requires more than elections. It requires accountable institutions, enforcement of basic rights, effective judicial systems, and civilian control over the military, which Egypt sorely lacked.

Transitions to democracy are rarely fast or smooth. It took decades—with many protests and failed uprising and much violence and backsliding along the way—for Communism to crumble and for democracy to begin to grow in its wake. Transitions in the Middle East are likely to follow a similar timeline, and perhaps take even longer.

DEMOCRACY AND DEVELOPMENT

So now we come to the final argument. Is democracy really so important for development? Some of the fastest-growing developing countries today are nondemocracies such as China, Vietnam, Uganda, Ethiopia, and Rwanda, following the pattern set in the 1970s and 1980s by South Korea, Taiwan, Singapore, and others. These countries have performed spectacularly well in facilitating income growth, poverty reduction, improved health, and better education, at least in recent years. They are an inviting model. I recently had dinner with one of the most widely respected financial leaders in the world. After hearing me talk about the emerging democracies and their good but not stratospheric GDP growth rates of (only) around 5 percent to 6 percent per year, on average, he wanted faster growth. He summed up the draw toward economically successful authoritarian governments this way: "I'd still rather have Lee Kuan Yew."

It's tempting to buy into the idea that a benign dictator is the best way for countries to develop. I saw this story line play out firsthand when I spent four years as a resident economic adviser in the Indonesian ministry of finance in the early 1990s. Indonesia's economic progress was undeniable: rapid growth, big reductions in poverty, and vast improvements in health care and education. However, there were brutal elements as well: strict restrictions on freedoms, disappearances and killings of political opponents, blatant corruption without consequences, and widespread political repression. For some people (typically those not at the wrong end of the torture rod), it seemed worth it. Many felt it was *necessary*. Someone had to instill order, even if it was harsh, to achieve development.

This belief was held widely across Asia in the 1970s and 1980s. At the time, the evidence seemed to back it up. Only a few developing countries were making rapid progress in those days, and most fit the model of benign dictator: Singapore, South Korea, Taiwan, Indonesia, Malaysia, and Thailand. India, the great example of a developing-country democracy, was floundering. Botswana and Mauritius were the only two developing-country democracies making much progress, and they were so tiny, they seemed irrelevant.

The argument that authoritarianism is superior to democracy at achieving development has a much older pedigree, of course, dating back to the beginnings of democracy, when it began to threaten monarchies and other authoritarian governments. During the Great Depression, critics in the United States on both the left and right assailed the economic meltdown as a consequence of failed democracy, and pointed to Italy and the Soviet Union as examples of the superiority of illiberal systems. In the 1950s and 1960s, the Soviet Union was seen as an economic juggernaut that was sure to outperform the West, just as China is seen today.

During my years in Indonesia, I regularly heard the story that people wanted development, and they didn't care much about democracy. But when the Asian financial crisis erupted in 1997, citizens seized the opportunity to rise up, at great personal risk, and throw out Suharto. It turned out, contrary to the old argument, that Indonesians cared a *lot* about personal freedoms and holding their leaders accountable. They had just been afraid to say so. They didn't see a trade-off: they wanted *both* democracy and development. Today that's what they're getting, as they are well into more than a decade of vibrant (imperfect) democracy alongside rapid (imperfect) development. Similar changes happened in Korea, Taiwan, and earlier in Japan—all societies in which the old line had been that the people cared only about jobs. But they wanted personal freedom and democracy, too.

There are three problems with the benign-dictator argument. First, from a simple strategic point of view, signing up with a dictator is a risky proposition. Because dictatorships put so few constraints on power, if you want a Lee Kuan Yew, you are at least as likely—in fact, far more likely—to get a Robert Mugabe, Ferdinand Marcos, Mobutu Sese Seko, Jean-Claude "Baby Doc" Duvalier, Idi Amin, Anastasio Somoza, or Islam Karimov. Not to mention the big three who grabbed power on promises that they would lead their countries to economic glory: Joseph Stalin, Adolf Hitler, and Mao Tse-tung. While there are a few exceptions—and Lee Kuan Yew is one of them—most dictators just get nastier over time, and economic performance deteriorates. Then you're stuck with political repression *and* economic disaster.

Second, for most people around the world, freedom is important in and of itself, as demonstrated in Indonesia, South Korea, the Philippines, Chile, Turkey, South Africa, Ghana, Bangladesh, and India. Amartya Sen made this case persuasively in his classic *Development as Freedom*. Sen defines development not in terms of income or poverty or health but as expanding human freedom. He sees the expansion of freedom as both the primary *end* and the principal *means* of development, and argues that because of its intrinsic importance, human freedom should be seen as development's preeminent objective. He sees personal freedoms—and the choices they provide—as the central means through which other dimensions of development are achieved.

Just as we view countries that are successful in achieving progress in some dimensions of development (improvements in health, say) but not in other areas (such as poverty reduction) as falling short in overall development progress, we should see those countries that achieve economic progress but suppress freedoms and participatory governance as less than fully successful. The idea that development does not include freedoms and the ability to select your government is, at best, an incomplete model of development. Personal freedoms and participatory governance are not just adjuncts to development—nice to have but not really necessary—they are central to human and societal development.

Third, the argument that authoritarian governments have achieved better economic performances than the democracies is increasingly hard to sustain. Some argue that there is a trade-off: that some authoritarianism is necessary (or at least advantageous) for securing growth. It is far from clear that there is any such trade-off, especially in the long run, and that rapid growth can come only with the sacrifice of freedom. Sure, China, Rwanda, Vietnam, and several other countries have recorded rapid growth rates in recent years, but so have many democracies, such as Botswana, Chile, Ghana, India, Indonesia, Latvia, Mauritius, Mongolia, the Dominican Republic, Panama, and Georgia. Perhaps their growth rates have not been quite as spectacular as China's, but, by any global historical standard, they have been extremely good. The growth rate for the developing-country democracies since 1995 has averaged 3 percent per capita; for the nondemocracies, it has averaged 2.9 percent—essentially identical. (As per capita growth rates, both of these are high by historical standards.)

While some dictatorships have shined, most others have been disasters. There are ten developing countries that have recorded negative per capita growth since 1995, and all are nondemocracies. Indeed, authoritarian governments are much more prone to disaster than democracies. As Professor Sen argued famously, "No famine has ever taken place in the history of the world in a functioning democracy." Putting aside the debate about whether there might be one or two exceptions to his basic rule (depending largely on how one defines famine), his point holds. He believed the reason was clear: democratic governments "have to win elections and face public criticism, and have strong incentive to undertake measures to avert famines and other catastrophes."[26] Such feedback links are weaker or nonexistent in dictatorships. China's current authoritarian government may be achieving record growth rates, but its predecessor authoritarian government managed to create economic disasters in the Great Leap Forward and the Cultural Revolution. Sen does not argue that democracies solve all the problems of hunger and weak social services automatically—they do not—but that they are much less prone to disasters.[27]

This debate has given rise to extensive academic research on the relationship between democracy and economic growth. During the 1990s and early 2000s, much of that research concluded there was little relationship—in other words, that democracies and nondemocracies tended to have about the same rates of growth after controlling for other factors. That finding is important, as it suggests there is no particular penalty for democracy, as some have argued. More recent research suggests that democracies outperform nondemocracies, especially in the long run. That has been the pattern in sub-Saharan Africa since the mid-1990s.[28] An extensive study by John Gerring of Boston University and his associates found that democracy—especially if it endured and strengthened over time—added about 0.7 percentage points to growth rates, on average, an important addition for countries averaging around 3 percent growth per year. Similarly, MIT economist Daron Acemoglu and his coauthors have concluded that countries that democratize tend to increase their GDP per capita by about 20 percent over twenty to thirty years.[29]

The old argument that authoritarian countries clearly perform better economically than democracies no longer holds up. It appears that the vast majority of people who want development *and* democracy can have both. This is extraordinarily good news. Against all odds, democracy has become the new norm.

PART TWO

THE CATALYSTS

Three major changes in the 1980s and 1990s sparked the great surge of development progress. First, the end of the Cold War and demise of the Soviet Union created a global environment that was much more conducive to development, including a shift toward more open markets, enhanced basic rights and freedoms, less conflict, and greater democracy. Second, globalization and the spread of new technologies opened a wide range of new opportunities for individuals and communities in developing countries to make economic and social progress. Third, new leaders emerged—political, business, social, community—to propel many developing countries to take advantage of these opportunities and move in new directions. This section explores each in turn.

SIX

GOOD-BYE COLD WAR, SO LONG COMMUNISM

If the owners of socialism have withdrawn from the one-party system, who are the Africans to continue with it?

—*Frederick Chiluba, chairman of the Zambia*
Congress of Trade Unions, December 31, 1989

WHEN MIKHAIL GORBACHEV TOOK OVER AS GENERAL SECRETARY OF THE COMMUNIST Party on March 11, 1985, the Soviet Union was in trouble. Its economy had been declining since the 1970s. Inefficient factories were producing poor-quality products that neither Soviet consumers nor foreigners wanted, worker productivity was falling, and agricultural production could not keep up with growing demand. The inevitable weaknesses of state control, central planning, and collectivized agriculture were showing through in nearly every corner of the economy. There were few incentives for hard work or innovation. A popular phrase at the time captured the mood: "They pretend to pay us, and we pretend to work." The government had sharply increased the production of military hardware in the 1970s and 1980s, leading to growing shortages of industrial and consumer goods. Increasing scarcities led to growing imports and mounting debt, and the embarrassment of the Soviets being forced to buy grain from the West. The ultimate failure of the 1979 invasion and long occupation of Afghanistan left the USSR bankrupt, and militarily and politically humiliated. The brief tenures of both Yuri Andropov and Konstantin Chernenko, each less than eighteen months, only added to the uncertainty and the downward spiral.

Gorbachev introduced a wide range of political and economic reforms, but it was too late. The deterioration accelerated following the 1986 disaster at the Chernobyl nuclear power plant. Gorbachev's efforts at reform seemed only to highlight the severity of the weaknesses of the entire system. Just as the USSR was sinking, China's shift toward more market-oriented systems in the 1980s after the death of Mao Tse-tung and the resulting surge forward underscored the message: China's new leaders had essentially announced to the world that its old system had failed. Mao's death was the beginning of the end of Communism. Gorbachev had the last watch.

Gorbachev's political reforms under *glasnost* ("openness") provided Soviet citizens with personal freedoms they had never experienced, including greater freedom of speech and less media control. In 1988 he announced that Moscow would abandon the so-called Brezhnev doctrine and allow Eastern bloc nations to determine their own internal affairs. Calls for change spread across the region. During 1988 and 1989, protest movements swept through Poland, Bulgaria, Hungary, Romania, Czechoslovakia, and East Germany. In August 1989 Hungary, acting on its own, opened its border with Austria. The forces for change could no longer be stopped. By November 1989, the game was up.

If one date marks the turning point in the transformation of low-income countries from decades of stagnation to the beginning of a breakthrough, it is November 9, 1989. East Germany opened its western borders, and the Berlin Wall came crumbling down. Earlier that same day, Deng Xiaoping resigned his last formal post in China's Communist Party leadership as chairman of the Central Military Commission, effectively marking an end to the Chinese imperial tradition (that had been continued by Mao) of leaders holding on to power until death.

Although Deng continued to wield power informally for several more years, a transition was under way. Amazingly, at the same moment the Soviet Union was falling into total disarray, China was beginning a relatively seamless transfer of power amid an economic boom. Unnoticed by all but a few on that same day, faraway South-West Africa—soon to be renamed Namibia—ushered in Africa's shift toward democracy by electing its first National Assembly and gaining its independence from South African rule. Apartheid was about to collapse as well.

The demise of Communism, the end of the Cold War, and the dissolution of the Soviet Union together created a decisive moment in world history: global power structures, economic relationships, and powerful ideas about governance and economics all changed substantially.[1] These tectonic shifts enhanced the global conditions for development, creating new opportunities for major transformation and affecting developing countries in ways that are continuing to play out today. Dictators supported by the superpowers began to fall. Civil wars and state violence began to decline. New leaders came to the fore determined to move their countries in more positive directions. New ideas and ideologies gained prominence. Communism and strong state control lost legitimacy; so did right-wing totalitarian dictatorship. A consensus began to emerge around more market-based economic systems and more accountable, transparent, and democratic governance.

Old barriers that had prevented the majority of people in developing countries from making significant progress were coming down. The gates to new opportunities were beginning to open.

To understand the full measure of what changed in the 1990s, we must go back further in history. Global conditions and power structures had been working against the people in today's developing countries for a long time—long before the Cold War, and, for that matter, long before the Soviet Union or the advent of Communism.

The enormous gaps between today's rich and poor countries emerged centuries earlier when some countries were able to capitalize on the ideas, technologies, and institutions that began to emerge from Europe in the fifteenth century and accelerated after the industrial revolution, while most other countries were not. These changes might have spread further and faster, but for more than two centuries, the vast majority of people living in developing countries were effectively shut out of the opportunities to take advantage of the West's surge because of the power structures of the time: colonialism, imperialism, monarchism, and totalitarianism. Each system was designed to control resources for the benefit of a few. They were rationalized by the predominant ideas of the inherent superiority of one group of people over another based on race, religion, ethnicity, or class, and always backed by military force. The vast majority of people were left out. In some cases, foreigners blocked the way, and in some cases, developing countries' own "leaders" and elites blocked progress. Either way, for most people, opportunities for progress were not available.

THE COLONIAL LEGACY IN INDONESIA

When I lived in Indonesia for four years in the early 1990s, the country was booming. Investment was pouring in, trade was expanding rapidly, the economy was growing, and extreme poverty was falling fast. However, it had not always been that way. For the vast majority of the previous four centuries, Indonesia had been controlled by colonial powers interested in extracting its rich natural resources for their own benefit. A few Europeans got rich, most Indonesians stayed poor, and there was little development.

The Portuguese arrived in 1512 and sought to control—from their newly conquered base of Melaka on the Malay Peninsula—the trade in nutmeg, mace, cloves, and other rare spices found in Indonesia's eastern islands. They set the stage for the Dutch, who took over at the turn of the next century. In 1602 the Dutch parliament gave a monopoly on trade, and on colonial management, to the Vereenigde Oostindische Compagnie (VOC), better known to English speakers as the Dutch East India Company.

The VOC's purpose was straightforward: to profit from the trade in spices and other commodities. Although a private company, it had extraordinary powers, including the authority to form its own army, wage war, create colonies, erect fortifications, appoint governors, and sign treaties in the name of the Dutch. There were, in effect, no constraints on its powers. It was business, law, military, and government all rolled into one. It used those powers ruthlessly, and on a larger scale than any other European organization operating in East Asia. Over the course of two centuries, the VOC sent a million Europeans to Asia on 4,785 ships and exported back home more than 2.5 million tons of Asian goods.[2] It wrested control over the seaport of Ambon in eastern Indonesia, then conquered the small trading town of Jayakarta on the north coast of Java and changed its name to Batavia, a name that remained until newly independent Indonesia renamed it Jakarta in 1949. The Dutch forced local leaders to sign exclusive treaties and to coerce local inhabitants to provide tribute and forced labor. There were no systems to protect individual rights, enforce the rule of law, protect individual or community property, or constrain the power of those wielding the guns. In effect, over the next two centuries, essentially all economic and political institutions were shaped to extract as much as possible from the islands to profit the Dutch.

The VOC went bankrupt in 1800 as a result of massive corruption—an unsurprising problem for an entity with unconstrained power—but the Dutch government was not ready to let go. It took over all of the VOC's possessions and territories and established the Dutch East Indies territory. Indonesia became a formal Dutch colony, and remained so for nearly 150 more years—the same years in which the industrial revolution took hold and spread throughout Europe. The Dutch continued to focus on extraction, with little investment in infrastructure, schools, health systems, or other institutions that might have laid the foundation for development for Indonesians. Their rule continued until the Japanese invasion of 1941 forced them out.

Japanese occupation was hardly better. For many Indonesians, the occupation was a time of torture, sex slavery, arbitrary arrest, and execution. More than 4 million Indonesians died in just four years as a result of the occupation. Just three days after Japan surrendered to the United States and its allies, Indonesia declared its independence on August 17, 1945. The Japanese were gone.

The Dutch, however, weren't finished. Convinced that Indonesia was rightfully theirs, they returned with a vengeance and tried to reestablish their rule, leading to four more years of bitter armed conflict and political struggle. Only in 1949, after intense international pressure, did the Dutch give up their lucrative holdings, recognize Indonesian independence, and head home.

Indonesia had its independence—437 years after the Portuguese first took control. However, Indonesians found that institutions based on four centuries of armed control, violence, unconstrained power, and extraction of rich resources don't change quickly.[3] The country moved essentially from a model of Dutch government control by blunt force to one of Javanese control over the archipelago through force imposed by the Indonesian army. Indonesia's first postindependence leader, Sukarno, tried to maintain control while balancing the power of Indonesian nationalists with the rising power of the Indonesian Communist Party (which, in the early 1960s, was the third largest Communist Party in the world, after those in China and the Soviet Union). He failed, and the country exploded into chaos in the mid-1960s. Major General Suharto took over and imposed even stronger authoritarian rule.

By this point, Indonesia's most valuable natural resource was oil, but even that had long been under Dutch control. In 1880 the colonial government gave exclusive rights to a large plantation in Sumatra to a Dutch tobacco planter named Aeilko Jans Zijlker, and five years later he discovered oil, just as the commodity was beginning to become valuable. He formed a small company that would evolve into the Royal Dutch Petroleum Company and, later still, merge with the British Shell Transport and Trading Company to form Royal Dutch Shell, which today is the single largest corporation in the world (measured by revenue).[4] The Dutch, not the Indonesians, controlled all the related oil facilities in Indonesia for eighty years until they sold them to the Indonesian government in 1965.

Suharto took over in the late 1960s, just as Vietnam was engulfed in war. With the large and growing Indonesian Communist Party, the chaos of the mid-1960s, and the example of Vietnam, Suharto's major objectives were to establish control and stop the spread of Communism. He did so brutally, with the support of the United States, throughout the archipelago and including Timor-Leste, which Indonesia invaded and annexed in 1975 in response to a perceived Communist threat.

Given the history of four centuries of colonial rule, coupled with the conflicts engulfing Southeast Asia in the 1960s and 1970s, it is not surprising that Suharto based his rule on the tried-and-true recipe of strong military power, absolute political control, exploitation of natural resources to benefit a small elite, and no substantive checks on his power. Perhaps a different leader might have opted for more broad-based political and economic systems, but there were few examples of leaders of other countries doing so. Critically, the United States (and, later, Japan) were fully supportive so long as the fight against Communism continued.

Economically, Suharto deserves credit for beginning to open up the economy and provide more broad-based opportunities beginning in the 1970s, far more so than the Dutch had done. Suharto's government built a network of rural roads, encouraged agriculture (especially rice production), and built schools and clinics across the country. When oil prices fell in the 1980s, the government refashioned economic policies to foster the growth in a wide range of labor-intensive manufactured products—shoes, textiles, clothing, furniture, jewelry, toys—that created jobs for millions of Indonesians. As agriculture thrived and manufacturing expanded, incomes grew, poverty plummeted, and health and education improved. The government, and a few select cronies, maintained strict control over oil, gas, gold, tin, timber, and other mineral resources, but it created more extensive opportunities in agriculture and manufacturing. Suharto's government followed the lead of South Korea, Taiwan, Thailand, and Singapore by stimulating economic growth while imposing firm political control. It was only in the late 1990s, with the threat of Communism (and unquestioned US support) waning and the Asian financial crisis exploding, that Suharto fell and Indonesian democracy took root.

Indonesia is just one example. The details of the story lines differ across other developing countries, but the themes are similar. Most of today's developing countries were under some kind of colonial rule until a few decades ago, and had been for a century or more. Those not under colonial controls were under local rule that often was similarly brutal, with a small ruling group extracting resources from the broader population, such as in imperial China. Colonial rule ended in Latin America and the Caribbean a century earlier, but Spanish and Portuguese settlers established local elite rule that seized resources and privileges for themselves and failed to create more widespread development opportunities. Some regimes were far worse than the Dutch in Indonesia, such as the Belgians in the Congo. The most brutal supported the slave trade, which destroyed local institutions and human capital in ways that continue to reverberate throughout Africa and elsewhere today.

One way or another, various institutions of exploitation spread around the world: Spanish resource extraction in Latin America, the British Raj in India, Portuguese and Dutch control of territories in Africa and Asia, French colonialism throughout West Africa and Southeast Asia, and, later, American control through its colonies, territories, and support of various strongmen. Most people in developing countries were stuck.

POSTINDEPENDENCE: MORE OF THE SAME

Even after independence, while a few countries began to move in new directions, most did not. The majority of the new governments—interested primarily in establishing control—adopted, with only slight modifications, the systems and institutions that the colonialists had left behind, just as Suharto did. George Ayittey's brilliant and devastating book *Africa Betrayed* recounts how new dictators took over, and in many cases intensified, the institutions of unchecked power and domination when the colonial powers left Africa. Daron Acemoglu and James Robinson make a similar point in *Why Nations Fail: The Origins of Power, Prosperity, and Poverty*.[5] In Latin America, the problem in the twentieth century was no longer colonialism, but rather that one dictator after another promulgated institutions designed to enrich a small elite.

Two forces bolstered this pattern. First, the departure of colonial powers left a power vacuum with no clear process for choosing new leadership. A variety of groups competed for power: independence leaders, nationalists, Communists, business leaders, and the military, among others. Many countries held elections, but they were elections without democracy—that is, without the critical institutions of rule of law, control over executive power, and mechanisms of accountability. Each group was far more interested in gaining power for itself than installing rules for a fair process. Whoever allied with the military usually won, and the first job was to establish control over other competing interests, and over the country more broadly. The institutions of control left behind by the colonial powers provided convenient means of doing so.

Second, the global superpowers of the 1960s—the Soviet Union and the United States—forced the leaders of the newly independent countries (or the elites controlling older countries in Latin America) to line up with one or the other. They were more than eager to support the military and provide financial might to back new authoritarian leaders, so long as they chose the "right" side. The Soviet Union took firm control in Eastern Europe, Central Asia, North Korea, Cuba, Ethiopia, and several other countries. The United States supported Marcos in the Philippines, Suharto in Indonesia, the military leaders in South Korea, Pinochet in Chile, the Duvaliers in Haiti, Mobutu in Zaire, the anticommunist apartheid government in South Africa, and many others. No one was pushing for open and inclusive governance, protection of basic rights and freedoms, or opportunities for broader economic development.

Where no one won out in the internal power struggles, the global powers backed competing sides that went to war—on the Korean peninsula, in Vietnam, across southern Africa, in Afghanistan, between Pakistan and India, and throughout Central America. In developing countries around the world, violence flared as different sides competed to gain power. Dictators ruled. Development stopped.

There were a handful of exceptions: some developing countries began to move forward, especially where effective leaders emerged, such as in Botswana and several countries across East and Southeast Asia (at least in terms of economics, if not politics). In many countries, it took a generation or more for new leadership to emerge (in Latin America, much longer). Indeed, the surge of development progress in the 1990s coincides with a generational change in the leadership of many of the countries that had gained their independence in the 1950s and 1960s. Many of the immediate postindependence leaders had gained power through their prowess on the battlefield or otherwise ending colonialism. It turned out that most of them were far less effective as political or executive leaders in the newly formed governments. After a generation of failure, it was time for new directions.

It should not be all that surprising, after centuries of dictatorial rule, that it took a generation or more for new systems and institutions to take hold. Throughout Western Europe and North America, the process of building effective institutions of governance took much longer. In the United States, it has taken centuries to create institutions that are only beginning to create equal opportunities for all citizens. When the founding fathers declared that "all men are created equal," they actually meant "all white men who own land." It took several decades for most of the new states to loosen property rules and allow poor men to vote. It took 144 long years for women to get the right to vote, and 188 years to establish full civil rights for black Americans. Along the way, the United States enslaved 13 percent of its population until 1865 (in at least six states, more than 40 percent of the population was enslaved), nearly wiped out Native Americans in what many consider to be genocide, fought a brutal civil war, established systems of uneven protection of basic rights and liberties, and suffered multiple incidents of massive corruption and abuses of power.

My point is not to disparage the United States. Rather, it is to underline that it is hard to establish systems of good governance based on the rule of law and protection of basic rights and freedoms. Centuries of institutions, power relationships, trading partnerships, and other arrangements do not change overnight.

But they do change. Which brings us back to 1989.

The collapse of the Soviet Union sparked some of the most important and dramatic changes in world history. While radical transformation was most obvious in Europe and Central Asia, these changes affected developing countries around the world, in several ways. First, the two superpowers stopped their unquestioned support for some of the world's nastiest dictators. One by one, those dictators began to fall. Second, and related, war and conflict in developing countries began to decline. Third, Communism and strong forms of state control lost all credibility, leading to changing ideas and ideologies, and major shifts toward more market-based economic systems and, in many countries, democracy.

DOWN WITH DICTATORS

Beginning in the 1980s, some of the world's worst dictators began to fall once they lost their unquestioned support from their patrons in the United States or the Soviet Union. Ferdinand Marcos had been losing favor with the United States since the 1983 assassination of longtime opposition leader Benigno Aquino. As the Soviet Union began to open up under Gorbachev and the threat of Communism began to wane, so did Marcos's usefulness to the United States. He was pushed into exile in 1986.

The big changes began in 1989, when dictators across Eastern and Central Europe started to fall. One of the first was Romania's Nicolae Ceauşescu, executed just a few weeks after the fall of the Wall, on Christmas Day 1989 (the only nonpeaceful transition in the region). On December 29 Czechoslovakia elected Václav Havel as its new president. Poland elected Lech Walesa as president in November 1990. Hungary elected a new parliament and sent a hundred thousand Soviet troops home. Within two years, new governments swept into power in Bulgaria, Georgia, Moldova, Ukraine, and several other countries.

The effects went well beyond Eastern Europe. In South Africa, within days of the fall of the Wall, President F. W. de Klerk called together his cabinet to discuss legalizing the African National Congress Party and freeing Nelson Mandela. They did so twelve weeks later. When Mobutu Sese Seko—one of Africa's most ruthless dictators—watched television coverage of Ceauşescu's execution, he reportedly concluded that his own regime was in trouble. He soon announced steps toward "democratization." Augusto Pinochet, who had grabbed power in Chile in a US-supported 1973 coup d'état against the Socialist-Marxist leadership of Salvador Allende, was forced to relinquish power to a new elected government in

December 1989. That same month, the United States invaded Panama, deposed its onetime ally (and former CIA operative) General Manuel Noriega, and put him in jail for drug trafficking. In Benin, Major Mathieu Kerekou, a Marxist who had taken power in a military coup in 1972, called elections after Soviet support disappeared, and in early 1991 he lost in a landslide to opposition leader Nicéphore Sogolo. Ethiopia's brutal dictator Mengistu Haile Mariam saw his power evaporate as the Soviets withdrew, and was driven from office in May 1991. Bangladesh's military dictator General Hussain Muhammad Ershad lost his Western support, and resigned in December 1990. In Mongolia, citizens demanded the resignation of the Communist government, and by July 1990, elections ushered in a new democratic government.

Many transitions took longer. In Indonesia, Suharto maintained his strong control during the early 1990s as the economy boomed. As the global Communist threat receded, however, he found his old friends would not come to his aid during the Asian financial crisis and ensuing economic collapse that began in 1997. He fell from power amid riots and street protests in May 1998. Indonesia shifted to democratic rule somewhat chaotically. Timor-Leste gained its independence from Indonesia a year later, after much conflict and bloodshed. It took a decade, but the events that started in Berlin in 1989 had pushed Indonesia to democracy and given Timor-Leste its freedom.

In some countries, new leaders brought dramatic changes in economic policies and perhaps some improvement in governance, but not democracy—at least not yet. China is the most obvious example, alongside Vietnam, Ethiopia, Uganda, and Rwanda, and others. I'll have more to say about these countries later. While they fall short of providing basic political rights to their citizens, they have created many new economic opportunities and forged income growth and poverty reduction, a major improvement over their predecessors.

The end of the Cold War did not bring leadership changes in all countries. Some of the old men hung on, such as Robert Mugabe in Zimbabwe, Fidel Castro in Cuba, Kim Il Sung (and, alas, his son and grandson) in North Korea, and the generals in Myanmar. In some places, there was a change in leadership, but hardly for the better. Moscow's strong control over Uzbekistan was loosened in 1991, only to be followed by two decades (and counting) of authoritarian rule and human rights abuses under Islam Karimov. Mobutu was pushed out in Zaire, but the new (and badly misnamed) Democratic Republic of the Congo has turned out to be far from either democratic or a republic, and has known little besides war, theft, and abuse since Mobutu's exit. Charles Taylor invaded Liberia in 1989 to topple Samuel Doe, but with the Cold War over, nobody outside the country seemed to care much, and Liberia fell into fifteen years of brutal civil war and destruction before emerging as a democracy in 2005.

There is little doubt: even with these exceptions, the end of the Cold War meant the fall of dozens of dictators—on both the right and the left—and the opening for democracy, much more effective leadership, and new economic opportunities in dozens of developing countries around the world.

OUT WITH CONFLICT

The second and related major effect of the end of the Cold War was a decline in conflict in developing countries. The two superpowers instigated and financed a long succession of puppet wars around the world, starting with Korea in the 1950s, followed thereafter in Vietnam, then reaching to Bangladesh, Mozambique, Chad, Guatemala, Honduras, Nicaragua, India and Pakistan, Ethiopia, and many others. One of the most bizarre wars was in South-West Africa—today's Namibia—in which Cuban troops supported by the Soviet Union fought alongside Namibian rebels attacking from Angola, lined up against South African troops supported by the United States.

In developing countries around the world, violence picked up in the 1980s and early 1990s with the uncertainty surrounding political transitions. But by the mid-1990s, it began to dramatically decline. As we have seen, the number of civil wars has been cut in half, and battle deaths have dropped by three-quarters. The decline in conflict was not universal. Somewhat paradoxically, in some places the political vacuum from the end of the Cold War led to greater conflict, such as the outbreak of civil war in Liberia and Sierra Leone, and Somalia's failure to build a government and its ensuing conflict. The ongoing war in Afghanistan (and its spillovers into Pakistan) is rooted at least partially in the failed Soviet invasion and subsequent withdrawal. Many countries in the Middle East remain mired in recurrent conflict, especially in Syria and Iraq (the latter sparked by the US invasion of 2003). And terrorism is a constant threat in many developing countries. However, the end of the Cold War brought with it a sharp reduction in wars, coups, and assassinations, which, in turn, improved the opportunities for development.

CHANGING IDEOLOGIES

Third, and perhaps most important, ideas and ideologies changed. Communism, totalitarianism, and strong forms of state control lost credibility. More liberal forms of economic and political systems moved to the forefront of world ideas and, for the first time, to the majority of developing countries.

In the early part of the twentieth century, liberal democracy, almost always paired with capitalism, was on the rise. By 1926, as many as twenty-nine countries had become democracies (Samuel Huntington's "first wave"). Other leading countries eschewed democracy and reinforced various forms of long-held authoritarian or state capitalism. Germany under Prince Otto Eduard Leopold von Bismarck, Japan following the Meiji Restoration, and many countries in Latin America following their independence in the nineteenth century all had adopted forms of authoritarian state capitalism that were maintained well into the twentieth century.

In the aftermath of World War I and the onset of the Great Depression, Mussolini's ascension to power, followed by Hitler's rise a few years later—both seemingly with the enthusiastic approval of many of their country's citizens—marked the beginning of the rise of Fascism and Nazism. At the same time, with the overthrow of czarist Russia a few years earlier, Communism was changing from a theoretical construct to an implementable idea. Democracy was in retreat, as intellectuals on both the right and left in the United States and Western Europe (and beyond) questioned the usefulness of both democracy and capitalism as the Depression deepened. By 1942, the number of democracies worldwide had fallen to just twelve. Most other countries had adopted some form of authoritarian capitalism, Fascism, or Communism. Totalitarianism, in one form or another, controlled most of the world.

With the Allied victory in World War II, Fascism and Nazism were defeated. It was at this point that most of today's developing countries began to emerge as independent countries. It should not be surprising that they did not see Western systems as attractive political or economic models. Countries emerging from colonialism, with all of its abuses and its extraction of resources, were not rushing to fashion themselves after the countries that had colonized them. Meanwhile, the Soviet Union was consolidating its power across Eastern Europe and Central Asia, and, in developing countries, attracting followers disillusioned with what they had seen of capitalism. The Soviets gained further credence with the launch of Sputnik in 1957 and their apparent rapid economic and technological transformation. China's 1949 revolution seemed to provide a further example of Communism on the rise (at least at first). Not all developing countries adopted full-fledged Communism, but many introduced systems that borrowed from it with strong political and economic controls. Those that rejected Communism did not see democracy as a viable alternative—many in the elite feared it—and so they introduced various forms of authoritarian or state capitalism. A handful achieved economic success, including South Korea, Chile, Singapore, Indonesia, Thailand, and, later, China and Vietnam, and hence state capitalism retains some legitimacy today. However, the vast majority of countries experienced only economic stagnation, growing poverty, political repression, and deepening human rights abuses.

After several decades of misrule and failure, by the 1980s, people in developing countries were fed up. On the economic side, the obvious failures of strong state control contrasted with the clear economic success in Hong Kong, Taiwan, South Korea, Singapore, and a few other countries, giving more credibility to capitalism and market-based approaches. With China's change in direction and the collapse of the Soviet Union, Communism and strong forms of socialism lost credibility. At the same time, the human rights abuses under so many dictators, including those who had achieved some economic success, led to increasing calls for greater political freedom.

With the Soviets and the Americans no longer backing them, totalitarian governments—both right wing and left wing—began to collapse. Increasingly, local civic, business, religious, and other leaders saw the old systems as intellectually, economically, and politically bankrupt, and began to speak out for change. These calls were echoed and reinforced by an increasing number of people in the West, where the old ideas of racial and cultural superiority that undergirded colonialism and segregation were giving way to broader ideas of equality and freedom. At a time of increased media coverage, global connectivity, and flow of information, the idea that a major transformation was possible spread fast. People around the world could watch in real time as Marcos boarded a plane to flee to Hawaii, Chinese protestors stood up in Tiananmen Square, the Berlin Wall fell, governments in Eastern Europe collapsed, and Mandela walked out of jail.

By the early 1990s, dramatic change had begun, as political scientist and author Francis Fukuyama described in his masterpiece *The End of History and the Last Man*:

> The most remarkable development of the last quarter of the twentieth century has been the revelation of enormous weaknesses at the core of the world's seemingly strong dictatorships, whether they be of the military-authoritarian Right, or the communist-totalitarian Left. From Latin America to Eastern Europe, from the Soviet Union to the Middle East and Asia, strong governments have been failing over the last two decades. And while they have not given way in all cases to stable liberal democracies, liberal democracy remains the only coherent political aspiration that spans different regions and cultures around the globe. In addition, liberal principles in economics—the "free market"—have spread, and have succeeded in producing unprecedented levels of material prosperity, both in industrially developed countries and in countries that had been, at the close of World War II, part of the impoverished Third World. A

liberal revolution in economic thinking has sometimes preceded, sometimes followed, the move toward political freedom around the globe. All of these developments [are] so much at odds with the terrible history of the first half of the century when totalitarian governments of the Right and Left were on the march.[6]

The vast majority of developing countries have launched fundamental shifts to more market-based economic systems, a smaller role for state ownership, fewer price controls, more competition, and much greater integration with global markets. There is much more encouragement of trade and investment, far fewer obstacles to agricultural production, and much greater emphasis (although still not enough) on creating economic opportunities for the poor. Many countries also began to introduce social safety net programs to protect those who did not benefit from more market-oriented approaches. These countries did not embrace full free-market orthodoxy (nor should they have), but in many countries there was a clear shift from strong state control toward market-based systems.

In most countries, the change in ideas and ideologies went deeper than just economics. Voices from developing countries around the world—Mandela, Wałesa, Havel, Aquino, Arias—were not just calling for economic change; they were calling for freedom and increased individual and political rights. Within developing countries, the idea of democracy paired with more market-based economic systems had won out over Communism and authoritarianism.

The change in the big debates is profound. When I first started working in developing countries in the 1980s, the major arguments in the cafés and market stalls were about Communism versus free markets, the lingering effects of colonialism, the risks of populist democracy, and the dangers of multinational corporations. Today the debates are about the best ways to attract foreign direct investment (FDI), how to increase exports and access technology, the most effective ways to reduce corruption and improve governance, and how to deepen and expand democracy. Most, although certainly not all, of the countries that have not embraced liberal democracy make public pronouncements that suggest (at least for show) they want to eventually move toward greater democracy. Across the majority of developing countries during the last two decades, the big debates have been about how to make democracy and market-based systems work better, not whether or not they are fundamentally right.

So the end of the Cold War and the demise of Communism removed some of the major obstacles that had prevented the majority of the world's poorest countries from beginning to make development progress. New ideas emerged about how to organize political and economic systems in ways that would benefit far more people. Some of the development "traps" that had confined progress for so long in developing countries were beginning to ease, unleashing a new era of positive self-reinforcing cycles of development progress.

However, changing the global context was not enough. Developing countries needed the *opportunities* and vehicles to help propel them forward, and strong leadership to drive the process. The big opportunities came from globalization and new technologies. It is to those issues that we now turn.

SEVEN

HELLO GLOBALIZATION, WELCOME NEW TECHNOLOGIES

At the particular time when these discoveries [of the East and West Indies] were made, the superiority of force happened to be so great on the side of the Europeans, that they were enabled to commit with impunity every sort of injustice in those remote countries. Hereafter . . . the inhabitants of all the different quarters of the world may arrive at that equality of courage and force which, by inspiring mutual fear, can alone overawe the injustice of independent nations into some sort of respect for the rights of one another. But nothing seems more likely to establish this equality of force, than that mutual communication of knowledge, and of all sorts of improvements, which an extensive commerce . . . carries along with it.

—*Adam Smith, 1776*[1]

ON JULY 11, 1405, CHINESE ADMIRAL ZHENG HE WEIGHED ANCHOR IN NANJING HARBOR and commanded his great Ming armada to sail southwest and commence a two-year, six-thousand-mile journey that would bring them to today's

Vietnam, Indonesia, Sri Lanka, and, eventually, the Malabar Coast of India. Zheng's fleet was massive, with 317 ships and twenty-seven thousand men, equivalent to the population of a small city. The fleet included 62 enormous *Băo Chuán*, or treasure ships, which measured four hundred feet long and were powered by as many as nine towering masts. European expeditions were paltry by comparison: the three ships that sailed with Christopher Columbus and the four ships that went with Vasco da Gama (both a century later) could have all fit on the deck of just one of the *Băo Chuán*. These huge vessels were the largest wooden ships ever built, and, along with the earlier breakthrough inventions of paper, printing, gunpowder, and the compass, made China the indisputable world leader in innovation and technology. Not to mention global exploration.

Zheng's armada completed seven bold expeditions between 1405 and 1433. The first three voyages crisscrossed East and Southeast Asia to Vietnam, Thailand, Malaysia, Java, Sumatra, Bangladesh, Sri Lanka, and the Maldives, all on the way to their main destination of southwest India. The fourth journey pushed farther, across the Arabian Sea to the Persian Gulf, the Strait of Hormuz, and southern Iran. The next three voyages went farther still, to the great cities of Aden and Mecca on the Arabian Peninsula and south to today's Somalia, Kenya, and Tanzania.

Zheng was not the first to sail these routes, but he was the first to sail them with such audacious scale and force. The ships left China laden with silks, porcelain, spices, gold, and silver, and returned stuffed with precious gems, rare woods, textiles, ivory, minerals, and exotic animals, including camels, giraffes, and zebras. They transported people in both directions, including many a sultan and prince bringing tribute to China. They also carried ideas and knowledge about architecture, religion, languages, plants and animals, food, social practices, systems of government, and many other topics. Frank Viviano of *National Geographic* magazine described the voyages as "a floating Encyclopedia-in-progress for Ming China—a compilation of all worth knowing between Nanjing and Africa."[2] Decades before Europeans launched their major explorations, Zheng had connected Zanzibar to Persia to Nanjing.

Then the voyages stopped. In 1424 the new emperor, Zhu Gaochi, ended the expeditions, persuaded by isolationist courtiers and Zheng's rivals that they were too expensive and that they were diverting attention from pressing domestic matters—especially the rising threat from Mongols to the north. There were also growing concerns that trade would begin to enrich a merchant class that would be hard for the government to control. The next emperor allowed Zheng to sail one last time, but then the great armadas came to an end.

China turned inward. Its maritime expeditions declined in the decades that followed, at the same time the European powers were setting out to explore the world. In 1647 the emperor reinstated the *hǎi jin* laws—literally meaning "sea ban"—that had been imposed and revoked a century earlier, outlawing private sea trade and prohibiting the building of any large ships. Then in 1661 he decreed that all residents along the southeast coast should move fifteen miles inland behind a new border to curb their trade links with rebels in Taiwan. The edict came with lots of rules: "Persons found a few paces over the border line shall be beheaded instantly." If you want to restrict trade, that's a good way to do it.

Liu Yingsheng of Nanjing University, a leading Zheng He scholar, believes that the reversal to isolationism "changed history, stopped short what might have been a very different future for Asia and the world."[3] As China receded into isolationism, Europe went out and conquered the world. By the late nineteenth century, Britain controlled much of the trade in and out of China. It had defeated China in the two Opium Wars, imposed the "unequal treaties," and forced China to sign a ninety-nine-year lease that ceded control of Hong Kong to the British from 1898 to 1997. Far from Zheng He's great armada that traversed the seas, China could not control its own territory.

With the upheaval of the early twentieth century—the end of imperial rule, the long civil war, the emergence of the People's Republic in 1949, the disasters of the Great Leap Forward and the Cultural Revolution—China made little development progress. While there was some slow income growth alongside larger improvements in health, it remained a poor country. In 1970 its income per capita was around $350 (in constant 2005 PPP prices)—less than today's Democratic Republic of the Congo, now the poorest country in the world. China, largely disconnected from the global economy, was no longer a source of innovation and technology. In 1970 its exports accounted for a paltry 3 percent of GDP, the lowest among all developing countries.

Today, just a few decades later, all has changed. China's per capita income is more than $8,000, twenty-three times higher than in 1970 (in constant prices). It has become one of the world's most important sources and destinations for commerce, and, along the way, it created tens of millions of jobs and reduced extreme poverty faster than any country in world history. China is resuming its role as a major incubator for innovation and technology, importing ideas and exporting innovations around the world.

Many factors have contributed to China's resurgence: the decollectivization and opening of the agricultural sector; investments in roads, irrigation, ports, and other infrastructure; high savings rates that encourage investment over consumption; a leadership focused on economic growth; and a high priority on education and health. But there is no doubt that one of the most important forces was its decision to integrate itself into the global economy.

China's exports have jumped from 3 percent to 30 percent of GDP, and its imports have grown nearly as much. It is increasingly buying and selling not just goods but also services, including design, marketing, engineering, architecture, financial, and other services. It is both a source and a destination of capital: foreign direct investment, bank lending, bonds, stocks, remittances, and foreign assistance. Chinese firms now invest in Asia, Africa, Latin America, Europe, and North America, while firms from around the world invest in China. Its boom has become a major impetus for growth in developing countries around the world. Through cell phones and the internet, Chinese citizens have far greater access to information and ideas, even if the government imposes tight restrictions on that access.

China also has reestablished itself as a world leader in innovation and technology. In 1985 there were about nine thousand patent applications in China, accounting for around 1 percent of the global total; by 2012, patent applications had soared above six hundred thousand, and China accounted for 30 percent of the global total.[4] In addition, the

Chinese people can now travel internationally much more easily. Up until the 1980s, it was difficult for Chinese to travel abroad, or for foreigners to visit. When I traveled through China in 1984, visitors had to register with local government officials in every city, who would assign them a hotel. Today Chinese travelers pack airplanes bound for Dubai, South Africa, and Brazil, as well as countless other destinations, and it is easier for foreigners to visit China than many other countries. China's hinterlands remain much less connected to the outside world than its coastal areas, but China's isolation from the global economy is now a distant memory.

CAPITALISM LEAVES ITS WESTERN ENCLAVE

At around the same time that China was beginning to connect with the global economy, dozens of developing countries began to integrate into global economic and political systems. Globalization began to accelerate in the 1980s, but it took off in the 1990s. The earlier experiments by South Korea, Taiwan, Hong Kong, and Singapore in outward orientation and openness were enormously successful, providing examples that contrasted with the failures of countries that had turned inward.

India, Poland, Hungary, Brazil, Chile, Ghana, Turkey, and many other developing countries began to encourage trade—some dramatically, others more gradually. Governments lowered tariff rates, reduced quotas, established export processing zones, streamlined customs clearance, and reduced red tape and bottlenecks, all aimed at making businesses more competitive in global markets. Some went further and subsidized exports, either through direct assistance to selected firms or through undervalued exchange rates that provided extra incentives to exporters. In the 1970s and 1980s most developing countries shunned foreign direct investment from multinational corporations, but in the 1990s they began courting investors.

Changes in the international economic architecture accelerated the process (and as we will see later in the chapter, so did new shipping technologies, especially containerization). Whereas the first seven rounds of trade negotiations under the General Agreement on Tariffs and Trade (GATT) between 1947 and 1980 included only the rich countries, the Uruguay rounds of 1986 to 1993 included, for the first time, the majority of developing countries. The North American Free Trade Agreement (NAFTA) gave a further push to increased trade, especially as it included Mexico as an equal partner. Regional trade agreements—always controversial but always deepening trade and financial links—sprang up in Central America, the Andes, Southeast Asia, and elsewhere.

Based on their previous experiences in the 1960s and 1970s that had brought little good, many people in developing countries were skeptical. Early globalization meant the arrival of foreigners with guns and cannons interested only in extracting resources. Fights over resources and territory led to wars and tragedy. Slavery and colonialism are among the worst manifestations of globalization. Adam Smith recognized the deep inequities in global income resulting from the imbalances in military power back in 1776. Globalization is not inherently a force for good, because unequal power meant that only a few benefitted from it.

But Smith also believed that, eventually, greater sharing of knowledge and increased commerce would begin to rectify those imbalances. After World War II, new opportunities opened for developing countries to begin to integrate into the global economy in more advantageous ways than in the past. Initially only a few countries did. Most were caught up in the power struggles, ideological battles, and physical conflicts of the Cold War. At the same time as the Soviet Union collapsed and more countries began to adopt market capitalism, globalization and new technologies opened major new opportunities for developing countries to begin to move forward.

Deeper global integration has taken many forms: trade in commodities and manufactured goods, outsourcing of financial and technical services, the diffusion of new technologies, much larger financial and investment flows, instantaneous access to information, opportunities for education abroad, improvements in health systems through disseminating knowledge and technologies, and the sharing of ideas—including ideas about political systems and governance and basic rights and freedoms. The spread of democracy is a clear manifestation of globalization.

Most developing countries are far more integrated into the global economy than they were just a few decades ago:

- Total trade as a share of GDP, on average, for developing countries jumped from 66 percent in 1990 to 95 percent in 2012, meaning that trade has increased about 50 percent faster than GDP. (Total trade as a share of GDP can approach or even exceed 100 percent, since it is the sum of exports plus imports.) In 1990 there were twenty-two developing countries in which total trade exceeded 75 percent of GDP; by 2008, the number had nearly tripled to sixty-three.
- International financial and investment flows to developing countries are twelve times larger than they were in 1990 (after inflation), and now exceed $1 trillion per year.
- Foreign direct investment—in which foreign companies make significant equity investments in local companies—in developing countries now exceeds $600 billion a year, up from just $26 billion in 1990.
- Patent applications in developing countries, excluding China and India, multiplied eight times between 1990 and 2012.
- By 2014, there were nearly 7 billion mobile phone subscriptions in the world—almost one for every person on the planet—and more than three-quarters of them were in developing countries. Between 2005 and 2014, mobile phone subscriptions in developing countries jumped from 1 billion to more than 5 billion.
- One in three people in developing countries had access to the internet in 2014 through either mobile broadband or fixed lines, double the number of just five years earlier.
- In 2014 there were 2.3 billion mobile broadband subscriptions in the world—five times more than just six years earlier—and more than half were in developing countries.
- The fastest-growing region for mobile broadband penetration is Africa, which leapt from 2 percent penetration in 2010 to 20 percent in 2014.[5]

THE GLOBALIZATION OF TRADE AND
FINANCE—AND VACCINES

When working well, global integration provides families and businesses in developing countries with more choices, options, and opportunities for progress. For poor people living on subsistence incomes, the availability of cheaper goods boosts their effective income. Whatever income they have goes further. At the same time, integration creates new markets for exports that can accelerate growth and raise incomes. Global supply chains allow firms to specialize more narrowly, build expertise in specific areas, and sell goods and services into larger global markets, all of which helps create jobs. Telecommunications technologies allow developing countries to provide services—such as backroom accounting or call centers—that didn't exist a few decades ago. Integration of capital markets allows firms to attract financing from abroad that they might not find at home. Perhaps most critically, global integration allows businesses and individuals in developing countries to import new technologies and ideas, which help build skills, increase productivity, and grow wages and incomes.

Much of the action of globalization is in trade and finance. Developing countries trade far more goods and services than they did two decades ago: food, pharmaceuticals, consumer goods, computers, machinery, oil, commodities, shoes, toys, clothing, semiconductors, automobile parts, banking and financial services, data entry, and a range of other services. Partly because of revolutions in transportation and telecommunications technologies, trade is much cheaper, and supply chains are now global, with various components of a single product made in different countries and assembled in another. A Barbie doll made in Indonesia may be assembled from plastic pellets from Taiwan, given nylon hair from Korea, and packed in a cardboard box from Thailand.

Developing countries accounted for just 24 percent of global exports in 1990, a share that had dropped during the 1980s as part of the economic malaise. But twenty years later, the share had jumped to 41 percent as businesses in developing countries began to penetrate markets around the world. At the same time, imports to developing countries jumped from 22 percent to 38 percent of the world total as markets at home grew and developing countries bought more from global businesses.[6]

By 2012, total trade involving developing countries was worth more than $14 trillion, compared with just $2.6 trillion in 1990 (in constant 2012 prices), a fivefold increase in two decades (figure 7.1). Once again, it's not just China. Excluding China, total trade quadrupled from $2.4 trillion in 1990 to $10 trillion in 2012. Trade in manufactured products in countries in Eastern Europe, the Middle East, and North Africa grew by 15 percent *each year* between 2000 and 2010, and sub-Saharan Africa's trade in manufactures grew 13 percent per year, both much faster than the world average.[7] Trade has become central to the economies of most developing countries. In 1986, exports from developing countries averaged 27 percent of GDP. By 2012, they averaged more than 40 percent, and imports have risen almost as quickly.

Investment and financial flows have also surged (figure 7.2). The total amount of all international private capital flows to developing countries—direct investment, portfolio investment, bonds, and bank lending—declined during the 1980s in real terms. They more than doubled from $91 billion in 1990 to $215 billion in 2000 (in constant 2012 prices), then expanded more than fivefold to $1.1 trillion in 2012, even after the global financial crisis. Total private capital flows in 2012 were twelve times larger than in 1990, after accounting for inflation.

Ethiopian companies are selling T-shirts in Sweden. Indian companies are buying iron ore mines in Liberia. The Abu Dhabi investment authority is building office towers in Rio de Janeiro. Peruvian mangoes are for sale in my neighborhood grocery store outside of Washington, DC. The American multinational firm General Electric is building a $250 million electrical equipment factory in Nigeria. Korean firms are investing in Mexico. Coca-Cola is available in just about every village of every country in the world. Ugandan flowers are sold on the streets of Rotterdam in the Netherlands. Companies in Cambodia, Bangladesh, Albania, and Costa Rica are competing on global textile and apparel markets. A Brazilian construction company is building a port in Mozambique. Rwanda is positioning itself as a services and information hub for East Africa. Chinese firms seem to be investing just about everywhere, in poor and rich countries alike.

FIGURE 7.1: TRADE IS EXPLODING . . .

Developing Countries Total Trade

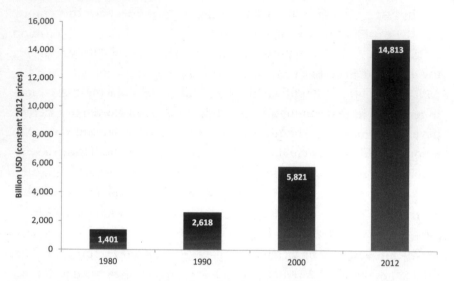

Source: Author's calculations, based on data from the World Bank's World Development Indicators.

FIGURE 7.2: . . . AND FINANCIAL FLOWS ARE RIGHT BEHIND

Private Capital Flows to Developing Countries

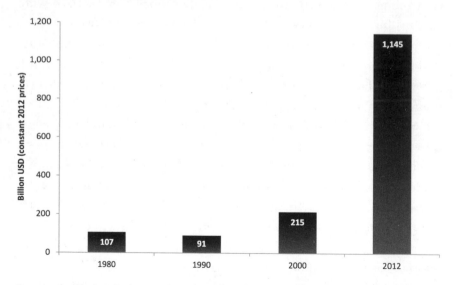

Source: Author's calculations, based on data from the World Bank's World Development Indicators.

Global integration goes well beyond these headline numbers for trade and finance. It includes a host of other global connections that affect health, education, water systems, literacy programs, news broadcasts, and the struggle for basic rights and freedoms.

One of the most important manifestations of globalization is the much greater availability of vaccines for the world's poor. In the early 1980s, vaccines for diphtheria, pertussis, tetanus, measles, polio, and tuberculosis were commonplace in rich countries but mostly absent in developing countries. The rich world had the knowledge and the technology, and the costs were tiny compared with the benefits. However, the vaccines weren't getting to poor countries, in part because rich countries didn't care enough to make it happen, but also because of lack of sufficient financing and, in some cases, obstruction or lack of effort in developing countries themselves. In 1980 only about 11 percent of children in developing countries were receiving the recommended three doses of the combined diphtheria, pertussis, and tetanus (DPT3) vaccine.

Today more than 80 percent of children are fully vaccinated.[8] This change is a direct result of globalization. Getting vaccines to children requires coordinating and connecting a wide range of actors: private businesses researching, developing, and manufacturing the vaccine; the global public health community spreading knowledge and information; a major international organization—the World Health Organization—launching a global campaign; committed public health officials in developing countries working hard to implement the programs; nongovernmental organizations like the Global Alliance for Vaccines and Immunizations (GAVI) connecting the actors; and willing funders in international aid agencies, private foundations (such as the Bill & Melinda Gates Foundation), and developing-country governments providing much of the financing. The result: the number of children in developing countries receiving vaccines jumped from 20 million in 1980 to 200 million in 2012. The globalization of the supply and delivery of vaccines saves millions of lives every year.

WINNERS AND LOSERS

Globalization, like capitalism and democracy, is inherently a disruptive force. It creates winners and losers, economically, politically, and socially. Many of these disruptions are positive: there are more job opportunities with firms engaged in global commerce, literacy programs are communicated via cell phones, ideas about human rights and justice move from one country to the next, knowledge and information spread faster than ever before through the internet, politically connected firms that have lived off of government subsidies must compete or shut down, and local monopolies that charge consumers outrageous prices can no longer do so.

Globalization brings many challenges as well. Both economic theory and abundant evidence show that while all countries gain from trade, all people do not. Workers in occupations that compete with imported goods often lose their jobs when countries open up to less expensive imports. Mexican corn farmers lost out to their American competitors when the border was opened as part of the North American Free Trade Agreement (NAFTA), in part because of the subsidies that the United States provides its farmers. Mexican automobile parts factories may have benefitted, but that provides little solace to Mexican corn farmers—or to US automobile workers. Similarly, firms producing blue jeans in Lesotho have had difficulty competing with firms from China, and many of them shut down. Bolivian shoe producers can't compete against imports. Ethiopian coffee farmers were hurt when Vietnam started growing coffee. Working conditions in factories and on farms can be difficult, whether businesses are globally integrated or not. Sweatshop atrocities are still all too common in both international and local factories, as exemplified by tragic fires in Pakistan and building collapses in Bangladesh. Across high-income countries, factories face stiff competition from emerging markets, and many workers have lost their jobs with little prospect of getting new ones. Even if the gains outweigh the losses, it's not satisfying for someone who has just lost his or her job because of foreign competition to hear that two new jobs were created in other industries.

Increased global trade in commodities and deeper global production processes raise important questions about energy use, resource extraction, and environmental damage, issues that I return to in chapter 12. Prices on global markets can be volatile, especially commodity prices, and businesses operating in these markets are affected by that volatility. A boom in cocoa production in Indonesia can undermine cocoa farmers in Côte d'Ivoire or the Dominican Republic. Developing countries that depend on mineral exports face the challenges of the well-known resource curse: the reliance on exports of a major commodity (such as oil) alters prices, wages, and the exchange rate in ways that undermine production of other exports, hurting workers in those sectors. Whereas economics research shows that developing countries that succeed in expanding exports of manufactures have achieved high rates of growth, those that rely on exports of minerals have recorded much slower (and more erratic) growth. Not all exports are the same, and global integration has different effects on different people.

Global financial markets can be especially volatile. Developing countries were hurt by the 2008 global financial crisis, even though they had nothing to do with creating it. Financial markets can be unpredictable and unstable, especially markets for short-term finance that can move around the globe in seconds. Poorly managed financial integration can wreak havoc, with devastating consequences for people in the middle.

These are big issues, and they are the reasons that people protest globalization, or at least they protest certain aspects of globalization. These concerns echo those that are often voiced correctly about capitalism more generally. While these concerns are often expressed about multinational corporations operating in global markets, many hold true for businesses operating domestically that have little to do with global markets. With capitalism, after centuries of experience, we have learned that while the gains outweigh the losses, many people lose out, and that completely open and free markets do not always lead to efficient, sustainable, or socially desirable outcomes.

Reaping the gains from globalization and minimizing the losses require adept economic management, pragmatism, and appropriate regulation and monitoring rather than strong ideological approaches. Encouraging globalization does not mean that completely free trade and open capital markets reign supreme. Sometimes moderate protection for domestic firms is warranted, so long as it is not pervasive and does not last too long. Competing in global markets requires strong investments in education and skills building. Because of the volatility in capital markets, higher reserve requirements on banks and modest controls on short-term "hot money" capital inflows can lead to better outcomes. People are right to fight hard for improved working conditions and better labor standards, and to be concerned about the environmental impacts of investments, whether those investments originate from domestic or foreign investors. Countries need to design social safety nets, such as unemployment insurance, that can protect workers from the worst effects of the economic dislocations that occur sometimes with global capitalism. Lots of countries talk about building safety nets, enforcing labor standards, and strengthening education and skills training, but few do it well. Opening to trade alone won't work, but opening to trade combined with prudent macroeconomic management, investments in health and education, building infrastructure, creating effective legal and regulatory institutions, and introducing social safety nets can propel progress over time.

Moreover, to some extent, global integration stirs forces that can help remedy issues around low wages and poor working conditions. Operating in global markets can help strengthen workers' skills, which helps increase wages over time as businesses move to more sophisticated products. In countries that are more globally integrated in manufacturing and services, wages tend to increase and working conditions improve over time. Wages have risen steadily since the mid-1990s for workers in traded goods and services sectors.[9] My Georgetown University colleague Ted Moran has shown that garment and footwear factories that are carefully monitored pay wages higher than the national norm. Pressure applied by consumers, such as student-faculty committees at Duke or Georgetown that oversee where college-logo T-shirts and caps are produced, can help improve both wages and working conditions. Today companies like Gap and Reebok pay much more attention to working conditions in the factories from which they buy their products than they once did, in part due to pressure from their consumers. Moran's research found that young women working in plants operated by Nike or Levi Strauss & Co. contractors were more knowledgeable about health issues (particularly reproductive health), tended to marry and have children later, and even enjoyed slightly greater "agency" in choosing their marriage partners as compared with women who remained at home.[10] Tufts University economist Drusilla Brown and her colleagues have found evidence of a "business case" for better worker treatment in developing countries: factories that comply with minimum wage and overtime regulations and have lower incidences of verbal and sexual abuse have higher productivity and earn higher profits than those with worse compliance.[11]

Increasingly the majority of foreign direct investment (FDI) in manufacturing and assembly is not in the lowest-wage sectors. The globalization of industry has become primarily a middle- and higher-skill phenomenon. FDI in emerging markets in autos and auto parts, electronics and electrical products, medical devices, industrial equipment, chemicals, and pharmaceuticals is ten times greater (and growing faster) than FDI in garments, footwear, and toys. In these sectors, foreign firms pay workers two to three times more for basic production jobs and ten times more for supervisory and managerial jobs than for low-skilled work.[12]

Globalization has been, on the whole, a major force for progress in developing countries during the last two decades, and has provided the opportunities for millions of people to begin to escape poverty, increase their economic opportunities and incomes, and improve their health. A good summary of the evidence comes from the Commission on Growth and Development, an international panel of leading economists and financial experts, including two Nobel Prize laureates (Michael Spence and Robert Solow), and nineteen other experts from around the world. This group examined the forces behind the fastest-growing countries over the last few decades. They observed that rapid growth sustained over decades was not possible before World War II, and concluded (in what they call "the central lesson of this report") that this rapid economic growth

> is possible only because the world economy is now more open and integrated. This allows fast-growing economies to import ideas,

technologies, and know-how from the rest of the world. One conduit for this knowledge is foreign direct investment, which several high-growth economies actively courted; another is foreign education, which often creates lasting international networks. Since learning something is easier than inventing it, fast learners can rapidly gain ground on the leading economies. Sustainable, high growth is catch-up growth. And the global economy is the essential resource.[13]

TECHNOLOGY GOES GLOBAL

Perhaps the most important manifestation of global integration for developing countries over the last twenty years has been increased access to technologies. Economists have long understood that technological innovation is the key to long-term growth. The industrial revolution was at its core a technological revolution. But, for reasons I have already discussed, much of that technology did not reach the majority of people living in developing countries.

Not this time around. As developing countries have become more integrated with the global economy over the last two decades, they have been able to take advantage of computers, the internet, cell phones, containerized shipping, cheaper and safer air travel, new plant varieties and agricultural techniques, and new medicines. Part of the importance of the recent global integration of developing countries is that it has taken place exactly when it did: during a period of some of the greatest advances in technology in the last two hundred years. Just as the industrial revolution can be traced to James Watt's invention of the steam engine, which drove innovations and changes across the economic landscape, much of the current technological revolution can be traced back to the semiconductor and the computer, a history that Erik Brynjolfsson and Andrew McAfee recount in *The Second Machine Age: Work, Progress, and Prosperity in a Time of Brilliant Technologies*.[14] There are multiple examples, but I will focus on technological advances in four areas that have been important to developing countries: transportation, agriculture, information, and health.

MOVING GOODS, MOVING PEOPLE

The most important development in integrating global trade during the last century was not the World Trade Organization (WTO) or global trade agreements or lower tariffs. The most important development was a box: a standardized shipping container. Up until the 1950s, goods were loaded and unloaded onto ships in individual boxes, barrels, sacks, and wooden crates, a process that was slow, cumbersome, and expensive, and resulted in a high rate of damaged goods and very inefficient use of space. An entrepreneur named Malcolm McLean developed an idea of how it could be done better. In the 1950s he converted an old World War II tanker into a customized ship with a reinforced deck designed to carry fifty-eight identical metal container boxes that could be loaded quickly and easily and stacked much more efficiently on deck, with little wasted space.

McLean's first trip from Newark, New Jersey, to Houston in April 1956 revolutionized shipping. It took some time to catch on and to standardize the size of the containers and build the port facilities needed to move them efficiently, but a decade later, containers went international, with trips between the United States and Europe. Shipbuilding companies began to build dozens of container vessels, and container ports began to grow. By the late 1970s, container shipping connected Japan with the US West Coast, and Europe with the US East Coast. By the early 1980s, shipping between Europe, Southeast and East Asia, South Africa, Australia, New Zealand, North America, and South America was largely containerized. A decade later, just as the major geopolitical changes were under way, most developing countries began to adopt containerized shipping. Sea-based trade took off.[15]

Shipping costs fell. On the first container ship, the cost to load one ton of goods dropped from $5.83 to $0.16, an astonishing 97 percent reduction. Because containers were sealed, losses from theft and damage also declined, as did insurance costs. Ships could be loaded much more quickly, from 1.7 tons per hour in 1965 to more than 30 tons per hour in 1970. The impact has been huge: one recent research paper found that in industrialized countries, containerization was associated with an eightfold increase in trade over twenty years, and that containers had boosted trade more than all trade agreements in the past fifty years combined.[16] For richer and developing countries alike, lower costs and faster shipping mean that far more goods of higher quality are available at lower prices, and businesses can integrate more fully into global markets.

Then there is air travel. Following World War II, air travel became much more common in North America and Western Europe, but it was the introduction of jetliners in the late 1950s that sparked a boom. The Boeing 707 and Douglas DC-8 doubled the speed and increased the productivity of air transportation, leading to steady declines in airfares. By the 1960s, jet service had been extended to most major world markets. Developing countries began to connect, although the long distances required multiple stops and transfers along the way. With the arrival of the Boeing 747 and other wide-bodied aircraft, that changed, especially with the development of the longer-range 747-400 in the late 1980s. Nonstop flights at reasonable prices could connect New York with Shanghai, London with Johannesburg, Tokyo with Istanbul, and Los Angeles with Santiago. Prices dropped: the price per mile traveled within the United Sates fell by more than half between 1980 and 2005 (figure 7.3), and prices for long-haul flights dropped by even more.

The air transportation revolution has helped connect people and markets in developing countries, albeit unevenly. Businesses that ship small, low-weight products have benefitted enormously. Intel, the world's leading manufacturer of computer chips, relies heavily on air transportation. Its operations in the Philippines receive their inputs and export their products almost exclusively by air. Similarly, horticulture producers in Uganda and Kenya rely on air transportation to fly fresh-cut flowers grown in greenhouses located near their airports to markets in Europe, where the flowers can be sold on the streets the next morning.

FIGURE 7.3: AIR TRAVEL IS MUCH CHEAPER

Real Cost per Mile in the United Sates

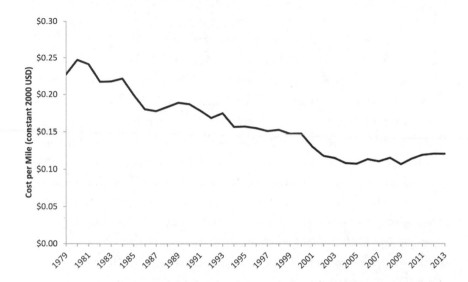

Source: "Annual Round-Trip Fares and Fees: Domestic," Airlines for America.

More important, cheaper airfares mean that people can move much more easily, and with them ideas and knowledge. Global supply chains benefit from managers and engineers connecting on the internet and by cell phones, but also from the ease with which people can move from one city to the next for planning and problem solving. Businesses are much more connected and integrated because people can move so easily. Inexpensive airfares also have been crucial to the growth of tourism. It took Theodore Roosevelt four weeks to get to Kenya to begin his famous safari for the Smithsonian Institution in 1909. Today I can travel to Kenya overnight, at a much lower cost.

However, not everyone has been helped by this transportation revolution. Millions of people live in geographically isolated areas connected only by poor roads or footpaths. The huge advances in global sea and air technologies stand in sharp contrast to the dilapidated roads that are the only means of connection for so many people and communities. These disparities are one reason why there has been so much development progress in some areas and so little in others. There has been huge progress, but there is tremendous potential for even more.

THE GREEN REVOLUTION CONTINUES

No other set of technological changes has been as important to developing countries as the Green Revolution, which continues to benefit the global poor today. In response to growing population pressures in the 1940s and 1950s, scientists and agricultural specialists under the leadership of plant scientist Norman Borlaug developed new seeds, fertilizers, and farming practices that transformed global agriculture, especially in Asia. These discoveries—triggered by cooperative efforts between private companies, the Rockefeller Foundation and the Ford Foundation, international organizations, national governments in developing countries, and international aid agencies (in particular the US Agency for International Development)—led to rapid expansions in food production and gains in nutrition that have been central to the improvements in health and economic growth in Asia.

During the last fifty years, cereal crop production in developing countries has *tripled*. Many countries went from chronic food deficits to self-sufficiency or even food surpluses, and dire predictions of widespread famine and death were largely proven false. By the late 1990s, more than 80 percent of agricultural land in Asia was planted with improved varieties of seeds. According to some estimates, without these efforts, food production in developing countries today would be 20 percent lower, food prices would be 35 percent to 65 percent higher, and average caloric availability would be around 12 percent lower.[17] Debates today about the origins of the Asian economic miracle tend to focus on trade, industrial policy, and macroeconomic management, but it all began with the Green Revolution and the increases in agricultural productivity and nutrition that came with it. Without these initial huge gains in food production, the subsequent gains in manufacturing and services would not have materialized.

Many people assume that the impact of the Green Revolution ended two decades ago, but advances in agricultural technology continue today, including in Africa. Improved varieties of sorghum, millet, and cassava began to emerge in the 1980s, and yields for roots and tubers grew 40 percent between 1980 and 2005.[18] The International Rice Research Institute (IRRI) has developed new varieties of rice with better tolerance to drought, flood, cold, salinity, and poor soils. The International Maize and Wheat Improvement Center (CIMMYT), a widely respected non-profit research organization, launched its Drought Tolerant Maize for Africa Project in 2006, bringing together farmers, research institutions, extension agents, seed producers, farm organizations, foundations (for example, the Bill & Melinda Gates Foundation), and aid agencies such as USAID. The project has already introduced sixty drought-tolerant hybrids and fifty-seven naturally pollinated seed varieties to smallholder farmers, with yield increases of 20 percent to 30 percent during moderate drought compared with traditional varieties. Enough new seeds have already been produced to sow more than 1 million hectares (equivalent to about 3 percent of the land planted to grow maize in all of Africa), benefiting 20 million people.[19]

Even cassava—a ubiquitous staple crop that provides a basic diet to half a billion people around the world—is on the rise. A stream of new improved cassava varieties, combined with new breeding and pest control efforts, have led to farm yield gains exceeding 40 percent—a change that has been dubbed "Africa's best kept secret."[20] Because the poor spend such a high percentage of their income on food, and because so many of the poor are farmers who depend on agriculture for their incomes, there's little doubt that the gains in agricultural productivity in the last several decades has been a major driver in beginning to reduce extreme poverty.

One of the most important agricultural technologies for developing countries for the future is genetically modified foods, or GMOs (the O stands for "organisms"). GMO crops have the potential to increase yields with less water in poorer soils; strengthen crop resistance to plant viruses, pests, droughts, and floods; and improve nutrition through vitamin enhancement. Unfortunately, GMO foods have engendered significant controversy, with opponents claiming that they have adverse health and environmental impacts, leading to marketing restrictions in Europe and a push for labeling in the United States. These reactions have reduced adoption of GMOs by farmers in developing countries, especially in Africa, where they could do much good, but where governments fear that their products will be banned from Western markets.

There is a strong scientific consensus that GMO foods are safe and impose no serious health or environmental risks. The board of directors of the American Association for the Advancement of Science—one of the world's largest and most prestigious scientific societies (and the publisher of *Science* magazine)—concluded that "the science is quite clear: crop improvement by the modern molecular techniques of biotechnology is safe." It determined that labels on GMO foods would "only serve to mislead and falsely alarm consumers."[21] The Research Directorate of the European Union found that "the main conclusion to be drawn from the efforts of more than 130 research projects, covering a period of more than 25 years of research and involving more than 500 independent research groups, is that biotechnology, and in particular GMOs, are not per se more risky than, e.g., conventional plant breeding technologies."[22] The World Health Organization, the American Medical Association, the US National Academy of Sciences, the British Royal Society, and other respected scientific organizations have all come to the same conclusion.

Developing countries are losing out on the potential benefits from a proven, safe technology. Wellesley College professor Rob Paarlberg lists some of the potential missed opportunities for developing countries:

> In Asia, poor consumers who currently don't get enough vitamin A from their rice-only diets could be better protected against blindness if their farmers had permission to plant so-called Golden Rice, which has been genetically engineered with high beta-carotene content. Farmers and consumers in India currently exposed to toxic insecticides when they grow and eat eggplant could reduce their exposure if farmers had access to a GMO eggplant, Bt brinjal, that needs fewer chemical sprays. Farmers and consumers in East Africa currently vulnerable to hunger and destitution when drought hits their maize fields would be more secure if growers had permission to plant GMO drought-resistant varieties of white maize.[23]

As with other safe and effective advances in agricultural technology throughout history, GMO crops can be an important part of the solution to increasing global food supplies, especially as developing countries face a future of declining yields from climate change.

MILLIONS SAVED: TECHNOLOGICAL INNOVATIONS FOR HEALTH

There are few technologies that have benefitted so many people around the world as have those for health. Basic medicines such as antibiotics are more widely available (to the point where, in many places, they are overprescribed), alongside oral rehydration therapy to stop childhood diarrhea, insecticide-treated bed nets and powerful drugs to prevent and treat malaria, vitamin-enriched foods, and antiretroviral drugs to suppress the progression of HIV/AIDS. Several decades ago, health technologies rarely reached the global poor; today almost everyone in developing countries has been affected by one or more of these advances.

One of the simplest and most potent is oral rehydration therapy (ORT), designed to stop childhood death from dehydration and diarrhea. ORT has been one of the most important medical advances of the last century. Diarrhea killed 5 million children every year just two decades ago. Today that number is down to 760,000.[24] A big reason for the decline is ORT. This simple salt, sugar, and water oral solution can be as effective as intravenous therapy, is far cheaper, and can be administered easily at home, with huge results. In Egypt, in 1980 about one in twenty children died of diarrhea before their first birthday, but after a massive countrywide campaign to introduce ORT—involving the Egyptian government, USAID, its implementing partner JSI Research and Training Institute (a US-based public health management consulting and research organization), and other donors—by 1987, child mortality due to diarrhea dropped by 62 percent.[25] That 760,000 children around the world still die every year from diarrhea is unacceptable, but it is an enormous improvement over the millions who died just two decades ago.

Vitamin A deficiency affects approximately 21 percent of pre-school-age children in developing countries and leads to the death of 800,000 women and children every year. Vitamin A deficiency compromises the immune system, increasing the risks of and deaths from measles, diarrhea, and malaria. Programs that combine the efforts of international organizations, aid agencies, and local actors have led to dramatic improvements in some cases. In 1993 the government of Nepal began to provide twice-yearly supplements of vitamin A to children. Child mortality fell by half in just five years. It cost just $1.25 per child annually.

For more than thirty years, the HIV/AIDS pandemic has decimated families around the world, especially in Central Africa and southern Africa. Across sub-Saharan Africa, nearly one in twenty adults carry the virus. In Swaziland, the prevalence among pregnant women has been as high as 42 percent. HIV/AIDS-related illnesses have killed an estimated 39 million people. But there is progress: new HIV infections fell from 3.4 million in 2001 to 2.1 million in 2013, and AIDS deaths dropped from 2.4 million in 2005 to 1.5 million in 2013.[26] Four out of the five countries in sub-Saharan Africa with the largest HIV epidemics (Ethiopia, South Africa, Zambia, and Zimbabwe) have reduced new infections by more than one-quarter.

There are many reasons for these improvements, including much stronger communication and educational campaigns, male medical circumcision, safe blood supplies, and a substantial increase in the availability of condoms. A major reason behind the decline in deaths has been the development and distribution of antiretroviral therapy (ART). As of December 2014, approximately 13 million people in low- and middle-income countries were receiving ART, *six times more* than in 2005. ART is also increasingly used prophylactically to prevent HIV infection in high-risk populations. In 2012 more than 60 percent of HIV-positive pregnant women in developing countries received combination antiretroviral prophylaxis during pregnancy, and 50 percent received it during breast feeding, which substantially reduced transmission to their newborn infants.[27] While these gains represent tremendous progress, it's not good enough. Only about a third of the people in developing countries who need ART receive the medication. Still, millions of people are alive today who would have been dead just a decade ago, because of ART.

There are dozens of other examples of new technologies and innovations saving lives. The eRanger "ambulance" is a motorbike with a sidecar modified into a stretcher used to transport people to health centers in rural Malawi. It has reduced delays by up to four hours at far less cost than an ambulance and has saved the lives of many women in labor. A company called Zyomyx has developed a simple kit to measure CD4 cell count, which is a critical test to determine when to start antiretroviral therapy for HIV/AIDS; the new test provides results in ten minutes using a finger prick of blood, and requires no electricity. In Nigeria, health workers are upgrading obsolete infant incubators with generic components sourced from the internet; the recycled incubators perform just as well as modern incubators, at a fraction of the cost, and have been credited with contributing to a fall in neonatal mortality rates. The list goes on.[28]

THE INFORMATION REVOLUTION

In 2000 there were four mobile cellular subscriptions for every hundred people in developing countries; by 2012, there were eighty-one per one hundred people. There are now an astonishing 5 billion mobile subscriptions in developing countries (figure 7.4), or four mobile subscriptions for every five people. Columbia University economist and leading development expert Jeffrey Sachs says that the mobile phone "has changed how everything about development is done."

Mobile phones and internet connections are creating jobs, reducing business costs, facilitating research, extending financial networks, strengthening health systems, improving information flows, and increasing transparency and accountability. In poor villages with bad roads, no landlines, no hope of a train, and unreliable postal services, mobile phones have opened the world and have created unprecedented access to information on prices, market conditions, banking services, legal advice, and medical care.

In rich countries, mobile phones are an important upgrade of an old technology (landlines), but in remote areas of developing countries, they are the difference between being isolated and being connected with the world. News and information travel much more quickly. Innovative text message schemes inform farmers about prices, market conditions, and the weather. Families send remittances by cell phones to relatives in remote villages. Literacy programs dictated over mobile phones help women learn to read. Thousands of poor rural women are using mobile phones to set up small businesses.

FIGURE 7.4: GETTING CONNECTED

Number of Mobile Cellular Subscriptions, All Developing Countries

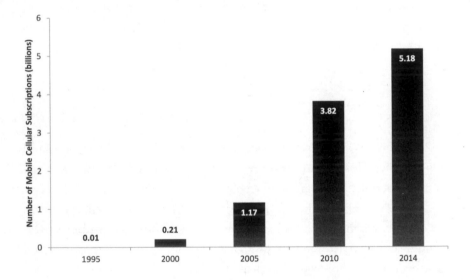

Sources: The data from 1995 through 2010 are from the World Bank's World Development Indicators, and the data for 2014 are from the International Telecommunications Union statistics page, Aggregate Data.

Sarah Arnquist of the *New York Times* described one use of mobile phones in the tiny Ugandan village of Bushenyi:

Laban Rutagumirwa charges his mobile phone with a car battery because his dirt-floor home deep in the remote, banana-covered hills of western Uganda does not have electricity. When the battery dies, Mr. Rutagumirwa, a 50-year-old farmer, walks just over four miles to charge it so he can maintain his position as communication hub and banana-disease tracker for his rural neighbors. In an area where electricity is scarce and internet connections virtually nonexistent, the mobile phone has revolutionized scientists' ability to track this crop disease and communicate the latest scientific advances to remote farmers. With his phone, Mr. Rutagumirwa collects digital photos, establishes global positioning system co-ordinates, and stores completed 50-question surveys from nearby farmers with sick plants. He sends this data, wirelessly and instantly, to scientists in the Ugandan capital, Kampala. "We never had any idea about getting information with the phone," Mr. Rutagumirwa said. "It was a mystery. Now our mind is wide open."[29]

On the other side of Uganda, great-grandmother Mary Wokhwale became one of the country's first "village phone" operators. She used a microfinance loan to buy a phone, a charger, and an antenna, and went into business selling phone time to other villagers. She paid back her loan, bought a second phone, and used the profits to set up a small shop selling food, beer, and videos. "My mobile phone has been my livelihood," she said.[30]

From taxi drivers, to bricklayers, to small shop owners, entrepreneurs are using mobile phones to spur their business. Shop owners place orders for delivery over the phone instead of shutting their doors to retrieve supplies. Construction workers order materials with their mobile phones instead of leaving their work sites. Farmers get much better prices because they can identify the best markets to sell their products.

Economist Robert Jensen of the University of California at Los Angeles (UCLA) found that with the introduction of mobile phones along the coast of Kerala in southern India, fishermen began calling several markets while still at sea to help determine where to sell their catch. The impact was substantial: a reduction in wasted fish, less variation in prices along the coast, an average 4 percent decline in consumer prices, and an 8 percent increase in profits. Mobile phones paid for themselves in just two months. Similarly, Jenny Aker of Tufts University found that mobile phones reduced price variations in grain markets in Niger by a minimum of 6.4 percent, and even more in remote markets, which contributed to both lower consumer prices and higher profits for farmers.[31]

And, of course, alongside mobile phones, increased internet connectivity has created new economic opportunities and transformed lives across developing countries—at least where it has reached so far. Call centers in the Philippines provide travel services, technical support to computer users, customer care services, and financial services to consumers around the world. There are now more than a thousand call centers in the Philippines, creating several hundred thousand jobs for semiskilled workers that didn't exist before. Data entry firms have sprouted up in Kenya, Ghana, Bangladesh, India, Colombia, Brazil, and dozens of other countries. The Song-Taaba Yalgré women's cooperative in Burkina Faso uses the internet to connect its shea butter producers with local and regional export markets. The internet has not penetrated as deeply as mobile phones in developing countries, but where it has, the impact has been huge.

The Mobile Alliance for Maternal Action—MAMA—is a mobile information program that provides mothers with mobile messages about health and nutrition. MAMA delivers information twice a week either as SMS text messages or as sixty-second "miniskit" voice messages, which allow mothers who can't read to take part in the program. The messages provide tips on immunizations, the importance of iron folate, breast feeding, and basic health care for infants and children. MAMA has reached more than five hundred thousand subscribers in Bangladesh, meaning that a half million pregnant women and new mothers and their families now have access to vital health information, helping them care for themselves, their babies, and their families.[32]

Mobile phones are also making promising inroads to improve education and literacy. Marshall Smith and Rebecca Winthrop of the Brookings Institution describe a program in the small village of Hafizibad in Pakistan's Punjab province:

A young girl is using her mobile phone to send an SMS message in Urdu to her teacher. After sending, she receives messages from her teacher in response, which she diligently copies by hand into her notebook to practice her writing skills. She does this from the safety of her home, and with her parents' permission, during the school break, which is significant due to the insecurity of the rural region in which she lives. The girl is part of a Mobilink-UNESCO program to increase literacy skills among girls in Pakistan. Initial outcomes look positive: after four months, the percentage of girls who achieved an A level on literacy examinations increased from 27 percent to 54 percent. Likewise, the percentage of girls who achieved a C level on examinations decreased from 52 percent to 15 percent.[33]

There are many more stories from around the world with countless applications of new technologies improving education, health, sanitation, job opportunities, agriculture, banking, and other aspects of life in developing countries.

Up until just a few decades ago, the majority of people in developing countries were shut out of global markets and isolated from information flows and new technologies. That has begun to change, especially in the last two decades. There's a long way to go. But the dramatic increases in global integration, access to knowledge and information, and spread of a wide range of incredible new technologies have created enormous opportunities and have been major forces behind the great surge in global development.

EIGHT

LEADERSHIP, CIVIL SOCIETY, ACTION—AND A BIT OF LUCK

Poverty is not an accident. Like slavery and apartheid, it is man-made and can be removed by the actions of human beings.

—*Nelson Mandela*

WHEN ZIMBABWE GAINED ITS INDEPENDENCE FROM GREAT BRITAIN IN 1980, THERE WAS great hope. The previous century had not been kind: in 1889 Great Britain set the stage for white minority rule by giving Cecil Rhodes and his British South Africa Company a mandate to colonize what became Southern Rhodesia. White settlers arrived from South Africa and crushed an uprising by the Ndebele tribe, the first of many rebellions to come. The government ruled by force and excluded the black majority from any meaningful political or economic opportunities. The Land Apportionment Act of 1930 formalized discrimination in land ownership: blacks were barred from owning most land, forcing many into wage labor working on white-owned farms. Guerrilla warfare against white rule intensified in the 1960s and 1970s, which led to a peace agreement in 1979 and independence in 1980.

Robert Mugabe was elected prime minister, and initially formed a government that included both Joshua Nkomo, the head of a rival opposition party, and Peter Walls, the white head of the army from the previous government. But Mugabe's interest in reconciliation and democracy was a charade. He pushed Walls and Nkomo out of the government, imposed a state of emergency, established a North Korean–trained security brigade to quell internal dissent, and later changed the constitution to eliminate the position of prime minister and give full executive power to the president. The government imposed strict controls over the economy, with Mugabe's tight circle of supporters reaping the benefits. Production, employment, and wages stagnated, then fell.

The country slid into a major economic crisis in 1998, which led to widespread riots and strikes. Zimbabwe's military adventurism in the Democratic Republic of the Congo's civil war made both the domestic and regional situations worse. The 1999 land reform program began ad hoc seizures of white-owned farms for redistribution to blacks. Mugabe refused to cede power, and the longer he remained, the worse the situation became. The government intensified its human rights abuses, imposed strict laws limiting media freedom, and rigged elections. Several government ministers who did not toe the line died in mysterious "accidents." In 2002 the government declared a state of disaster from worsening food shortages that threatened famine. The economy went into free fall, with widespread foreign-exchange shortages, a dual exchange rate, and extreme hyperinflation. The Reserve Bank of Zimbabwe reported that inflation reached 2,800 percent *during the month of July 2008 alone*. Inflation almost certainly accelerated further in the months that followed, but the government stopped measuring it.

Today the average income in Zimbabwe is a paltry $430 per person, about one-third *lower* in real terms than it was at independence in 1980. Economic "growth" per person has averaged -2 percent per year since 1995, the worst performance of any country in the world. Freedom House ranks Zimbabwe near the bottom of its global rankings on political rights and civil liberties. As of this writing, the ninety-one-year-old Mugabe still clings to power, thirty-five years after first taking control. Zimbabwe's dreams for prosperity and democracy are in ruins.

Then there is Nelson Mandela. When Mandela won the 1994 presidential election in South Africa that ended apartheid, tensions were extremely high. Blacks were split between those who wanted reconciliation and those who wanted retribution. There were huge rifts (and regular violence) between the African National Congress and the Inkatha Freedom Party, and the latter pushed hard for autonomy for KwaZulu-Natal province. Many white South Africans were set against the new government, and there were regular attacks from white supremacist groups. Many others were much more in favor, but there were widespread fears that the divisions would deepen and that South Africa might be headed for civil war.

Mandela focused on reconciliation and inclusiveness. He appointed a broad coalition government, including several whites and members of opposition parties. He worked to assure white South Africans that they would be protected and represented in the "Rainbow Nation." Against the wishes of some members of the ANC (who preferred a tribunal), he established a Truth and Reconciliation Commission to investigate crimes committed under the apartheid government and offered generous amnesty for those who testified about crimes they or others committed during the apartheid regime. He rejected demands to confiscate land or businesses owned by whites. Whereas Mugabe rewrote Zimbabwe's constitution to give himself more power, Mandela pushed through a new constitution that checked his own power and created limits on administrative authority within a constitutional democracy. He remained in office for just one term, rejecting calls to run for a second term or remain in office indefinitely. When he left office in 1999, the economy was on the rebound, South Africa was near the top of Freedom House's political rights and civil liberties rankings, and the country was at peace.

Mandela was far from perfect, and he admitted that he made many mistakes during his presidency, not least moving too slowly to fight HIV/AIDS. South Africa's early success was hardly due to his efforts alone—he had a lot of help from civil-society, religious, and business leaders. The country has faced many challenges since then, some of which are rooted in the hostilities and injustices of the apartheid era and some in the weaknesses of Mandela's successors. There has been less progress than many had hoped for in creating an inclusive political system and generating economic progress. Growth in GDP per capita has averaged just 1.5 percent per year in the twenty years since the mid-1990s. While that rate is slow by global standards, it is far better than the 0 percent per capita growth recorded during the last twenty years of the apartheid regime. Infant mortality and extreme poverty are on the decline. There is no question that Mandela's leadership was critical to fostering peace and setting the country on a new path for democracy and development—one that many thought impossible in 1994.

LEADERSHIP AND ACTION

Why did most developing countries begin to move forward over the last several decades, while others did not? The forces I discussed in the previous two chapters—the end of the Cold War, the demise of Communism, the acceleration of globalization, and the spread of new technologies—created much better global conditions and generated big opportunities for development. But while around two-thirds of developing countries began to change direction and take advantage of those opportunities, others did not. Why?

The answer lies primarily in differences in decisions and actions taken within developing countries, and the leaders that guided the process: heads of state; senior government officials; business, community, civil-society, and religious leaders; and others who made the choices and took the actions that began to move countries in new directions. In countries that progressed, leaders forged change, built more effective institutions, introduced new policy directions, and installed good governance.

In addition to governance and leadership, another factor that partially distinguishes country performance is geography: access to global shipping routes (and with it, greater access to the benefits of globalization and technology), soil quality, climate, and natural resources. Countries or regions with more favorable geography had more options and opportunities and tended to make more progress. It's a lot harder to make progress in remote, arid countries with heavy disease burdens.

The most important factors are leadership and governance. Leadership matters, particularly at critical moments during historical transitions. Sometimes the fate of a nation rests with individual leaders and the choices they make, for good or for ill. The end of the Cold War created the opportunity for change, and globalization created an important set of mechanisms for progress, but neither guaranteed that capable leaders would emerge who would make the right choices. Many did: along with Mandela, there were Lech Wałesa in Poland, Václav Havel in the Czech Republic, Corazon Aquino in the Philippines, José Ramos-Horta in Timor-Leste, Oscar Arias in Costa Rica, Ellen Johnson Sirleaf in Liberia, and many others who led their countries in new directions and began to build more effective institutions and new systems of governance and accountability.

Effective leadership tends to spread from one country to another. When the leaders of one nation establish new political and economic directions and begin to show progress, citizens and leaders of neighboring countries take notice. Success tends to create peer pressure, as citizens expect to see matching success, and good leaders can become models for others to follow. (However, Fascism and Communism showed that bad leaders can also become models, unfortunately.) When I lived in Indonesia in the 1990s, government officials regularly wanted to know what South Korea and Singapore had done on a particular issue. South Africa's peaceful surge became a model for many other African countries. During the past twenty years, there clearly has been some contagion effect at work: the more a country makes progress, the more others look to it as an example. Good leadership in one country helps throughout the neighborhood.

However, over the last two decades, effective new leaders did not always emerge. In some countries, the old leadership clung to power, as with Kim Il Sung in North Korea, the Communist government in Laos, the generals in Myanmar, the notorious Teodoro Obiang Nguema Mbasogo in Equatorial Guinea, and most of the leaders across the Middle East (at least, so far). In some cases, the end of the Cold War created a vacuum not yet filled, as in Somalia. In some countries, global changes allowed new leaders to rise to power who either have been ineffective (as in Haiti) or are old-style brutal dictators, as with Mugabe, Islam Karimov in Uzbekistan, Omar al-Bashir in Sudan, Alberto Fujimori in Peru, Alexander Lukashenko in Belarus, and Laurent Kabila in the Democratic Republic of the Congo. The protests in Egypt pushed Hosni Mubarak from office in 2011, but that did not lead to improved governance or democracy.

To some extent, some countries are just lucky about who emerges and takes the helm, especially during critical moments of historical transition. Leadership (good or bad) is not simply fated by history and institutional characteristics: particular individuals can emerge that move their country in new directions. There was nothing fated about Deng Xiaoping emerging to take power in China. Had the Gang of Four—the notorious group led by Mao Tse-tung's wife that controlled the Communist Party in the latter stages of the Cultural Revolution and that were later convicted of treason—gained power and sidelined Deng, history would have been much different. After Marcos, someone other than Corazon Aquino could have wrested control of the Philippines (and several people tried) and continued a tradition of dictatorship. In Liberia, there was no guarantee that Ellen Johnson Sirleaf would win the 2005 elections, defeating several former warlords (all claiming to have been "rehabilitated"). There is little question that Liberia would have made much less progress (if any at all) with someone else at the helm.

Individual political leaders are not the complete story. They don't act alone. They cannot succeed without the support of business, civil-society, labor, religious, and social leaders who help drive their agenda forward, set precedents, and shape institutions for those who follow. Political change cannot happen without broad civil-society coalitions pushing for it. The deeper and wider these leadership circles, the greater the likelihood that the country will build the institutions necessary for progress. Mandela worked with Archbishop Desmond Tutu, won over (somewhat grudgingly) Mangosuthu Buthelezi of the Inkatha Freedom Party, and gained the support of white business owners and other political leaders, in addition to the widespread support he had from national and community leaders in the ANC. The supporting cast deserves at least as much credit as the leader. A country needs both.

Fernando Cardoso, the former president of Brazil, made the point about the importance of coalitions in 1973 when he was a well-known academic, long before his political career. He argued that overthrowing the Brazilian military would require a "reactivation of civil society . . . the professional associations, the trade unions, the churches, the student organizations, the study groups and the debating circles, the social movements."[1] Corazon Aquino had widespread support through the People Power Revolution. Lech Wałesa had labor unions and many other groups behind him, not to mention a Polish pope.

But it starts at the top, with the decisions that political leaders make and the examples they set. Francis Fukuyama described the importance of leadership this way: "Stable liberal democracy cannot come into being without the existence of wise and effective statesmen who understand the art of politics and are able to convert the underlying inclinations of peoples into durable political institutions."[2] Stanford's Larry Diamond makes a similar point: "The fate of democracy is not simply driven by abstract historical and structural forces. It is a consequence of struggle, strategy, ingenuity, vision, courage, conviction, compromises, and choices by human actors."[3] It took *both* the historic opportunity created by the end of Communism and effective leadership to move countries forward.

In 1993 Brazil was an economic mess. After a short-lived stint of rapid growth in the late 1960s and early 1970s, the combination of the global oil price shocks, a mismanaged exchange rate, growing trade deficits, and mounting debt led to a downward spiral. The military junta that had been in control since a 1964 coup gave way to a civilian government. In 1989 Fernando Collor de Mello became the first democratically elected president in nearly three decades, but the economic trouble continued: a series of ill-fated economic reform programs failed to halt crippling hyperinflation (exceeding 1,000 percent in 1989 and 1990) and economic contraction (the economy shrunk 6 percent in 1990). It didn't help when Collor de Mello was impeached in 1992 for corruption.

The new president, Itamar Franco, appointed Fernando Cardoso as minister of finance—the same Cardoso who had so well understood the importance of forging a broad coalition for democratic change. Cardoso

and his successors at the ministry brought in a skilled economic and finance team and implemented wide-ranging economic reforms centered
around the Plano Real (or "Real Plan"). The government introduced a
new currency (the real), cut the budget deficit, established strong supporting monetary policies, and, over time, began to liberalize trade and
privatize state-owned enterprises. The economy stabilized and began
to grow, albeit slowly at first. Over time, growth accelerated, especially
after 1994. Critically, the government did more than just push for stability and growth: it took actions to ensure much wider participation and
greater economic opportunities for the poor. Brazil invested in education
and health, introduced new minimum-wage laws, strengthened the social
security system, and established the Programa Bolsa Família to provide
cash grants to poor families in return for their children going to school
and getting vaccinated. The results were not just economic stability and
faster growth but also a reduction in poverty and marked improvement
in income distribution. These changes did not occur automatically or
simply because of global economic and political systems: they were the
result of decisions and actions by Brazil's leaders.

Individual leadership has also been central in the countries that have
made substantial economic progress but with fewer advancements in
basic rights, personal freedoms, and democracy. China, Vietnam, Ethiopia, Rwanda, Uganda, Jordan, Morocco, and a few other countries fit this
pattern, following broadly the example of South Korea, Taiwan, Indonesia, and Chile in the 1970s and 1980s. China's leaders today are a vast
improvement over Mao, Ethiopia's government is much better than the
Derg, and Uganda's Yoweri Museveni, for all his faults, is not Idi Amin.
King Abdullah II has brought steady economic and social progress to Jordan, as did his father, King Hussein I. Chile made substantial economic
progress under Pinochet, as did Indonesia under Suharto, registering impressive declines in poverty and gains in income and health. Citizens of
these countries today are better off than they were twenty or thirty years
ago. In terms of political governance, in many countries, people have
more freedoms than they did once. Here as well, the key difference between these countries and the dictatorships that have made no progress
(or are sliding backward) is leadership.

TURNING POINTS AND NEW DIRECTIONS

The actions and choices that leaders make are especially important when countries face critical moments of change: at these junctures, they can have substantial impact in establishing effective institutions, precedents, and policy directions, for good or bad, for years to come. In developing countries, institutions—the rules, laws, precedents, and organizations that structure economic, political, and social interactions—tend to be weak or favor a small elite. Many developing nations are quite young by historical standards and are still building their national identities. Others are in transition from authoritarian rule, and new systems are not yet established.

Existing institutions, on their own, do not dictate the outcomes. Rather, decisions, events, and choices create and change those institutions, which, in turn, influence future decisions and choices. People create institutions, and people can change them; they need competent and sustained leadership to become more effective and inclusive over time. The Commission on Growth and Development observed, "Developing countries often lack these market and regulatory institutions. Indeed, an important part of development is precisely the creation of these institutionalized capabilities."[4]

There is a self-reinforcing cycle at work: strong leadership, smart decisions, and fair rules create the precedents and expectations that begin to build stronger institutions, which help countries achieve progress; this progress, in turn, helps build more capacity and reinforce the tendency for better decisions and choices in the future. It takes time, and building effective institutions can take years—indeed, generations, as it has in the West, Japan, and elsewhere. And, of course, the self-reinforcing cycle can work in the opposite direction: decisions that centralize power, reduce accountability, and distort economic incentives can create rules and precedents that are more difficult, although not impossible, to change in the future. Poor governance can lead to a downward cycle and a poverty trap, as Paul Collier described in *The Bottom Billion*.

Jerry Rawlings, Ghana's head of state and president from 1981 to 2001, did not start out as an inclusive, democratic leader: He was a thirty-one-year-old air force flight lieutenant in May 1979 when he joined six other soldiers in an attempted coup against the military government of General Fred Akuffo. The coup failed, and Rawlings was arrested and sentenced to death. He managed to escape and mount a successful coup one month later. He handed power over to a civilian government, but two years later seized leadership again in another coup. This time he held on to it for a while. By that point, in 1983, Ghana was an economic and political mess. Rawlings's second coup was the last of a long series of coups and countercoups that had led to eight different heads of state during the previous fifteen years, alongside scores of assassinations, disappearances, and flagrant human rights abuses. The economy was a disaster: government revenues had collapsed, inflation skyrocketed to more than 100 percent, and GDP per capita fell by a stunning one-third between 1970 and 1983.

Rawlings's first set of critical decisions was on economic policy. He brought in one of Africa's most talented finance ministers, Kwesi Botchwey, to design an economic recovery plan. The strategy was bold, and cut against much of the conventional wisdom of the time. The government cut the budget deficit, removed trade restrictions, devalued the currency, raised the farm price for cocoa, and privatized many state-owned enterprises. The results were striking: inflation ground to a halt, the black-market premium for foreign exchange dried up, shortages disappeared, and the economy began to grow, sparking one of sub-Saharan Africa's longest periods of sustained growth. Average incomes have more than doubled since 1983, and the share of people living in extreme poverty has fallen from 56 percent to 18 percent.

The second set of decisions, which came later, related to the political system. Rawlings's military roots, combined with his economic success, meant that he could have decided to stay in power for the rest of his life. Instead, he made the extraordinary decision to step down and let his vice president, John Atta Mills, run for president in the 2000 elections. Mills lost to opposition candidate John Kufuor. Under these circumstances, many leaders in Rawlings's position might have stuffed the ballot boxes, annulled the elections, or found some other way to keep his man and his party in power. But he made a second decision to let the results stand, allow Kufuor to take power, and reshape his party as the loyal opposition. These two decisions set the foundation for Ghana to become a vibrant democracy, which has now experienced several competitive and fair elections, the transfer of power back and forth between parties, and the peaceful and seamless constitutional transfer of power when Mills, who was later elected to the presidency in 2008, died in office in 2012. Democracy has taken hold.

SKILLS, CAPACITY, AND THE ABILITY
TO GET THINGS DONE

Of course, it's not enough just for smart leaders to announce new policies and strategies. They need broad coalitions of support and some basic capacity to implement their ideas. Here we come to another key factor that has begun to change during the last two decades. Slowly, developing countries are building the skills and the capacity needed at all levels of society to implement policy changes, build institutions, and make progress in economic growth, health, education, and governance.

The skill base used to be weak. The legacy of colonialism in many countries left few people with adequate education, skills, training, or experience. When Botswana gained its independence in 1966, it had just twenty-two college graduates. The situation was even worse in the Democratic Republic of the Congo: only sixteen people—out of 13 million—had college degrees. There were zero Congolese physicians or engineers.[5]

While I was living and working in The Gambia in West Africa in the mid-1980s, only two senior economics officials—the minister of finance and the chief economist at the Central Bank—had graduate degrees, and only a handful of others had an undergraduate education. The skill base was so weak that the government hired British expatriates to temporarily fill the roles of the governor of the Central Bank and the accountant general in the Ministry of Finance. The previous Gambian incumbents of these positions had performed so poorly that the government had to look abroad—rather horrifyingly, back to the colonial power that had so limited educational opportunities in the first place—to find people with the skills to do the job.

FIGURE 8.1: THE EDUCATION BASE IS GROWING

Share of Adult Population That Has Completed Secondary or Tertiary Education

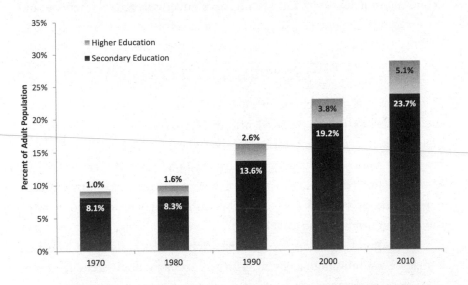

Source: Robert Barro and Jong-Wha Lee, "A New Data Set of Educational Attainment in the World, 1950–2010," working paper 15902, National Bureau of Economic Research, Cambridge, MA, April 2010.

In 1980 only 10 percent of adults in developing countries had completed either secondary school or higher education (figure 8.1). Less than 2 percent had a college degree. By 2010, the share had almost tripled to 29 percent. Of course, just being in school does not translate into skills, but it is indicative of steady progress. Across the majority of developing countries, there is stronger capacity to implement government policies, manage local community programs, run successful businesses, and hold governments accountable.

I see this change regularly in central banks and ministries of finance: the skill and experience level is significantly greater than it was two decades ago. And it shows. When the most recent global financial crisis struck in 2008, most developing-country policy makers responded adroitly—much better than their predecessors had twenty-five years earlier during the 1980s global recession—and developing countries generally navigated the crisis with minimal damage. In addition to finance, ministries of health, education, and agriculture typically have many more skilled people than they once did, even if not yet enough. In both economic policies and efforts to improve governance, the difference between the 1970s and 1980s and today are stark.

THE TURNAROUND IN ECONOMIC POLICIES

Deng Xiaoping took China in an entirely new economic direction in the early 1980s. Indian finance minister Manmohan Singh began implementing deep economic reforms in July 1991. The reforms introduced in Brazil were mirrored in different ways across Latin America. In Ghana, Mozambique, Tanzania, and many other countries across Africa, economic policies changed. Eastern European countries introduced some of the most dramatic reforms of all.

Four sets of economic policies have changed significantly. The first is macroeconomic management. Thirty years ago, dual exchange rates, overvalued currencies, and foreign exchange shortages were common, leading to widespread black markets and crippling disincentives for exporters. Today the shortages and black markets are rare. It's hard, outside of war zones such as today's Ukraine and a few disasters like North Korea, to find countries that mismanage their exchange rates so badly that there are widespread currency shortages and black markets (Argentina is a sad exception). Most countries keep much higher levels of foreign exchange reserves, which help maintain stability and reduce the risk of sudden crises.

Similarly, in the 1980s, many countries ran large budget deficits and printed lots of money to finance them, leading to high inflation. Today few countries do so. As recently as 1994, fifty countries recorded inflation rates of 20 percent or more (and that's not counting the many countries that didn't report the data). In 2013 there were just five (figure 8.2).

FIGURE 8.2: MACROECONOMIC MANAGEMENT IS MUCH STRONGER

Number of Developing Countries with Inflation Exceeding 20 Percent

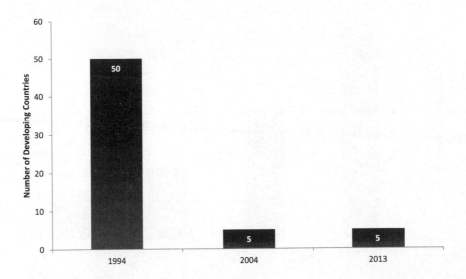

Source: World Bank, World Development Indicators.

Many countries also amassed large external debts in the 1970s and 1980s. In 1990 external debt averaged more than 100 percent of GDP across all developing countries. Today, due to a combination of donor debt relief initiatives and much better economic management, debt levels have fallen to around 40 percent of GDP.

Second, countries are much more open to trade and more integrated into the global economy than they once were. There are many policies that influence trade: exchange rates, quotas, subsidies, industrial policies, directed credit, and so forth. One of the most important is import tariffs. In the early 1980s, tariff rates across developing countries averaged around 38 percent. As ideas changed about the importance of trade and global integration, tariff rates began to fall, and in 2010 they were down to an average of just 9 percent (figure 8.3).

FIGURE 8.3: COUNTRIES ARE MORE OPEN TO TRADE

Average Import Tariff Rate, All Developing Countries

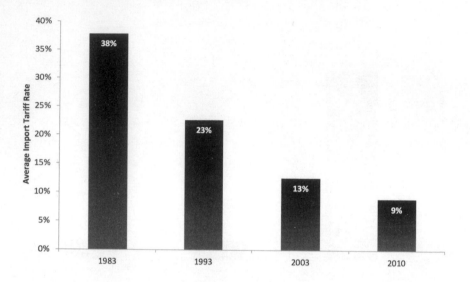

Source: "Data on Trade and Import Barriers," World Bank, last modified December 2012.

Third, agricultural policies have improved in most countries. In the 1980s, it was common for governments to control farm prices and keep them low for consumers, at the expense of farmers. Today the worst of those controls have been removed, and farmers can sell their products for much better prices. State-owned agricultural marketing boards that had near-exclusive power to buy farm products at depressed prices are largely gone. Taxes on agricultural production are much lower, especially for export products. A team of World Bank researchers has tallied up the total financial penalty against farmers from heavy taxes, export restrictions, and price controls, and the results are striking. In the early 1980s, the penalty was equivalent to 12 percent of the total value of their products, as shown in figure 8.4. By 1995, distortions had been eliminated in the aggregate through deregulation of farm gate prices, lower taxes, fewer export restrictions, and far fewer marketing boards. In 2010, farmers enjoyed a net subsidy equivalent to 4 percent of the value of output.

Farmers have responded to the changes in policies and incentives:

agricultural production has grown about 3 percent per year since the mid-1990s, and total farm output today is 75 percent more than it was twenty years ago. In some countries, performance has been much better. In the 1980s, state-owned farms in Mozambique controlled more than 50 percent of production, and private farmers had to sell all their output to state-owned marketing boards at below-market prices. It was a disaster: agricultural production fell 30 percent between 1975 and 1982. Starting in 1987, the government sold several state-owned enterprises, liberalized prices, eliminated the overvalued exchange rate, and allowed private traders to enter the market. With the penalties gone, farmers responded. Agricultural production has grown by more than 6 percent per year since the early 1990s—double the rate for other developing countries—and production has more than doubled.[6]

FIGURE 8.4: DISTORTIONS TO AGRICULTURAL INCENTIVES BROADLY HAVE BEEN ELIMINATED

The "Nominal Rate of Assistance" to Agriculture Shifted from a Net Penalty (Negative) to a Net Advantage (Positive).

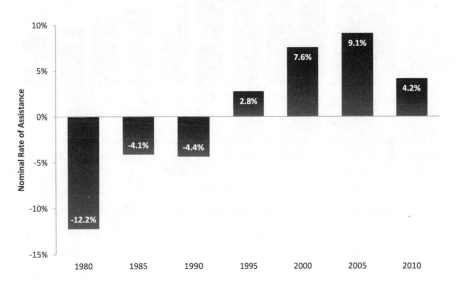

Source: Kym Anderson and Signe Nelgen, *Updated National and Global Estimates of Distortions to Agricultural Incentives, 1955 to 2011* (Washington, DC: World Bank, June 2013).

Fourth, the operating climate for private businesses is much better. Many governments were hostile to private business (unless it was owned by a friend or relative); today governments are much more welcoming. There are far fewer licenses, permits, and registrations needed to start and operate a business. In many countries, it is much easier to register property, which helps reduce land disputes and facilitates using property as collateral.

FIGURE 8.5: BUSINESS COSTS HAVE FALLEN SHARPLY

Costs to Start a Business as a Share of Average Income

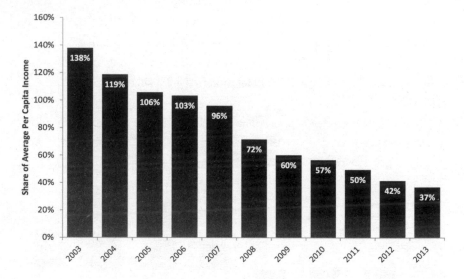

Source: *Doing Business 2014: Understanding Regulations for Small and Medium-Size Enterprises* (Washington, DC: International Bank for Reconstruction and Development/ World Bank, 2013).

One indicator of the improvement is the overall cost of starting a business. Sometimes promising entrepreneurs are knocked down at the starting blocks: they find that it's just too expensive to launch a business because of the morass of permits, signatures, and processes they need to wade through, not to mention the high fees (and accompanying bribes) at every step. The World Bank's data on the costs to start a business go back only to 2003, but since then, there has been a dramatic change (figure 8.5). In 2003 it cost the equivalent of 138 percent of average income to start a business—way too high for most entrepreneurs (and the costs were almost certainly higher in the 1980s and 1990s). By 2012, the cost had dropped to 37 percent of average income—a decline of three-quarters in just ten years.

Current economic policies are hardly ideal in many countries. It is still difficult to start a business, farmers face too many obstacles, infrastructure is weak, and red tape and unnecessary costs add to the burden. Nonetheless, economic policies are far better than they once were.

IMPROVED GOVERNANCE

Across the majority of developing countries—although far from all— citizens can choose their leaders, governments are much better at upholding basic rights, legislatures are more effective, and civil-society and citizen groups are much more involved in political processes. As with changes in economic policies and institutions, the transformations in political systems—some more advanced than others—were not a fait accompli.

Whether a new democracy succeeds or fails is not predetermined by history, culture, religion, poverty, mineral wealth, social divisions, or ethnic fragmentation. Those factors are important, but perhaps the most decisive force is the actions taken by new leaders at key moments. Young democracies in developing countries are in a particularly fragile position: with a new government and a new system, it is difficult to deliver progress fast enough to build support for deepening democracy. If new governments don't succeed, citizens may come to believe the democratic experiment has failed. Samuel Huntington observed, "New democracies are, in effect, in a Catch-22 situation: lacking legitimacy they cannot become effective; lacking effectiveness they cannot develop legitimacy."[7]

Perhaps the best ways for a new democracy to build credibility are to stimulate broad-based economic growth, begin to reduce poverty, and improve health and education services by increasing school enrollments and opening clinics. Brazil's democracy sputtered initially, but its progress in delivering social progress and renewed growth alongside improvements in income distribution has gone far to strengthen its legitimacy.

In addition, the leaders of the countries that have been most successful in consolidating democracy have worked to strengthen democratic institutions. Ethan Kapstein and Nathan Converse, in their book *The Fate of Young Democracies*, concluded that "democracy builders serve their countries particularly well when they establish institutions that place effective constraints on executive authority."[8] The best leaders were wise enough to establish rules and institutions that limited their own power and that of their successors, as Mandela did, to minimize the abuses of a strong executive. Taking steps to limit one's own power requires exceptional leadership.

Elections—when they are free and fair—are the most widely recognized and effective mechanism to limit power. A strong legislative body, a well-functioning judicial system, transparency in government financial accounts and decision-making processes, an active civil society, and a free press are all important complementary mechanisms. So is limiting the power of the military and ensuring that the military serves citizens, rather than the other way around.

One of the most important ways that leaders begin to limit executive power is to strengthen political rights and civil liberties and give more voice and power to citizens. Doing so creates great risks, as it subjects political leaders to criticism, allows people to speak against the government, and gives people the freedom to live their own lives. Whereas in the early 1980s only twenty-two developing countries met a modest threshold of upholding civil liberties (specifically, a score of 4 or better on Freedom House's 7-point scale), today sixty-five countries do so. The same change is evident in strengthening basic political rights (figure 8.6).

These kinds of changes can set off a positive self-reinforcing cycle that establishes the norms, expectations, and rules around how societies govern themselves. Once basic rights are extended to citizens, it is much harder (although not impossible) to take them away. Establishing freedom of speech, religion, assembly, and the press creates the expectation that those freedoms will be not just upheld but also deepened. Free and fair elections, even if they don't always work well, build the expectations and norms among citizens that they have the right to choose their leaders, rather than the leaders choosing themselves. Once citizens' groups, labor unions, youth groups, and other civil-society associations are allowed to organize and operate, citizens begin to expect and demand that they will continue to have that right in the future. At critical moments in history, leaders must be willing to take those risks, put constraints on power, and take the steps necessary to build the institutions of personal freedoms, transparency, accountability, and overall good governance.

FIGURE 8.6: MORE COUNTRIES SUPPORT POLITICAL RIGHTS AND CIVIL LIBERTIES

Number of Developing Countries with Scores of 4 or Lower on Freedom House's Indices of Political Rights and Civil Liberties (out of 109 countries)

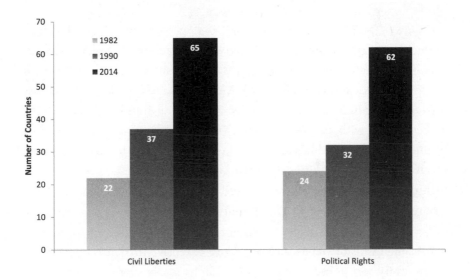

Source: Freedom House, "Freedom in the World Comparative and Historical Data Series, Individual Country Ratings and Status 1973–2015," Freedom House, Washington, DC.

LOCATION, LOCATION, LOCATION

We have seen how global political forces, ideas, globalization, technology, institutions, and leadership all matter for development. There is another factor that influences the opportunities for progress: geography. A country's location relative to major global markets, the quality of its soils, the prevalence of disease, its climate, and its abundance of natural resources all affect the process of development, sometimes positively and sometimes negatively.

Geography is not destiny, and geographical characteristics do not dictate success or failure on their own. Nevertheless a country's geography matters: it affects the extent and range of economic opportunities, the ability to take advantage of globalization and technology, and the incentives that influence institutions and governance. Geographical characteristics have influenced which developing countries have begun to make progress in recent decades and which ones have been left behind.

One of the most powerful ways that geography affects development is through a country's location and its access to global markets. The old adage says that the three most important things about business are location, location, and location. Most of today's global trade occurs through sea-based shipping, as it has for several hundred years. Cities and countries with greater access to the sea have lower shipping costs, so businesses and individuals are much better positioned to take advantage of all of the opportunities afforded by trade, including access to new technologies. Adam Smith recognized the importance of global access through sea-based trade in *The Wealth of Nations*:

> As by means of water-carriage a more extensive market is opened to every sort of industry than what land-carriage alone can afford it, so it is upon the sea-coast, and along the banks of navigable rivers, that industry of every kind naturally begins to sub-divide and improve itself, and it is frequently not till a long time after that those improvements extend themselves to the inland part of the country.[9]

True to Smith's insights, as development spread from Europe over the last two centuries, coastal cities—or cities with direct access to the sea through rivers—became the major centers of commercial activity around the world: London, Rotterdam, New York, Los Angeles, New Orleans, Tokyo, Seoul, Sydney, Shanghai, Istanbul, Rio de Janeiro, Buenos Aires, and many others.

The same is true with today's developing countries. All of the fast-growing "miracle" countries of Asia have used their location to take advantage of sea-based trade to drive job creation and development. Singapore boomed because of its port location on the busy Strait of Malacca, halfway between Middle Eastern oil supplies and Japan. South Korea and Taiwan moved forward by producing manufactured goods in export processing zones in major port cities. The Philippines converted the Subic Bay Naval Station into an electronics hub. In Indonesia—where it was often said that its thirteen thousand islands spread across the sea showed that "God meant Indonesia for free trade"—factories near the major seaports helped launch the country forward.

Over the past two decades, China's economic powerhouses have been the cities on the coast or on major rivers that produce shoes, clothing, toys, electronics, refrigerators, and a wide range of other goods. To be sure, China's rural areas have made huge progress, with major gains in income, improvements in health, and reductions in poverty. But people living near the coast have made much bigger gains because they have had far more opportunities for economic advancement because of their location. Coastal cities in Brazil are far better off than those in the hinterlands, and coastal Ghana prospers more than the arid and isolated north.

Of course, these countries' success wasn't just about geography. (A few skeptics of geography try to discredit its role by claiming that anyone who points to the importance of geography is claiming that geography is the sole determinant of development, which it is not.) Leadership, good governance, and smart policy choices matter more. The successful Asian countries invested in education and health, established strong institutions, maintained high savings rates, built strong public infrastructure, and invested in agriculture. However, their access to sea-based trade also was central to their success.

The reason is simple: costs. Landlocked countries typically pay around 50 percent more for shipping compared with their coastal neighbors, because once goods arrive in port, they have to be transported inland by road or rail. The higher costs act like a big, fat tax: less purchasing power for consumers, lower profits for businesses, lower wages for workers, less investment, and lower standards of living. As a result, some types of investments simply don't happen, such as for low-cost manufactured products like shoes and computers that are so central to jump-starting development. The factories that produce Nike shoes and Panasonic televisions are *never* going to relocate to where there is no direct, easy, and cheap access to sea-based trade.

Landlocked countries such as Nepal, Afghanistan, Burundi, Niger, Bolivia, and many others have a major disadvantage compared with their coastal neighbors. They simply don't have the same range of economic options and opportunities. It doesn't necessarily mean that development can't happen, but it's a whole lot harder.

To be clear, the constraint is the cost and difficulty in accessing global markets, which is not necessarily the same as being landlocked. Not all landlocked countries are cut off from world markets, and not all countries with limited geographical access to global markets are landlocked. Switzerland and Austria are both landlocked, but since they are located in the middle of the European Union, they have easy access to markets. Botswana is landlocked, but it has direct access to global markets via excellent roads through South Africa. This situation is what Paul Collier had in mind in *The Bottom Billion* when he referred to countries that are "landlocked with bad neighbors" being in a development trap. If you are in a bad neighborhood with no direct access to global markets, development is more difficult.

At the same time, some countries that are surrounded by ocean have little access to global markets if they are small and far away. I spent two years as a Peace Corps volunteer in Western Samoa, where there was nothing but two thousand miles of open sea between Samoa and New Zealand, and more than five thousand miles to Tokyo or Los Angeles. Samoa and other island countries are the opposite of landlocked, but they are just as isolated from global markets.

Access to global trade—or lack thereof—can have a huge impact on prospects for local development. Several years ago, I was on the border between Nepal and Tibet at the Mitteri Bridge over the Bhote Koshi River, one of the few places where a road actually crosses that remote border. Nepal's only real access to global trade comes through the other side of the country to the south on overland routes through India—and even that is a long, difficult, and expensive journey. The capital city of Kathmandu is five hundred difficult miles from Kolkata (formerly known as Calcutta), the nearest major port city, on the Bay of Bengal in India. On the border to the north, the country is rimmed by the great Himalayas, making transport difficult for just about anything. Over this border, "shipping" does not happen by ships, trucks, carts, or even donkeys. Most of it happens on the backs of Sherpas. Distance is measured in the number of days walked.

When I arrived at the river, the bridge had been washed out, so people were crossing by jumping from one rock to the next. It was a busy—if tiny—international trade route. A continuous stream of Sherpas appeared out of nowhere on the Tibet side with huge loads of consumer goods on their backs—shoes, clothing, soap, matches—all manufactured in China, transported across the country and through Tibet, and carried by foot into Nepal. As the Sherpas made their way across the rocks, they had to take care to not bump into the Sherpas coming the other way, carrying loads of rice, vegetables, and other foodstuffs from Nepal into Tibet. They hopped across the river, hiked up the trail, and melted into the mountainside.

Because of its remote location, and despite this little stream of trade, the nearby village of Kodari has almost no chance for any kind of sustained development: investment and job opportunities aren't going to happen. Even in Kathmandu, location makes development much harder than in most places. Since India is the only way out, Nepal is completely dependent on keeping up good relationships—and open borders—with India for its economic survival. This situation gives India enormous leverage over Nepal. When relations between the two countries soured in 1989, India simply closed the border. Just like that, Nepal's economy crashed: shortages emerged for food, fuel, and basic supplies; road traffic (and internal trade) came to a standstill; businesses closed; and people stripped the forest (even faster) for cooking fuel. India tightened the screws for fifteen months, reminding Nepal of who was boss. If Nepal had its own seaport—or an alternative land route; say, directly through Bangladesh—none of this would have happened.

Many businesses that might help jump-start development in Nepal simply won't consider investing there. Why would they? Better to locate in Kolkata on the Indian coast and save the enormous cost and time of overland shipping, not to mention the risks of an embargo. That's bad news for Nepal: less investment, fewer jobs, lower incomes, less technology, and slower development. It doesn't mean development can't happen, but it is a lot harder.

Other geographical factors also strongly affect development prospects. Soil quality and rainfall are critical to agricultural development, food production, and nutrition, and therefore long-term development. Jared Diamond showed how some of these factors have affected income levels around the world for centuries in his classic *Guns, Germs, and Steel*. The most salient points echo today in understanding why some developing countries have begun to move forward while others have remained behind.

Indonesia's most populous island of Java has some of the world's richest soils, together with plentiful rainfall. When these advantages were combined with better technologies—the new seed varieties and fertilizers introduced as part of the Green Revolution—and effective economic management, the result was an agricultural boom that laid the basis for rapid economic growth and poverty reduction.

Contrast Javanese farmers with their counterparts in Niger—a landlocked country on the southern edge of the Sahara Desert with little arable land and not much rainfall. Parts of Niger get less than an inch of rain a year. It's so hot in some areas that raindrops evaporate before they reach the ground. It's pretty hard to grow much on the edges of the desert, even under the best of circumstances.

Indeed, countries like Niger are doubly disadvantaged: most of the country is desert or semiarid, and it is also landlocked and isolated from major trade routes. Since agriculture and trade are so foundational to development, it's hard to get started when there are obstacles to both. It's all about options and opportunities: the good people of Niger have far fewer options for productive investment, job creation, and economic growth than the people of Indonesia. It's little wonder that some of the most difficult development challenges occur in countries that are both landlocked and predominantly desert or mountains: Niger, Burkina Faso, Chad, Mali, Afghanistan, Nepal, Tajikistan, Kyrgyzstan, and, on the other side of the world, Bolivia with the Uyuni Salt Flat.

There also is the impact of geography on health and disease, about which Jeffrey Sachs has written extensively. Disease burdens differ by country, and while some of these differences stem from income levels, public health systems, institutions, and policy choices, much can be attributed to geography and climate. Disease burdens tend to be much greater in tropical countries, especially the wet tropics, where ecological conditions favor killer diseases such as malaria, dengue fever, tuberculosis, schistosomiasis, hookworm, and many others. Countries across sub-Saharan Africa tend to have particularly high disease burdens, a point underlined during the last several decades with the epicenter of the HIV/AIDS pandemic in Central Africa and southern Africa and the more recent outbreak of Ebola in West Africa. Where disease burdens are more severe, development is more difficult: workers are less productive when they are sick or caring for the sick, investment is more limited (or may not happen at all), education is less beneficial when children are weakened cognitively by disease or malnutrition, and more public spending must be diverted to tackle health challenges.

Finally, a country's mineral resources have an enormous impact on development. At first blush, it might seem that the more minerals, especially oil, the better for development. But, as is now widely understood, this is far from the case. Some of the greatest development successes have few natural resources, including South Korea and Taiwan; at the same time, some of the world's largest oil exporters have been development disasters. Paul Collier describes the detailed working of the "natural resources trap" in *The Bottom Billion*, as have Jeffrey Sachs, economist Alan Gelb of the Center for Global Development, and others. Developing countries that have abundant mineral resources are prone to the "resource curse," which I described briefly in chapter 7. Resource-rich countries are more likely to mismanage their currencies and their economies more broadly, more likely to have poor governance and institutions that enrich only the elite, and much less likely to become democracies. It is striking that *none* of the major developing-country oil exporters is a democracy.

Resource-rich countries also are more likely to go to war. Many of the countries that have made the least development progress are precisely those in which enormous mineral deposits have only engendered war and conflict. The Democratic Republic of the Congo, for example, has been engaged in one of the longest civil wars of the last two centuries, with control over diamonds at the root of the conflict. The conflict in Darfur in western Sudan is, at its core, a fight about water rights. The civil wars in Liberia, Sierra Leone, and Guinea during the 1990s were to a large extent fights over controlling valuable timber, diamonds, and other resources.

The good news is that geographical advantages and disadvantages can change, albeit slowly, with new technologies, appropriate investments, new discoveries, and more effective institutions and policy choices. The most favorable locations for access to global markets, for example, have changed over time with technology. Up until around seven hundred years ago, almost all trade was conducted overland by foot, horse, donkey, or camel. Places such as Timbuktu, Marrakesh, Cairo, Istanbul, Kathmandu, and Kabul all rose to prominence because their geographical locations favored overland trade, some of them along the old Silk Road.

Timbuktu (in the central region of today's Mali) exists because it lies at the intersection of the northern reach of the Niger River and the southern edge of the Sahara Desert. It flourished by connecting trade on river canoes with overland trade across the desert in gold, salt, ivory, and slaves. But when the new technology of seaworthy vessels arrived in the fifteenth century, the major mode of trade began to shift to the sea, and, for the first time, coastal regions became the place to be—an advantage that remains. Timbuktu today is a fraction of its original size, and deeply impoverished.

With new technologies, the mechanisms for trade continue to change. An increasing amount of trade today takes place on airplanes or via the internet. As a result of these new technologies, the geography of trade is changing, and countries have a wider range of options. Bolivia can send fruits, vegetables, and flowers by air to markets in the United States. Landlocked Rwanda is attempting to become a regional hub for services via the internet, mobile phones, and air travel. They may succeed, although there is a long way to go, and ultimately their options are more limited than they would be otherwise because of their geography. For the time being, port cities enjoy a sizable geographic advantage.

The best combination is to have good governance and favorable geography. Botswana has benefitted from strong leadership and sound institutions since its independence, features that make it stand out from other countries in Africa. Even though it is landlocked, it had two geographical advantages: abundant diamonds and a border with South Africa. Its effective institutions allowed it to manage its diamonds well and to work with South Africa to build the infrastructure to export them efficiently. Without effective institutions, Botswana would not have made nearly as much progress and might have gone to war over its diamonds. On the other hand, even with its institutions and strong leadership, had it not had diamonds or a border with South Africa (imagine, for example, if Zimbabwe lay between Botswana and South Africa), it would not have been nearly as successful.

The great surge in global development during the last two decades was spurred by the enormous changes in global power relationships that swept across the world in the 1980s and early 1990s. These changes removed a wide range of obstacles and constraints that had impeded progress for centuries, and led to global conditions that were much more conducive to development. At the same time, the acceleration of globalization and the development of new technologies created a wide range of new opportunities and provided the vehicles through which countries could move forward.

Some developing countries have failed, so far, to take advantage of these opportunities, especially where either old dictators have been able

to hang on (for example, North Korea and Myanmar), or new dictators took advantage of the moment of change to seize power (such as
Zimbabwe, Tajikistan, and Sudan). Geographical constraints have made
the challenge more difficult for many countries, including Nepal, Niger,
Malawi, and Afghanistan.

However, the majority of developing countries have been able to
begin to seize these opportunities through a combination of strong and
focused leadership, better policies, more effective institutions, greater
freedoms, and improved governance. None is perfect, of course, and they
all face challenges in the years ahead, but they have made considerable
progress in creating the foundation for sustained growth and expanded
prosperity.

NINE

FOREIGN AID: BLESSING OR CURSE?

Liberia's recovery from its long civil war was driven by the determination and courageous action of the Liberian people. But we would not have made it this far without the strong support of the international community, and foreign aid was central to that effort.

—*Ellen Johnson Sirleaf, president of the Republic of Liberia*

FOR CENTURIES, THE SCOURGE OF MALARIA HAS KILLED MILLIONS OF PEOPLE AND DEBILI-tated tens of millions more. During the twentieth century alone, the disease killed nearly 200 million people.[1] It is particularly lethal in children: 60 percent of all malaria deaths worldwide involve children under five years old. It is especially threatening to the poor, who are much more likely to live in places where malaria thrives (such as slums or the countryside) or have housing that doesn't protect against mosquitoes, and are less likely to be able to afford bed nets or treatment when malaria strikes. Even when it doesn't kill, malaria means missed days of work, lost jobs, and less time in school. It means reduced farm and food production, and less investment from international businesses that can go elsewhere. Economists John Gallup and Jeffrey Sachs estimated that the severe incidence of malaria reduces the rate of economic growth by about 1.3 percent per year, which, over the course of decades, is huge. Countries with severe malaria had just one-third the income level of other countries, after controlling for other factors.[2]

But there is good news. Because of the combined efforts of governments, committed citizens in developing countries, and foreign aid programs, malaria is in retreat, and millions of lives are being saved. Since 2002, malaria deaths have fallen by 47 percent worldwide. More than 4 million lives have been saved, most of them children under five years old. Foreign assistance programs alone cannot claim full credit for this progress, but there is little doubt that these lives would not have been saved without aid.

Many people forget that malaria was widespread throughout the world until just a few decades ago. At the end of World War II in 1945, malaria was present on every continent except Antarctica and was found in all but a handful of countries. It reached as far north as Canada, Finland, and the Soviet Union, and as far south as Chile and Australia. Malaria was endemic across the southern United States.[3] The US Centers for Disease Control and Prevention (CDC) was originally founded in 1946 primarily to fight malaria—it was the successor to the World War II Malaria Control in War Areas program. The CDC was located in Atlanta specifically so that it would be in the midst of the United States' major malarial zone.[4] In fact, my father contracted malaria in Texas in October 1941 while serving in the US Army Air Corps at Sheppard Field, just north of Wichita Falls. Over the next eight months, he suffered through three nasty bouts with it and was hospitalized for six weeks. Fortunately, it didn't kill him, and it had the rather positive side effect of keeping him in Texas training other officers rather than fighting in Europe or the Pacific.

Throughout history, malaria has wreaked havoc on individuals, families, societies, and economies. For centuries, no one knew where it came from or how to control it. It was blamed on swamp fumes or bad air (the word *malaria* comes from the Italian *mala aria*, meaning "bad air"). It wasn't until French military physician Alphonse Laveran discovered in 1880 that malaria was carried by a parasite, and British physician Ronald Ross recognized in 1897 that it was transmitted by mosquitoes, that it was possible to control the disease.

These discoveries had immediate impacts. The first attempt to build the Panama Canal failed in the 1880s after more than twenty thousand workers died from malaria or yellow fever. As the second attempt started in 1906, malaria again threatened to stop it: of the twenty-six thousand people working to build the canal, twenty-one thousand were hospitalized for malaria. Six years later, after malaria and yellow fever control efforts were put in place, the number of workers hospitalized fell by three-quarters to five thousand, even as the total number of workers more than doubled to fifty thousand. The health benefits spread far beyond the canal to all of Panama. Across the country, deaths from malaria fell by a factor of *six* in just three years between 1906 and 1909.[5] Of course, the economic benefits from the canal were, and continue to be, profound.

The Global Malaria Eradication Program, launched by the World Health Organization in 1955, was the first major international effort to combat the disease. The program aimed to wipe out malaria in all countries outside of sub-Saharan Africa. In Africa, where the challenge was much greater, the goal was control rather than eradication. By 1978, a total of thirty-seven countries that had been endemic were malaria free—mostly richer countries in more temperate climatic zones.[6] Even where it was not eradicated, stronger control efforts helped support development. The reduction of malaria allowed farmers to work new lands in Malaysia, Sri Lanka, and the Terai area of northern India, all of which had been effectively off-limits to development because of rampant malaria. Singapore's economic prosperity was made possible partly because widespread malaria was brought under control.

Despite the gains in richer countries and in a few pockets in developing countries, the scourge continued in most poor tropical countries, particularly in Africa. Unfortunately, the success in richer countries had a major adverse consequence: malaria fell off the global public health agenda. The Global Malaria Eradication Program was abandoned in

1969 when funding dried up. Many people seemed to think that since malaria was under control in rich countries, it was under control worldwide, which was a big mistake.

For the next three decades, global funding to fight malaria in developing countries remained small, while international agencies focused their attention on other issues, and developing countries—many run by dictators—made little effort to fight the disease. At the same time, resistance to the major antimalarial drugs began to rise. When the United States banned the use of DDT in 1972—by far the most effective insecticide to battle mosquitoes—because of the effects from widespread aerial spraying, most other rich countries, the United Nations, and many poor countries followed this overreaction with their own bans, even of small amounts, where there was little evidence of harmful side effects. As a result, the number of malaria-related deaths in developing countries continued to rise.

However, a dramatic change began in the late 1990s. International organizations and researchers began to turn their attention back to malaria. The World Health Organization's Commission on Macroeconomics and Health showed how investments in fighting malaria could reap big benefits. Global efforts to fight the disease expanded beginning around 2000, and malaria deaths began to fall—fast. The new worldwide effort brought together international organizations and aid agencies including the World Health Organization; the US government; the Roll Back Malaria Partnership; the Bill & Melinda Gates Foundation; the Global Fund to Fight AIDS, Tuberculosis and Malaria; national governments; and committed local actors. Foreign assistance aimed at tackling malaria increased from $149 million in 2000 to almost $1.2 billion in 2008.[7] At the same time, governments in developing countries increased local funding to fight the disease.

The increase in funding led to a significant scaling up of malaria control efforts, including greater distribution of bed nets, stronger public education programs, controlled use of DDT and other chemicals in safe indoor spraying, community-based case detection and treatment, and more widespread availability of malaria medicine. Whereas in 2004 only 3 percent of households in sub-Saharan Africa owned insecticide-treated bed nets, by 2013, 49 percent of households had them, and the share of households protected by indoor residual spraying doubled.[8] In addition, the development of new inexpensive diagnostic tests and new treatments to fight the disease, such as artemisinin-based combination therapies (ACTs), with distribution financed primarily by aid agencies, have saved hundreds of thousands of lives.

After rising for several decades, malaria deaths began to fall. The global malaria map is shrinking. Whereas once malaria transmission occurred in almost every country in the world, today 108 countries are malaria free, and transmission is declining in dozens more.[9] Remarkably, between 2000 and 2013, deaths from malaria fell 47 percent. The World Health Organization estimates that 4.3 million malaria deaths were averted between 2001 and 2013, and that children under five years of age made up 3.9 million, 92 percent, of those saved.[10] These gains were not the product of aid alone: they required the combined efforts of aid agencies, international organizations, scientists, committed governments, and local actors. But they would not have been achieved without foreign aid.

Foreign aid is one of the most contentious issues in all of development. Over the decades, critics such as economists Milton Friedman, Peter Bauer, William Easterly, and Angus Deaton have leveled stinging critiques, charging that aid has enlarged government bureaucracies, perpetuated bad governments, enriched the elite in poor countries, or just been wasted. They cite continued widespread poverty in Africa and South Asia despite three decades of aid, alongside countries that have received substantial aid yet have had disastrous records such as the Democratic Republic of the Congo, Haiti, Papua New Guinea, and Somalia. In their eyes, aid programs should be reformed, curtailed, or eliminated altogether.

Supporters counter that these arguments are misleading and overstated. Jeffrey Sachs, Joseph Stiglitz, Paul Collier, Nicholas Stern, Bill Gates, and others have argued that although sometimes aid has failed to achieve its goals, overall it has helped improve global health, provided urgent humanitarian relief, increased food production, and supported economic growth, especially in countries with strong economic policies and good governance. They point to a range of emerging countries where aid has contributed to development progress (among them Botswana, Indonesia, South Korea, and, more recently, Tanzania, Vietnam, Mozambique, and Rwanda), along with successful initiatives such as the Green Revolution, childhood vaccine programs, and the campaigns against tuberculosis, guinea worm, river blindness, smallpox, HIV/AIDS, and other diseases.

The critics make important points. Aid programs do not always work (nor, by the way, does private investment), there is too much bureaucracy and too little local input, some funds are wasted on bad ideas and badly designed programs, and at times (especially during the Cold War) aid has been used to prop up dictators and bad governments.

But the critics overstate their cases, based largely on sweeping statements and outdated evidence. Despite the shortcomings, the bulk of the evidence shows that, overall, aid has helped support development progress. Foreign aid is not the main driver of development success. It does not always succeed, and there are several ways its efficacy can be improved. Nevertheless, on the whole, it has helped developing countries advance education, increase agricultural productivity, and accelerate economic growth. And it has saved millions of lives.

Even the fiercest critics have had to backtrack on some of their earlier critiques, as it has become clear that aid has played a huge role in global health advances. Essentially all the major programs to fight specific diseases and increase immunization rates in developing countries have been supported by foreign assistance, working in conjunction with international organizations, philanthropists, local governments, and committed citizens. My former colleague from the Center for Global Development Ruth Levine (now at the William and Flora Hewlett Foundation) and her team documented many of the advancements in health and the role of aid in supporting them in *Case Studies in Global Health: Millions Saved.*[11] Donor-financed programs have helped increase the number of children receiving basic vaccinations from 20 million in 1980 to 200 million today. Tuberculosis infections have fallen by 25 percent just since 2002. AIDS-related deaths have fallen by more than one-third in just seven years because of donor-financed antiretroviral therapy programs.

Smallpox—one of the world's greatest killers—was completely eradicated through a global effort financed partly by foreign assistance in developing countries. Since 1988, the number of polio-endemic countries has fallen from eighty-eight to just three, and the world is on the brink of eradicating polio once and for all. Child deaths from diarrhea have fallen by more than 80 percent in just two decades, due in large part to donor-financed programs that helped develop and distribute oral rehydration therapy.

Foreign aid has also supported progress in education, especially girls' education. In Afghanistan, fewer than 1 million children attended schools in 2002, and almost all of them were boys. Girls and women were excluded. Since then, the Afghan government and international donors have built more than 13,000 schools, recruited and trained more than 186,000 teachers, and increased net enrollment rates for school-age children to 56 percent. Just one decade later, in 2012, there were 8 million children in school—more than eight times the number in 2002—including 2.5 million girls.[12]

Many of the big advances in agricultural production and technologies that I discussed in earlier chapters were supported by foreign aid programs. The Green Revolution is probably the greatest success of all aid programs, as it has saved millions of lives, improved the nutritional status of millions more, and helped set the foundation for Asia's economic rise. More recently, aid-funded programs have helped develop new varieties of rice, maize, and cassava that can better withstand drought, flood, cold, salinity, and poor soils. Rinderpest, an infectious disease known as "the cattle plague," killed huge numbers of cattle for thousands of years. An international effort bringing together aid agencies, local governments, private farmers, scientists, and international organizations eradicated the disease, saving millions of cattle and improving the lives and livelihoods of thousands of cattle farmers in developing countries around the world.[13] New rice varieties developed by the International Rice Research Institute (IRRI)—an international research and training organization based in the Philippines and funded by a consortium of donors, governments, and foundations—boosted yields by an average of 11 percent between 1985 and 2009 in the Philippines, Vietnam, and Indonesia, increasing the value of rice produced by farmers in these countries by $1.46 billion *every year*.[14]

Aid projects have also financed extensive amounts of infrastructure, including roads, school buildings, electricity generation facilities, airports and seaports, and water and sanitation facilities. Many of Cairo's water and sanitation facilities were built with funds from USAID. Many of Indonesia's primary schools were built with aid funding. Infrastructure investment helped rebuild war-torn Mozambique, Liberia, Uganda, and Timor-Leste. As one example, the Millennium Challenge Corporation— a US government foreign assistance agency—worked closely with the government of Benin to design and finance a $188 million investment in the Port of Cotonou. The volume of merchandise flowing through the port increased by 75 percent in just six years, from 2004 through 2009, helping to stimulate growth and wider development progress.

Some of the most successful developing countries have been large aid recipients, starting decades ago with South Korea and Taiwan, both of which launched their remarkable postwar development with the support of foreign assistance. Two of Africa's most successful countries— Botswana and Mauritius—have been supported by large amounts of aid. Botswana received assistance averaging more than $150 per person per year (in today's dollars) for more than thirty years, more than *triple* the average for the rest of the continent, which helped build infrastructure and support health and education programs. Mauritius received aid averaging more than $65 per person per year for thirty years, which helped it build some of the infrastructure and services that made it successful. Since 1993, Mozambique's GDP has grown more than 7.5 percent per year, and its poverty rate has dropped substantially, supported by assistance averaging $60 per person annually. Rwanda, Tanzania, Uganda, and several other countries have achieved rapid growth since the mid-1990s while receiving significant amounts of aid. Although many other factors have contributed to growth in these countries, the bulk of the research evidence suggests that aid helps spur growth, as we will see later in the chapter.

Donors are coordinating more with one another and with developing-country governments to achieve specific goals and make aid more

effective. The Millennium Development Goals (MDGs), which were established by donor and recipient governments following the Millennium
Summit of the United Nations in 2000, specify targets for poverty reduction, health, education, gender equity, environmental sustainability,
and other development issues, with commitments by both donors and
recipients. These goals have helped concentrate efforts among donors
and local governments in fighting disease, reducing infant and maternal
mortality, and getting more girls in school, thus contributing in important ways to the progress that has been achieved in many developing
countries. Bill Gates refers to the MDGs as the world's "report card"
because they measure performance and act as a force for change by focusing attention on critical development issues.[15] A new set of objectives,
called the Sustainable Development Goals, will take effect in 2015 with
the aim of helping focus projects and programs around agreed-upon development goals for the next fifteen years.

Oxford University economist Paul Collier argued in *The Bottom
Billion* that aid can be particularly helpful in postconflict situations
in support of reformist governments trying to turn around countries.
Liberia was torn apart by a brutal fifteen-year civil war that killed an
estimated 270,000 people—about 1 in 12 Liberians—and destroyed
families, communities, infrastructure, and social institutions. Since peace
returned in 2003, there has been a remarkable recovery. Children went
back to school, roads were rebuilt, businesses reopened, and from 2005
through 2013 the economy grew 8 percent per year. Liberia has held
two open, free, and fair elections; strengthened personal freedoms; encouraged greater press freedoms; and taken other steps toward establishing a vibrant democracy. The country still faces many challenges. The
2014 Ebola outbreak was a huge setback, and shows that despite the
significant postwar achievements, there is still a long way to go in building strong and resilient institutions. Nevertheless, Liberia has made far
more progress than anyone imagined was possible as conflict still raged
in 2002. President Ellen Johnson Sirleaf sees foreign aid as central to
those achievements. "Without international support," she has said, "Liberia would not have made nearly as much progress, and might have even
plunged back into conflict."[16]

THREE RED HERRINGS

There are many criticisms leveled against aid, some of which are valid, but three common misleading arguments distract attention from far more important issues.

First, many critics claim that aid flows have been massive (with the implication that they should have had much greater impact), when, in fact, they have been quite modest. In 2012, sub-Saharan African countries received $30 billion in foreign aid from all donors. With a population of around 930 million people, this works out to approximately $33 per person per year, or less than ten cents per person per day. It isn't much, so we should hardly expect miracles.

From the donor's point of view, the amounts are also relatively small. Across all major donors, official (government) development assistance is the equivalent of less than one-third of 1 percent (0.3 percent) of national income. In the United States, foreign aid accounts for less than two-tenths of 1 percent (0.2 percent) of national income, and about 1 percent of the federal budget. Yet most Americans have a perception that aid spending is huge. Multiple surveys show that Americans believe that foreign aid accounts for 15 percent to 30 percent of the federal budget. When asked how much they think the United States *ought* to spend on aid, they say it should be much lower—only around 5 percent of the budget.[17] In other words, Americans think they should be spending five times more than they actually do, while believing they are spending fifteen times more than they do.

The second red herring is the claim that aid should solve global poverty by itself, and if it doesn't, it's a failure. This criticism often appears as the second half of a statement that begins with the claim that aid amounts are huge: "Donors have spent three trillion dollars over sixty years, and there are still one billion people living in poverty." Or "and there are still people dying of malaria." Or "and most Africans are still poor." Or "and there still is not enough clean water." The faulty logic is clear: problems still exist, so aid has obviously failed.

Princeton University economist Angus Deaton, whose work I admire greatly, recently relied on this line of reasoning to attack aid. He criticized what he called "the aid illusion, the erroneous belief that global poverty could be eliminated if only rich people or rich countries were to give more money to poor people or poor countries."[18] He goes on to show, in some detail, that aid alone cannot possibly solve global poverty. That conclusion is no surprise—of course it cannot. The real illusion is the idea that there is anyone that claims that aid—by itself—can eliminate global poverty or that the total elimination of global poverty is the appropriate standard against which the effectiveness of aid should be judged. There is no silver bullet for development and no single approach that can solve global poverty—not trade, foreign investment, a better business climate, improved health, better education, democracy, better governance, or lower population growth. The test of whether aid can solve poverty all by itself is an impossible standard.

Although some aid proponents make strong statements about its potential benefits (especially charities trying to raise money), no one in donor organizations or in the academic community claims that aid—by itself—can eliminate global poverty. Critics often point to Columbia University's Jeffrey Sachs, one of the strongest proponents of aid. (Over the years, critics have claimed that Sachs believes that macroeconomic "shock therapy" alone is the key to igniting growth, or that open trade alone is responsible for growth, or that geography alone explains growth, or that the natural resource curse alone explains failure, or that aid alone can solve poverty.) While Sachs argues that aid can have big benefits, he does *not* claim that aid alone is the solution. He has written extensively on the importance of macroeconomic management, trade policy, private investment, institutions, technology, and many other factors in reducing poverty. He wrote recently:

> Of course, I do not believe that aid is the sole or main driver of economic development. I do not believe that aid is automatically effective. Nor should we condone bad governance in Africa—or in Washington, for that matter. Aid is one development tool among several; it works best in conjunction with sound economic policies, transparency, good governance, and the effective deployment of new technologies.[19]

The wrong standard is to test whether aid alone can eliminate poverty. The right standard is to judge whether aid is helping countries achieve tangible development progress.

The third red herring goes back to the British economist Peter Bauer, who in 1971 wrote famously:

> If all conditions for development other than capital are present, capital will soon be generated locally, or will be available to the government or to the private businesses on commercial terms from abroad . . . If, however, the conditions for development are not present, then aid . . . will be necessarily unproductive and therefore ineffective.[20]

This is a beguilingly seductive line of thinking: if the conditions are right, aid is not needed; if the conditions are not right, aid is a waste. It's a great line that typically elicits knowing nods and approving applause from the skeptics.

However, it's not accurate. The first half of the statement claims, in effect, that domestic and international capital markets operate perfectly: if the conditions for development are right, private markets will be ready and willing to provide all the financing poor countries need. Of course, capital markets are far from perfect. They are reluctant to provide funding to poor countries even when the conditions for development are favorable. There is little private capital available in postconflict countries that are beginning to move forward, such as Timor-Leste or Sierra Leone, and the private companies that are willing to invest in these countries usually demand government subsidies and guarantees. Private markets will not fund investments in social sectors that are important to development but provide little cash return, such as vaccination programs, antiretrovirals, or agricultural research stations. Governments in low-income countries, especially those where growth is just beginning to accelerate, typically cannot generate sufficient tax revenues to finance all productive investments. So let's not claim that capital markets are perfect and that the private sector will provide all of the necessary financing. It just isn't true.

What about the second half of his statement: that if conditions are not right, aid is a waste? This claim is at best partially true, but as a blanket statement, it is incorrect; it depends on the purpose of the aid and how it is delivered. Conditions for development are not right in Zimbabwe. It is correct that large amounts of aid aimed at triggering broad-based growth and development would be a waste as long as Robert Mugabe remains in power. That does not mean that all aid is a waste. Aid given through non-governmental organizations (NGOs) is helping to support antiretroviral treatment for people living with HIV/AIDS and to fight malaria, and is managing to help individual Zimbabweans despite their government's dysfunction. It may be true that this aid would be even more effective in better circumstances, but that does not mean it cannot save lives. When circumstances are adverse for broad-based development, it means typically that smaller, more narrowly targeted aid programs focused on social services and humanitarian assistance might be appropriate, with funds provided through NGOs. It does not mean that aid can't be effective at all. Let's put Peter Bauer's overused platitude to rest.

CRITICISMS OF AID

Putting aside some of the broadsides, there is no question that aid programs do not always work, and there are many shortcomings in how they are managed and delivered. The critics make several valid points, many of which have been the basis for recent reform efforts within donor agencies. Donor organizations have plenty of room for improvement.

First, some aid programs are poorly designed, with little input from local citizens and others with knowledge of local context. They may overlook obstacles, ignore underlying incentives, or otherwise design programs in ways that undermine results. Second, donor and recipient views of the highest priorities are not always aligned, and sometimes what donors want to fund does not match the community's highest needs (a common challenge for many charities and philanthropies). If donors want to fund textbooks when recipients actually need teacher training, aid will be less effective than it could be. Third, since money is fungible, aid directed at a commendable goal can allow governments to divert more money to other, less desirable goals. Aid financing for vaccination programs could allow governments to spend less on vaccines and more on limousines. Fourth, some donor programs are expensive to manage, with layers of bureaucracy, contractors, and others between the original funders and the intended beneficiaries. There are good reasons for some of these functions, such as ensuring financial oversight so that funds are less likely to be stolen, or including funding for people with special expertise and knowledge that may not be available locally. Nevertheless, sometimes there are far too many cumbersome processes and layers of bureaucracy between the funders and the ultimate recipients, which can add costs, create inefficiencies, and reduce the impact of each aid dollar. Fifth, donors do not always monitor and evaluate their programs. Targets and goals are sometimes poorly specified or nonexistent, making it more difficult to understand what works.

One common criticism of aid is that it keeps bad governments in power. There is no question that over the years—especially during the Cold War—rich countries provided large amounts of funding to some of the world's nastiest dictators, including Mobutu Sese Seko in Zaire, François "Papa Doc" Duvalier in Haiti, Ferdinand Marcos in the Philippines, and Jean-Bédel Bokassa in the Central African Republic, among others. In these countries, the objective of donor governments actually *was* to keep the dictators in power. The practice continues today with funding that goes to authoritarian governments that are helping to fight terrorism, combating drug trafficking, or otherwise aligned with the priorities of rich-country governments. In countries with unaccountable governments, it may not matter what the aid is intended for. Since money is fungible, aid can help free up other money for dictators to do with as they please.

These are legitimate concerns. However, at their core, they are less about aid per se than about the policies and intentions of rich-country governments wanting to keep their allies in power. Today the United States, the European powers, Russia, and China use a wide range of tools to keep friendly dictators in power: diplomacy, trade preferences, military support, private investment guarantees, loans, information campaigns, and—yes—foreign aid. Aid is a tool, and like any tool, it can be misused. Since the purpose of aid in these situations is not development, it should be no surprise that it fails to spur development. It is valid to criticize the rich countries for using their powers to prop up dictators, but that does not imply that foreign aid is a failure across the board any more than it implies that trade preferences, diplomacy, and loan guarantees are always failures because they have been used to keep dictators in power. Private investment has been at least as powerful in propping up dictators—United Fruit Company across Latin America, timber companies in Indonesia, oil companies in Equatorial Guinea, and many other examples—but that does not mean private investment has been a failure.

Nevertheless, these concerns should be taken seriously. Today some aid still goes to countries run by autocrats, but less than in the past. As many developing countries have moved from dictatorship to democracy, more aid has gone to support legitimately and democratically elected regimes in countries such as Ghana, Senegal, South Africa, Turkey, Timor-Leste, Indonesia, Mongolia, Costa Rica, and the Dominican Republic. Recent empirical research suggests that the relationship between aid and democracy changed after the end of the Cold War. Since then, foreign assistance appears to have helped support democratic transitions, both by reinforcing broad development progress in these countries and by supporting civil-society organizations, stronger judicial systems, and multiparty elections. University of California at Berkeley political scientist Thad Dunning found that foreign aid had a positive effect on democracy in Africa after the Cold War, and concluded that "the end of the Cold War marked a watershed in the politics of foreign aid in Africa." Duke University political scientist Sarah Bermeo found that after 1992, foreign aid from democratic donors was associated with an increase in the likelihood of a democratic transition. (Aid from nondemocratic donors, such as China, did not have this impact.) Similarly, Simone Dietrich at the University of Missouri and Joseph Wright of Penn State University showed that over the past two decades, donors have increasingly linked foreign aid to democracy objectives in Africa. They concluded that "economic aid increases the likelihood of transition to multiparty politics, while democracy aid furthers democratic consolidation by reducing the incidence of multiparty failure and electoral misconduct." These studies did not find support for the idea that aid as a general matter undermines democracy or keeps autocrats in power.[21]

As a recent example, donor pressure in Senegal—in support of the majority of local voices—had a big impact in thwarting former president Abdoulaye Wade from changing the constitution and seeking a third term in office in 2012. Far from supporting dictatorship, donor pressure helped the citizens of Senegal achieve an open and fair election for a new president. Many programs that support civil society seem to be effective, at least judged by the reactions of authoritarian governments. In 2012 Russia banned US assistance to a wide range of prodemocracy civil-society groups because of what it saw as American "meddling" in its internal affairs. President Vladimir Putin clearly did not see these programs as supporting dictatorships—he saw them as strong voices for democracy and accountability, and he wanted to squelch them.

Still, significant amounts of aid go to countries that are not democracies. Donors provide substantial amounts of food aid and assistance to Somalia, Sudan, Syria, and other countries affected by disasters and humanitarian crises. They provided significant aid to Haiti following the massive earthquake there in 2010, even though it is not a full-fledged democracy. They also provide substantial aid to Uganda, Ethiopia, Rwanda, Vietnam, and other countries to fight disease and support other development initiatives.

There are myriad challenges—and no easy calls—in providing assistance to countries that are progressing in some areas of development and not in others. A legitimate critique of current aid allocation is that more aid should go to countries that are democracies, and to supporting civil-society voices in nondemocracies. Doing so would make aid more effective in achieving development goals, help support democracy, and improve its legitimacy. But the strong claim that, at a broad level, aid's main impact is to keep autocrats in power and undermine democracy doesn't hold up.

WHAT ABOUT AID AND GROWTH?

The negative views of the effectiveness of aid center largely on the claim that aid has had little impact on economic growth. This view has its roots in the years from the mid-1970s to the mid-1990s, when, outside of a handful of countries, there was almost no growth in developing countries. The reasoning was straightforward if superficial: growth (and development) had largely failed; therefore, aid aimed at supporting development had failed. Critics assert that academic research shows conclusively that there is no evidence that aid stimulates growth, but this claim is incorrect. While some studies do reach that conclusion, the bulk of the research—especially in more recent years—shows a modest positive relationship between aid and economic growth.

Among the studies that find no relationship between aid and growth, perhaps the most frequently cited is a 1996 paper by economist Peter Boone that concluded that aid had no impact on investment (and by extension, on growth). In 2000, World Bank economists David Dollar and Craig Burnside concluded that aid did not stimulate growth overall but did have a positive impact on growth in countries with better economic policies and institutions. In 2008 Raghuram Rajan and Arvind Subramanian found no relationship between aid and growth in a paper that was cited widely, since, at the time, Rajan was the chief economist of the International Monetary Fund.[22] (He is now the governor of the Reserve Bank of India.)

Each of these results is fragile. I spent several years working with three colleagues—Michael Clemens of the Center for Global Development, Rikhil Bhavnani of the University of Wisconsin, and Sami Bazzi of Boston University—trying to untangle the relationship between aid and growth. In our most recent paper, we looked at each of the three famous papers that I just described. We found that, by making a few small but sensible uniform adjustments to their underlying assumptions, the results in each case were reversed and became positive. With respect to Peter Boone's article, upon closer examination, we found that his original research actually found a positive relationship between aid and investment. He reported briefly this positive result, then—oddly—dropped fourteen observations from his sample—observations with the largest amounts of aid. It was only in his truncated sample that he found no relationship between aid and investment. So, stated correctly, Boone's original study, with the full sample, found that aid had a *positive* relationship with investment in developing countries.

However, we went further. We made three straightforward adjustments in the assumptions behind the studies. First, we included the standard economic principle of diminishing returns—that is, that the impact of aid on growth would diminish with larger amounts of aid—instead of the dubious assumption in each of these studies of a constant, linear relationship, in which each additional dollar of aid would continue to have the same impact on growth forever. Second, we allowed for the impact of aid to materialize with a lag of around four years (to provide time for the investments to be completed and take hold) rather than test for an immediate impact, as these studies had assumed. Third, we recognized that it doesn't make sense to look at the relationship between *all* foreign aid and economic growth, since significant amounts of foreign aid are not intended to spur growth, including humanitarian assistance, or health and education programs that might not impact growth for decades, if at all. A country in distress (say, from a major flood) would attract more aid flows just when its growth rate falls, which, in terms of basic statistics, would suggest that aid correlates with poor performance. To get a better understanding of the true relationship between aid and growth, we focused on the subset of aid intended to support economic growth.

After making these simple adjustments (and otherwise keeping the studies in their original form), we found that the same data used in all three of these influential studies yielded a *positive* and significant relationship between aid and economic growth. We did not find that aid always worked in every country. There was wide variation in the relationship across countries, with some positive and others much less so (and even negative). But overall, we found that aid showed a modest, positive, statistically significant relationship with growth. The paper went through long, extensive review before its publication in 2012 in the *Economic Journal*. It won the Royal Economic Society prize for being the journal's best article that year.[23]

Of course, no single piece of research is definitive, and not everyone is swayed by these results, but our work is consistent with a growing body of other research that reaches similar conclusions by academics such as Henrik Hansen, Finn Tarp, Robert Lensink, Howard White, Sandrina Berthault Moreira, Channing Arndt, Markus Brükner, and many others, all published in respected academic journals (but rarely, if ever, mentioned by skeptics).[24] A new working paper by University of Maryland economist Sebastian Galiani and three coauthors from the World Bank found a statistically significant positive impact of aid on growth in a group of thirty-five countries that had graduated from World Bank concessional aid eligibility (concessional aid includes grants and subsidized loans).[25] Indeed, at this stage, far from the claims that all the academic evidence shows that aid does not bolster economic growth, the preponderance of recent research shows the opposite, with aid having a modest positive impact on growth.

More and more leading economists are reaching that conclusion. Nobel laureate Joseph Stiglitz states: "Foreign aid . . . for all its faults, still has brought benefits to millions, often in ways that have almost gone unnoticed." Georgetown's Martin Ravallion, one of the world's foremost experts on poverty, concluded after a careful review that "the recent macro evidence is more consistent with the claim that sustained aid commitment to poor countries is good for their economic growth over the longer term." Oxford's Paul Collier found that "a reasonable estimate is that over the last thirty years aid has added around one percentage point to the annual growth rate of the bottom billion." Former secretary of the Treasury Lawrence Summers says, "It makes fiscal sense to support smart and effective foreign aid programs that are saving millions of lives." And Channing Arndt and his coauthors at the University of Copenhagen found that "an inflow [of aid] on the order of 10 percent of GDP spurs the per capita growth rate by more than one percentage point per annum in the long run."[26]

Fortunately, the debate on aid has begun to move beyond the simple and unhelpful extreme views to focus on better understanding when and where aid can work, and how assistance programs can be strengthened to support development. I'll discuss some of these ideas in the final chapter. Foreign aid has not been the major driver of development progress over the last twenty years, nor will it be in the future. But despite all the rhetoric, the evidence shows that aid has been a positive force in supporting the surge of development progress.

PART THREE

THE FUTURE

Can the great surge be sustained? Can it spread to other countries and regions that so far have been left behind? Or will progress begin to slow, or even be reversed? In the chapters that follow, I explore three possible futures for developing countries that capture broadly the range of likely possibilities: (1) progress continues and spreads; (2) progress subsides in a world of small gains and missed opportunities; and (3) progress is derailed by poor leadership, increasing environmental pressures, and a return to major conflict. In the final chapter, I examine the key actions upon which these outcomes will depend.

TEN

FUTURE 1—
PROGRESS EXPANDED: A NEW
AGE OF GLOBAL PROSPERITY

We are at an auspicious moment in history, when the successes
of past decades and an increasingly favorable economic outlook
combine to give developing countries a chance—for the first time
ever—to end extreme poverty within a generation.

—World Bank president Jim Yong Kim, April 2, 2013

BEGINNING IN THE EARLY SIXTEENTH CENTURY—FOR ALMOST FIVE CENTURIES NOW—THE
West has been ascendant in the world economy. Western Europe, the
United States, Canada, Australia, and New Zealand accounted for 25
percent of the world economy in 1820, but by 1950, following the end
of World War II, their share had soared to 55 percent, even though they
accounted for less than 20 percent of world population.[1] Their economies grew steadily over this period at just less than 2 percent per person
per year, a pace that seems modest but was enough to power an eightfold increase in average incomes. Extreme poverty all but disappeared;

life expectancy doubled; and personal freedoms, respect for basic rights, and democracy took hold steadily. Yet, for the other 80 percent of the world's citizens, there was almost no progress at all. The vast majority of the world's people continued to live in or near extreme poverty, with poor health, inadequate nutrition, little access to education, and low income.

Starting in the 1960s, major changes in the patterns of global income began to unfold. A small number of developing countries, primarily in Asia, began their rapid ascent. China awoke and began to reemerge in the 1980s. In the 1990s, the breadth and the pace of change expanded, with accelerated growth in more than seventy developing countries, a doubling of average incomes for hundreds of millions of people, a spectacular reduction in extreme poverty, and huge improvements in human welfare and well-being.

The good news is that there is significant potential for these dramatic changes to continue in the decades to come. Most mainstream projections suggest that developing-country economies could grow at a pace that would nearly double average incomes—again—in dozens of countries in the next twenty years. If so, hundreds of millions more people will be lifted out of extreme poverty. Child deaths will continue to fall, and fewer people will face hunger or famine. Three-quarters of adults will have at least a secondary education, including an equal share of women. Democracy—imperfect, as always—will continue to spread, slowly and unevenly, but eventually becoming deeper and stronger in the majority of countries.

These may sound like naïve projections about a fairy-tale future, but they are based on relatively modest assumptions: economic growth for the majority of developing countries averaging around 3 percent per capita per year, improvements in health and education spreading more widely, and democracy continuing to expand its reach around the world. These outcomes are far from guaranteed, but they are eminently achievable.

If a future along these lines is achieved, the great surge of development progress that began in the 1960s and accelerated in the 1990s would be just the beginning of a decades-long transformation for hundreds of millions of people in developing countries, from deep poverty to modest prosperity. Millions more people will have incomes that will allow them to take care of their families, with less poverty, better health and education, and a wider range of basic freedoms. Far fewer countries will be failing states, and the world will be a far better place because of it.

As I write in early 2015, there are many dark clouds forming on the horizon that could impede further advances. The global economy has not recovered fully from the 2008 financial crisis, and there are growing concerns as to whether the world's leading economies and emerging markets can return to the pace of growth achieved before the crisis. Growth has slowed in both China and India. The global shift toward democracy has stalled, and in some countries reversed, raising questions about a more widespread democratic recession. After a decade of unprecedented global peace, conflict is on the rise. Russia's invasion of Ukraine, several skirmishes along China's borders, Syria's implosion into civil war, and terrorist attacks around the world may signal the beginning of a new era of hostilities. Population growth, increased urbanization, greater resource demands, and climate change are creating enormous risks and challenges, especially for many low-income countries.

Alongside these challenges come many opportunities. Technological advances continue to unfold, creating new possibilities for alternative energy sources, improved health, water conservation, and greater food production. Even just expanding the reach of existing technologies—such as electricity, paved roads, vaccines, and the internet—would improve the welfare of hundreds of millions of people. Developing countries have a much wider array of options for financing development, from their own growing domestic savings and tax revenues to global financing networks. Interest rates around the world have been at historically low levels since the financial crisis, providing an opportunity for developing countries to finance major infrastructure projects and attract other investments. Most developing countries have a much larger skills base and talent pool from which to draw, and most are only beginning to deepen trade, financing, and information networks among themselves, with considerable potential for further expansion.

Continuing the great surge of development will depend on actions in three main areas, as I discuss in the final chapter. First, it will require strong leadership from the United States, Europe, and Japan, working much more closely with the emerging countries, to establish and maintain the global conditions necessary for continued progress. Global leaders must fix some significant problems at home, including slow economic growth following the global financial crisis and political gridlock that raises major questions about the effectiveness of democracy. In addition, the traditional powers will need to include, to a much greater extent, the rising powers—such as China, India, South Africa, Brazil, and Turkey—in shaping global institutions, exerting leadership, and making key decisions.

Second, sustaining progress will depend on deeper and more effective integration of trade, finance, information, ideas, and—critically—vigorous investments in new technologies. Advances in energy, transportation, health, information flows, and agricultural technologies will be vital to propelling progress, both globally and in developing countries, and in overcoming the threat of climate change and the challenge of feeding a growing population. These technologies will not emerge without commitment, innovation, and investment.

Third, skilled leadership in developing countries—from all across society—will be central for building effective institutions that can sustain progress. Continued advancement will require action on infrastructure investments, trade, financial systems, energy, natural resource management, economic diversification, health and education systems, social safety nets, inclusion of women and minority groups, governance, corruption, and human rights and accountability. There is no single formula for success, but all developing countries will have to wrestle with these issues—just as most of today's higher-income countries did and continue to do.

None of these challenges will be easy to meet, but with the right choices and decisive action, the prospects for continued development progress are strong.

THE GROWTH SURGE CONTINUES

Brazil, China, India, Indonesia, Mexico, South Africa, Turkey, and other large emerging economies will be central to continuing and expanding widespread development progress. Their continued advancement will be important for their own citizens but also will help drive economic activity in other developing countries. China is the most important. The Chinese economy has been growing extraordinarily fast during the past several decades, but the pace of growth has begun to slow. In the five years preceding the global financial crisis (2003 through 2007), the Chinese economy grew 11.7 percent per year. During the next four years, growth slowed to 9.6 percent, then it decelerated even further to 7.7 percent in 2012 and 2013, and 7.4 percent in 2014. The IMF expects slower growth in 2015 and 2016, and a further deceleration to around 6.3 percent by 2019. Some observers, such as Harvard University economists Lant Pritchett and Lawrence Summers, think that China's growth rate could slow even more.[2]

China faces some major headwinds that are likely to gradually slow its spectacular growth but not bring it to a halt. Three stand out.

First, China's savings and investment rates have been huge, but their impact on growth is beginning to decline. This change is the familiar pattern of diminishing returns on investment: as the total amount of capital expands—roads, power supplies, factories, machines—each new investment tends to increase production by a smaller amount. China's investments have been filling big gaps in roads, ports, energy supplies, and housing, but those gaps are shrinking, so there are now fewer investments that will bring big returns. Longtime China expert and Harvard professor Dwight Perkins reports that in 2011–12 alone, China completed 3.8 billion square meters of housing space, enough to house more than 100 million people comfortably. That kind of investment adds to economic growth, but China can't keep building that many new houses year after year—even in China, there won't be demand for new housing for 100 million people every year into the future.[3]

Second, an important part of China's rapid growth has come from its shifting agricultural workers to manufacturing, where the average worker's productivity is much higher. At the same time, China has been able to import technologies developed elsewhere and adapt them to manufacturing. Both of these forces have contributed to rapid productivity growth and, hence, GDP growth, but they are likely to slow: fewer workers are moving from agriculture to manufacturing, and more are beginning to shift from manufacturing to services, where productivity gains tend to be harder to achieve. China also is moving slowly from importing other countries' technologies to becoming more of an innovator in developing technologies itself—an important shift for long-term growth, but one that tends to translate into slower growth rates, since this is harder and more costly than simply adopting someone else's ideas.

Third, China's changing demography will begin to work against it. Over the last few decades, China has enjoyed the benefits of a "demographic dividend." A large share of its population has been of working age, with a smaller share of children and senior citizens. Economic growth is faster when more people are working and there are fewer nonworking dependents. As China's population ages, there will be fewer workers relative to dependents. As a result, its growth rate per person will slow.

The deceleration from spectacular growth is what happened to Japan in the 1980s and 1990s and, more recently, has begun to take hold in South Korea, Taiwan, Botswana, and other countries that surged ahead a few decades ago. South Korea's annual growth slowed from nearly 8.5 percent from 1966 through 1990, to 6.2 percent between 1991 and 2000, to 4.1 percent over the last decade. Economist Barry Eichengreen from the University of California at Berkeley and his coauthors studied dozens of cases of "When Fast Growing Economies Slow Down." They found that while there is significant variation across countries, slowdowns in growth of around 2 percent are most likely to occur when per capita income reaches around $17,000 (in 2005 PPP terms), a level that China is likely to reach in 2015.[4]

While the Chinese juggernaut will begin to slow, it is hardly likely to crash. Most estimates suggest that the economy will grow 6 percent to 7 percent or more per year over the next decade, which is still very fast.[5]

Given its overall size, this growth will have a major impact on the world economy, pulling with it the economies of many developing countries that trade with China, and helping to continue to propel the global surge of development progress.

India is not as far along as China, either in accumulating capital or in approaching the turning point in its demographic structure. Its GDP growth averaged a strong 6.4 percent between 1996 and 2005, and accelerated to 8.3 percent annually for the five years from 2006 through 2010—even through the global financial crisis. However, its growth sputtered, slowing to around 5 percent per year in 2012 and 2013, owing to a sharp decline in new investment, before accelerating somewhat to 5.8 percent in 2014. Raghuram Rajan, formerly an economics professor at the University of Chicago and now the governor of the Reserve Bank of India, attributes the slowdown to institutional bottlenecks in facilitating investment, especially around land, mining rights, and the allocation of the wireless spectrum, alongside challenges in managing the domestic economy in the aftermath of the global financial crisis. He is upbeat about India's future growth prospects, and believes that with the right reforms and investments in infrastructure, India's growth can again reach 8 percent.[6]

Others are not quite as optimistic but still see relatively rapid growth. A recent study by the Organization for Economic Cooperation and Development (OECD) projects GDP growth in India to average 6.7 percent until 2030 and slow afterward. The IMF expects growth in India to average 6 percent to 7 percent per year over the next five years. Others are more pessimistic, such as Pritchett and Summers, who foresee India's growth falling to around 4 percent for the next ten years, and even lower thereafter.[7] Much will depend on the policy actions and institutional reforms enacted by the Indian government.

Since India's and China's populations combined exceed 2 billion, what happens in those two countries will have an enormous impact on the future of human prosperity and the global poor. India is home to the largest number of people living in extreme poverty—more than 300 million in 2011—so its growth will be central to the continued reduction in extreme poverty at the global level. But progress will hardly be limited to the two giants: many other developing countries are also likely to continue robust growth, including Indonesia, Vietnam, Bangladesh, Panama, Colombia, Turkey, Tunisia, Georgia, Tanzania, and Ethiopia, among others. Developing countries will increasingly become more interdependent, with growth in the larger economies pulling along some of the others, and deeper trade and investment ties. Trade between developing countries is likely to increase from about 20 percent of the global total to 35 percent or more by 2035. More than one-third of foreign direct investment in developing countries today is from other developing countries, and that share will rise steadily.

FIGURE 10.1: CAN THE GROWTH SURGE CONTINUE?

Number of Developing Countries with Different per Capita Growth Rates, Historical Data and IMF Projections for 2015 to 2019

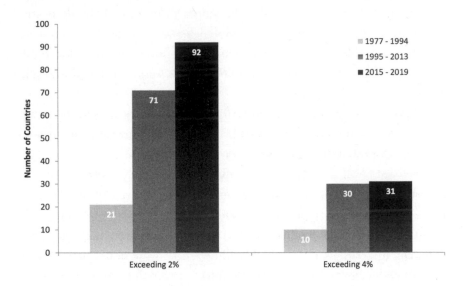

Sources: World Bank's World Development Indicators and *World Economic Outlook: Legacies, Clouds, Uncertainties* (Washington, DC: International Monetary Fund [IMF], October 2014), p. 188.

Most projections suggest that developing countries as a whole could grow by 3.5 percent to 4 percent per capita annually. Some countries will grow slower as rapid bursts of growth begin to lose momentum, but others can grow faster as policy and institutional reforms implemented in recent years begin to take hold. Critically, the forecasts suggest that this growth will include dozens of countries, not just a few. Between 1977 and 1994, just 21 developing countries (out of 109) recorded growth exceeding 2 percent per person per year. Between 1995 and 2013, the number grew to 71. The IMF projects that between 2015 and 2019, fully 92 out of the 109 developing countries will do so. It projects that 31 developing countries will achieve per capita growth exceeding 4 percent, about the same number as in the last two decades (figure 10.1).[8]

To be clear, the IMF projections are only for the next five years. They are mere projections, and they may prove to be overly optimistic, as many IMF projections have been in the past. Nevertheless, they indicate the potential for widespread continued growth, at least in the near future. While growth in some countries will slow, many others have considerable opportunities to grow even faster in the future. Investments in electricity generation, road networks, internet and cellular access, and education systems—alongside efforts to continue to deepen and strengthen institutions—can pay off in many countries. If average growth continues to proceed at anywhere close to the pace of the last two decades, and even if it is somewhat slower, the vast majority of developing countries—and the hundreds of millions of people who live in them—will make significant advances.

Consider the case in which per capita growth averages 3 percent per year for the next twenty years, equal to the average growth over the last two decades. In effect, this scenario assumes that growth in some countries will naturally slow, but in others, it will accelerate as policy and institutional reforms take hold. If something along these lines occurs, average incomes in 2035 in developing countries will be almost twice as high as in 2013, and three and a half times higher than in 1994 (figure 10.2). Even with a far more modest average growth rate of 2 percent per capita per year over the next two decades, average incomes would be almost triple their 1994 levels.

FIGURE 10.2: INCOMES CONTINUE TO CLIMB

Average Income in Developing Countries, Population Weighted, Excluding China (Constant Prices)

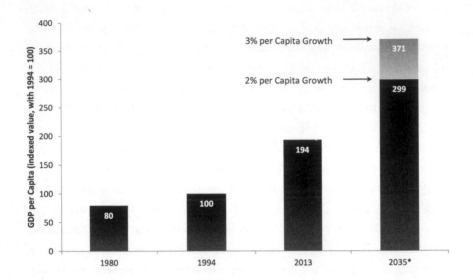

Source: Author's calculations, based on data from the World Bank's World Develop-ment Indicators. The figures in the graph are indexed values, with the original GDP per capita figures recalculated to equal 100 in the base year of 1994 for all countries. The 2035 figures are projected based on annual growth of 2 percent and 3 percent per person from 2013 to 2035.

The impacts would be substantial. Tanzania has 47 million people, including 28 million still living with incomes below $1.25 a day. With growth projected to exceed 4 percent per capita per year,[9] its 2013 per person income of $1,700 (in PPP terms) will more than double to around $4,000 per person by 2035, allowing most Tanzanians to live in better housing, send more of their children to school, and access better health care. Extreme poverty would fall substantially.

Millions more people in developing countries will begin to enter the middle class. Homi Kharas, an economist at the Brookings Institu-tion, has explored these trends in depth. While there is much debate about what constitutes the middle class in developing countries, he uses a standard of daily income between $10 and $100 (in PPP terms), a higher level than most other researchers. (Note that the bottom level is eight times higher than the extreme poverty line of $1.25 a day.) By this definition, in 2009 the world middle class included about 1.8 billion people, or about 25 percent of the global population. He finds, based on reasonable assumptions, that the world middle class will expand rapidly to nearly 5 billion people by 2035 (about 60 percent of global population), with the majority of those people living in today's developing countries.[10]

Higher incomes also mean greater savings and tax revenues, so that developing countries will be in stronger positions to make the investments and build the institutions necessary to sustain growth. Banks, insurance companies, stock exchanges, pension funds, and other financial institutions will grow, creating larger pools of finance to drive investment. Larger tax revenues will mean that countries can invest more in infrastructure, judicial systems, health, education, police, and other public sector institutions. In other words, developing countries will be able to ignite a reinforcing cycle between higher incomes, stronger institutions, and greater public and private investment, which will help drive continued growth and improvements in human welfare.

These changes will have profound effects on the global economy. After more than two centuries of divergence in incomes between the world's richest and poorest countries, we have entered a period where many poor countries are beginning to close the income gap. Kishore Mahbubani, the dean of the Lee Kuan Yew School of Public Policy at the National University of Singapore, has referred to the process of developing countries—especially those in Asia—beginning to catch up as "the great convergence."[11] If growth proceeds along these lines, developing countries' share of the global economy could reach 55 percent or more by 2035 (in PPP terms), up from 41 percent in 1995.

LIFTING 700 MILLION MORE PEOPLE
OUT OF EXTREME POVERTY

As we have seen, between 1993 and 2011, the share of people living in extreme poverty in developing countries was slashed from 42 percent to 17 percent, and the absolute number fell by half from 2 billion to 1 billion. The first Millennium Development Goal—to reduce the share of people living in extreme poverty by half between 1990 and 2015—was achieved several years early. The world has never seen such a rapid reduction in extreme poverty.

The success in reducing the share of people living in extreme poverty by 25 percentage points in less than twenty years has led some to ask an obvious question: Can we reduce it by another 17 percentage points by 2030, and eliminate extreme poverty? It's a tantalizing goal. Both the World Bank and the US government have set a target to eliminate extreme poverty by 2030, as World Bank president Jim Kim called for in his quotation at the beginning of this chapter. There is a small caveat: by "eliminate," they mean reduce to around 3 percent of the world's population, or about 300 million people. Putting aside whether the word *eliminate* is the best choice to describe getting to 3 percent, it's still an ambitious goal. It would imply *lifting another 700 million people out of extreme poverty by 2030*. If achieved, the decline in extreme poverty between 1993 and 2030 would surely rank as one of the greatest achievements in human history.

Continuing to reduce global poverty at the same pace for the next two decades will be much harder, for three key reasons. First, there is only so much more poverty reduction that can be squeezed out of China. Between 1993 and 2011, 560 million Chinese were lifted out of extreme poverty, accounting for more than half of the global reduction. There are only about 84 million extreme poor remaining in China (as of 2011), so continued global progress will depend on other countries, especially India, where 300 million people live in extreme poverty. It will require significant continued progress in large countries such as Bangladesh, Indonesia, the Philippines, and dozens of countries across Africa.

Second, the biggest challenges will be in several countries with large and growing numbers of poor that have not yet begun to stimulate rapid growth and poverty reduction, including Nigeria, Pakistan, Somalia, North Korea, and the Democratic Republic of the Congo. In these countries, continuing past trends is not good enough—they need a more fundamental change in direction. Eliminating extreme poverty will be possible only if the trajectories change in these more difficult countries.

Third, as the number of poor declines, those remaining tend to be the most difficult to reach: people who have incomes far below the $1.25-a-day standard, are geographically isolated, have few assets (such as land), confront significant discrimination (women and minorities), or live in countries riven by conflict and poor governance. As the global total falls, additional declines get harder.

So, is lifting another 700 million people out of extreme poverty and getting to 3 percent possible? Laurence Chandy and his colleagues at the Brookings Institution have looked at this question.[12] They explore three sets of poverty projections (baseline, optimistic, pessimistic) for each country around the world for the next several decades. They point out—echoing other poverty experts, such as Martin Ravallion of Georgetown University—that future poverty reduction will depend on both the rate of economic growth and changes in income distribution. The intuition is straightforward: if distribution worsens and most of the benefits of growth accrue to the rich, the impact on poverty will be muted. By contrast, if distribution remains neutral or improves, poverty falls faster for any rate of growth. Global poverty has fallen rapidly over the last two decades because of relatively rapid growth and because income distribution has changed relatively little in most countries.

According to Chandy's estimates, if growth proceeds consistent with most projections, and if distribution does not change appreciably, the share of the world's population living in extreme poverty could fall to 5.4 percent by 2030 (and even more by 2040, although they do not project that far—see figure 10.3). The number of extreme poor would fall to around 386 million. This outcome would be a huge achievement.

To place it in broad historical perspective, it would mean that the number of people living in extreme poverty—after rising steadily from the beginning of human history until its peak at around 2 billion people in the early 1990s—would have fallen by more than 80 percent in the remarkably short period of just forty years. It would mean that hundreds of millions of people around the world would move from near destitution to being able to better feed, clothe, and educate their families, and having the foundation to achieve further progress well into the future.

FIGURE 10.3: THE BEGINNING OF THE END OF EXTREME POVERTY? THREE PROJECTIONS

Percentage of People with Incomes Less Than $1.25 a Day

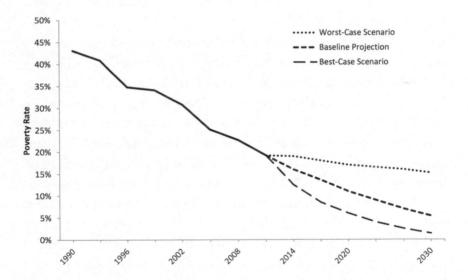

Source: Laurence Chandy, Natasha Ledlie, and Veronika Penciakova, "The Final Countdown: Prospects for Ending Extreme Poverty by 2030," policy paper 2013-04, Global Economy and Development Program, Brookings Institution, Washington, DC, April 2013.

However, if growth slows or distribution deteriorates, poverty reduction will be much slower, and could be concentrated in just a few countries such as China and India. In this pessimistic scenario, the share of people living in extreme poverty would still continue to fall, but slowly and only to around 15 percent of the world's population. Because of population growth, the total number of people would fall only slightly. This outcome would be a major disappointment.

On the other hand, even better outcomes are possible than Chandy's baseline suggests. If growth in developing countries accelerates and income distribution improves slightly—through the combination of greater advances in technology, deeper global integration, smart policy choices, and some large countries (such as Nigeria and Pakistan) shifting toward more rapid growth—poverty could fall to what they describe as "tantalizingly close to zero" at around 1.4 percent of global population, or about 100 million people.

Finally, all of these projections are for 2030, which is not far into the future. Even if the baseline or more optimistic scenarios are not achieved exactly in 2030, they could be achieved more easily by 2040 or 2050. Over the next several decades, we could indeed be getting close to ending extreme poverty.

BETTER HEALTH, BETTER EDUCATION

Developing countries have made unprecedented gains in health and education. The share of children dying before their fifth birthdays fell from 22 percent to around 5 percent from 1960 to 2012, life expectancy increased from forty-nine to sixty-five years, and 80 percent of girls now complete primary school. But as important as these gains are, there is still a long way to go before people living in developing countries can enjoy the same quality of health and education as those in rich countries. With the combination of strong global leadership on health and education issues, continued economic growth, advances in technology, and robust social sector investments financed by both developing countries and the donor community, the next few decades hold the promise for continued rapid advancements in health and education.

Sustained progress in health is hardly a given, as the world faces emerging threats from antimicrobial resistance, new pandemics, emerging infections, and climate change. The British medical journal *Lancet* recently assembled the Global Health 2035 Commission, a distinguished panel of twenty-five world-renowned scientists, physicians, public health experts, and economists, chaired by Lawrence Summers and University of Washington professor Dean Jamison. The commission found enormous potential for continued progress: with strong leadership in developing countries and in global health organizations, robust investments in research and development, and continued development assistance for health, people living in developing countries can look forward to dramatic gains in health well into the future.[13] Specifically, both child and maternal mortality rates could be slashed by an additional 75 percent. The share of children dying before their fifth birthdays would fall to around 2 percent, an almost unbelievable decline from the 22 percent that prevailed in 1960. *Instead of one out of five children dying young, it would be one out of fifty*. New cases of tuberculosis would be cut by two-thirds, and new HIV/AIDS infections could drop by 85 percent. Taken together, these achievements would prevent about 10 million deaths *per year* by 2035. Early versions of several tools to fight malaria are under development—including a vaccine to reduce transmission, a single-dose cure, and a rapid diagnostic test—which, if successful, would save millions more lives.

These improvements won't happen spontaneously. The commission describes how achieving these gains will require investments in family planning, maternal and neonatal health, immunization, malaria, tuberculosis and HIV/AIDS treatment, health systems, and improved technologies. The panel estimates that it will cost $20 to $24 per person per year. But it also estimates that the economic benefits will be nine to twenty times higher than the costs. Moreover, these investments will be easier to finance in the future, since developing countries will have larger economies and larger tax bases. As a result, most of these investments can be financed at home, with complementary investments from donors focusing on the development and delivery of new health technologies and curbing antibiotic resistance.

Similarly, as incomes grow, developing countries will see continued improvements in schooling. Over the next two decades, as development progress continues, educational systems in most developing countries are likely to change in three important ways. First, the *quality* of schools will improve as families push harder for better teachers, stronger curriculums, and a better match between what children learn in school and what they need in the job market. More private schools will emerge, creating some tensions as wealthier families shift more to private schools, but also competition and higher quality. At the same time, as tax revenues increase, local funding for public education will rise, allowing for better-trained teachers, better supplies and facilities, and smaller classroom sizes.

Second, as more children complete secondary school, more countries will begin to expand and strengthen their university systems. Many promising institutions of higher education were hit badly during the economic and political crises of the 1980s. Hundreds of universities in developing countries were forced to close because of war, economic instability, funding cuts as tax revenues plummeted, and other challenges. This is beginning to change, and over the last decade, many universities have begun to rise again, including China's Peking University and Tsinghua University, Turkey's Boğaziçi University and Istanbul Technical University, South Africa's University of Cape Town and University of Witwatersrand, the National University of Singapore, Brazil's University of São Paulo, Colombia's University of the Andes, Poland's University of Warsaw, and the Indian Institute of Technology, to name a few. By 2035, it's likely that some of these universities will rank among the world's finest, and that there will be many more universities in developing countries, all creating more opportunities for students to gain a high-quality education at home.

Third, traditionally excluded groups—women, minorities, the rural poor—will gain much greater access to education. Girls are already catching up around the world in terms of their access to formal education, and in some regions, such as in Asia, they will probably forge ahead. Minority groups are also gaining greater access to education. Higher national incomes will allow for an expanded reach of formal education systems to more remote areas, providing many of the rural poor an initial chance at basic education. Building the skill base of previously excluded groups will help spur economic growth, better health, and increased political participation in the decades to come.

A NEW EXPANSION OF DEMOCRACY

The rapid spread of democracy that began in the late 1980s and early 1990s slowed around 2005, and there is growing concern that democracy is in retreat. But if anything like the future scenario described in this chapter comes to fruition, individual empowerment and liberal democracy—or something similar to them—will continue to expand and deepen in developing countries over the next twenty-five years. Higher incomes, improved technologies to enhance information flows, deeper trade links, a continued reduction in poverty, an emerging middle class, and a healthier and more educated citizenry will all help strengthen and broaden democracy. Countries such as Singapore, Malaysia, Tanzania, Mozambique, Armenia, Cuba, Haiti, Kosovo, and Zimbabwe could become full-fledged democracies, among many others, and those that have recently teetered, such as Thailand and Venezuela, could rebound. Under this scenario, democracy will not reach everywhere, to be sure, but it will spread.

As progress continues, the majority of people in developing countries will expect their leaders to deliver *both* prosperity and personal freedoms and political accountability. Women, minorities, and other historically excluded groups will increasingly gain freedoms and enjoy greater political participation. Increased education, expanded access to information, better access to health services, and more women with formal sector employment will facilitate much greater political participation.

Democracy also will be strengthened in the countries in which it has already been adopted. John Gerring and his associates at Boston University examined the history of democracies around the world and their longevity. They found that the longer a country remains a democracy, the stronger and deeper its democratic institutions become, and the less likely it is that there will be a reversal. The norms, rules, laws, and expectations about personal freedom, elections, political accountability, and civilian control over the military become more strongly held over time, passing from one generation to the next. Many developing countries have been democracies now for twenty years or more, and as time goes on, democracy is more likely to become institutionalized and more permanent. They also found that the longer a country remains a democracy, the stronger the positive reinforcing relationship between democracy and development.[14]

There will be setbacks to democracy's expansion. In some countries, authoritarian leaders or armed rebel groups may seize power and reverse democracy. In a world of growing incomes and an emerging middle class, these will be the exceptions rather than the rule.

THE DRAGON IN THE ROOM

What about China? Just as it has over the past three decades, China will have major impacts—economic and political—on development for three reasons: its importance as a huge developing country itself, its economic and political relationships with other countries, and as an example for other countries to emulate.

There are three broad views on China's future. First, China could continue to march forward much as it has for the last three decades, with robust (albeit slower) economic growth alongside some increases in personal freedoms, but with little systematic political change. This model is the hope of the Communist Party leadership: a future in which it can maintain control and power with continued material progress and limited political reform. It's not just the leadership: some Chinese citizens and many private investors would be quite content with this future, fearing that political change could undermine economic and social progress.

Second, China's authoritarian rule could continue, but economic growth will slow more sharply or even stall. Many economists and political scientists argue that this scenario will be the case, including Daron Acemoglu and James Robinson in *Why Nations Fail*. Under the current heavily state-controlled economy, property rights and contract law remain limited and weak, undermining long-term incentives for innovation and risk taking and weakening future growth prospects. Old and inefficient companies (and banks) are allowed to remain operational, limiting the room for "creative destruction"—the great Austrian economist Joseph Schumpeter's term for how dynamic economies are constantly rebuilt, with new, more innovative, and more efficient businesses replacing the old. Feedback loops from citizens and business leaders to government leaders weaken over time as officials focus on maintaining power and control.

There are many examples of authoritarian countries that were seen for a time as economic superstars, but where dictators held on to power for too long and progress slowed considerably or even came to a halt, including Argentina over the last century, the Soviet Union (and Russia today), and Japan and Germany in the late nineteenth and early twentieth centuries. It is worth remembering that in the late 1950s and 1960s, the Soviet Union was seen as an economic juggernaut that could take over economic leadership from the United States, and that supposedly provided a viable economic and political model for developing countries. Nikita Khrushchev's admonishment to Western ambassadors in November 1956, "We will bury you," followed a year later by the astonishing launch of the Sputnik satellite, generated widespread concern that he might be right, and that authoritarian Communism might prevail over democratic capitalism. However, the system collapsed.

If China continues with heavy state and party control, growth will slow, and citizen unrest will rise. The only way for the party to stem the tide will be through increased control and greater force, which will undermine its legitimacy and threaten continued growth. Like the Soviet Union before it, China will never match the prosperity of the world's most advanced countries.

Third, China's political system could evolve to greater democracy—or something like it—with greater individual freedoms and more pluralistic and accountable political institutions. This kind of change has been the pattern across much of Asia for the past several decades. Most of the old authoritarian governments—which many pundits said would never change—have moved toward democracy, including Japan, South Korea, Taiwan, the Philippines, and Indonesia, and even to some extent Malaysia and Singapore (although neither is there yet).

No country in history has been able to sustain the Chinese Communist Party's preferred model of continued economic progress under authoritarian rule. History shows that under authoritarian rule, economic

growth begins to stall, and once it does, citizens begin to demand political change and greater freedoms. At this point, one of two scenarios
unfolds: either the government cracks down with greater restrictions
(leading to even slower growth), or it begins to facilitate political change
with greater rights, accountability, and a stronger foundation for sustained innovation and growth.

China has the weight of history against it. Inevitably, either rapid
growth or authoritarian rule will have to give. But neither necessarily has
to give soon. The Soviet economy grew for five decades before it began
to crack, and it took two more decades for it to collapse. China could
last longer. Unlike the Soviets, it is not trying to support a multitude of
satellite states or to build as big a military. Since it was so poor when it
started, it still has a lot of room for relatively easy "catch-up" growth, and
it is much more of a market economy than the Soviet Union ever was.
The current system could last for many years.

Perhaps the most likely outcome is that a political transition will
happen, but only some years in the future: as incomes continue to grow,
and a larger middle class emerges, the inevitable cracks will begin to
appear in the state-run system. The demands for political change will
increase, and the political system will evolve into something much closer
to democracy. That is unlikely to happen soon: the current Chinese leadership shows little interest in even gradual political evolution. When
it comes, the change could be sudden and abrupt, and possibly messy.
Whatever happens, there is no doubt that China's economic and political evolution will be central to the future of sustained progress for developing countries around the world.

If the great surge in development that began twenty years ago continues in the years ahead—and even if it slows somewhat—the average
income of people in the world's poorest countries will nearly double
again by 2035. More than 700 million more people will be lifted out
of extreme poverty, child death will continue to fall, and more children
will obtain a better education. Democracy will continue to deepen and
spread, perhaps even to China. There is much skepticism about this kind
of future, just as there was—incorrectly—in the early 1990s about the

future prospects of developing countries. These kinds of positive outcomes are not just possible, but feasible and achievable. I believe that
something along these lines is what *will* happen in the future, despite the
pessimism—if rich and poor countries take actions along the lines that
I propose in the final chapter. History will show that we are in the early
stages of what will be the largest and most widespread transformation in
the world's poorest countries in human history.

However, it may not turn out that way.

ELEVEN
FUTURE 2—
PROGRESS DIMINISHED:
STUCK MUDDLING THROUGH

The years immediately following the end of the Cold War offered a tantalizing glimpse of a new kind of international order, with nation-states growing together or disappearing, ideological conflicts melting away, cultures intermingling, and increasingly free commerce and communications . . . But that was a mirage. The world has not been transformed.

—*Robert Kagan*, The Return of History and the End of Dreams

THE MOOD IN THAILAND IN 2001 WAS BUOYANT. THE ECONOMY WAS RECOVERING RAPIDLY from the disastrous Asian financial crisis, which had ignited in Bangkok in July 1997. Investment was pouring in, trade was booming, and business was expanding. Thailand was again feeling like an "Asian miracle" economic juggernaut. A new constitution was taking root, bringing with it many new rights, freedoms, and institutions to monitor the government and hold it more accountable. The 2001 elections were among the freest in the country's history, with robust participation throughout the country. Thailand was seen as an economic and political example for developing countries to follow. As US assistant secretary of state James Kelly declared in 2002, "Thailand's freedom, openness, strength, and relative prosperity make it a role model in the region for what people can achieve when they are allowed to."[1]

The new prime minister, Thaksin Shinawatra, had won an overwhelming victory with strong support from rural areas based on his populist platform for economic growth and development. However, the political situation started going downhill fast. Corruption charges dogged Thaksin from the start, dating back to his time as a telecommunications tycoon. He began to show disdain for many of his urban-based political opponents and for democratic institutions more broadly. He used his "war on drugs" as an excuse for extrajudicial killings that went well beyond the drug trade. Most horribly, in October 2004 Thai security forces rounded up hundreds of young men after antigovernment demonstrations, and eighty-five of them suffocated while being transported on military trucks. Despite these deepening problems, the economy continued to hum along, especially in rural areas, and Thaksin was reelected the following year. But corruption charges continued to mount, and the urban middle class became disenchanted. Massive anti-Thaksin protests began to paralyze the country. The military threw him out in a 2006 coup.

Unrest and instability have come and gone in waves ever since. The military pushed through a controversial new constitution in 2007 and allowed elections and a return to civilian rule later that year. Thaksin's party regained control of the parliament with strong support from rural areas. (Thaksin himself was not part of the new government but was widely seen to be controlling it from the sidelines.) Urban protests escalated again in 2008, especially after Thaksin's wife was found guilty of corruption. A constitutional court disbanded the ruling party in 2009 for electoral fraud, and an opposition party took over. Almost immediately, new protests erupted, this time from the other side, with Thaksin's supporters taking to the streets. Security forces killed ninety protestors at a rally in 2010. In 2011 Thaksin's party swept back into power, this time with his sister Yingluck Shinawatra as prime minister. The protests continued, first from one side and then the other. The economy began to suffer: GDP growth in the five years before the 2006 coup averaged 5.7 percent per year, but by 2009, growth had plunged to -2.3 percent, and it has recovered only to around 2 percent per year since.

Protests intensified throughout 2013 and early 2014, and efforts to broker some kind of viable path forward all failed. In May 2014 the military took over once again, dissolved the government, and imposed martial law. Democracy has faltered, conflict has risen, and economic growth has sagged. Thailand's development progress— once among the fastest in the world—has nearly halted. In some ways, it has gone in reverse.

Growth has slowed in both China and India. Brazil's economy has sputtered, Argentina is once again facing a financial crisis, and economic growth in Latin America as a whole barely exceeded 1 percent in 2014. The Arab Spring of 2010 has turned into an Arab Winter, with greater political instability across the region, increased violence, slower economic growth, and no clear shift to democracy except in Tunisia. Syria is in flames. The global advance of democracy has plateaued, and reversed not just in Thailand but in Venezuela, Armenia, Mali, Sri Lanka, and several other countries. Turkey seems to be shifting toward more authoritarian rule, and the prime minister of Hungary— a NATO country and a strong democracy since the end of the Cold War—has championed illiberalism. Vladimir Putin has tightened his grip, and his invasion of Ukraine seems to signal a new era of confrontation with his neighbors and with the West. Ebola has devastated West Africa. Meanwhile, Western Europe has yet to recover from the global financial crisis, Japan's economy has stalled again, and the US recovery, while better than in other leading countries, remains lukewarm. The clear weaknesses in the world's leading democracies and the inability of their political leaders to reach consensus on key issues and take action has raised questions around the world about the attractiveness and effectiveness of democracy.

Is the great surge of development progress about to stall?

It's entirely possible. With the world facing so many challenges, the pace of development progress could diminish considerably in the years ahead. If the global economy continues to languish, growth in developing countries could drop to around 1 percent to 2 percent per person per year, less than half the rate of the last two decades. A handful of countries might continue to expand more quickly, such as China and India, but growth in the majority of developing countries would deteriorate. With weaker growth, extreme poverty will decline much more slowly, and in some countries the number of extreme poor could begin to rise again. Income inequality, already deteriorating in some countries, could worsen in many more. The progress in global health will slow if new diseases emerge or microbial resistance expands and global leaders and developing countries fail to react. With economic and social progress faltering, democratic progress will stall as citizens lose faith in the democratic process and more leaders take advantage of the opportunity to rig the system and consolidate power. In short, twenty years from now, developing countries as a whole may look only modestly better than they do now, with significant advances in only a few countries alongside setbacks in others.

Many people believe that something along these lines is the most likely future. The view that progress is bound to slow is partly a result of our natural tendency toward pessimism, as I discussed in the opening chapter. The problems ahead always seem bigger than the opportunities. However, there is more to this perspective than misplaced pessimism. It is based in the reality that developing countries face significant challenges: a global economy that has not yet recovered from a major crisis, the difficulties in creating new jobs in high-skilled manufacturing and services, the possibility of greater isolationism and withdrawal from global engagement by the United States and Europe, and threats to democracy from unmet hopes or rising religious fundamentalism. Population pressures, resource demand, and climate change are increasing environmental and ecological stresses. There are rising threats of conflict from a more militant Russia, a stronger China, and a combustible Middle East.

Taken together, and without an adequate response, these forces could significantly slow the great surge of development progress.

GLOBAL HEADWINDS

The global financial crisis of 2008 was a major turning point for the world, both economically and politically. Although policy makers managed to avoid the catastrophic collapse that many feared, the recovery has been sluggish. Economic growth in the advanced economies dropped from 2.8 percent per year in the decade before the crisis to about half that rate since 2011. Across all developing countries, per capita growth averaged around 4.4 percent in the five years before the crisis, but slowed afterward, and was just 2.6 percent in 2013. The economies of both China and India have cooled considerably, and as their growth rates have decelerated, others have followed. Global trade collapsed in 2009, rebounded in 2010 and 2011, but then grew very slowly in 2012 and 2013. Whether these changes are a temporary setback in the wake of the crisis or represent a more fundamental shift is unclear. If they are more permanent, and especially if growth in China and India decelerate more abruptly than expected, economic growth in developing countries that depend on these markets will slow in tandem.

Former secretary of the Treasury and Harvard professor Lawrence Summers worries that the United States and other leading economies may be entering a period of "secular stagnation," with structural changes in the global economy such that a return to past growth rates might not be feasible. Economic growth has rebounded much less quickly than many expected, and output remains far below its potential. Japan is in its second decade of slow growth, with a GDP today far lower than anyone would have predicted twenty years ago. Global investment and aggregate demand have remained tepid despite low interest rates. Summers does not argue that secular stagnation in the advanced economies is inevitable but that it could become the reality if policy makers do not take steps to heighten demand such as increasing public investment in infrastructure and changing regulations to spur private investment in alternative energy sources.[2]

Northwestern University economist Robert Gordon sees other forces working to slow long-term growth in the United States. One is simple demographics: the baby boomers are retiring, so the labor force is growing more slowly than the number of retirees, a dynamic that is not going to change anytime soon. He also points to the plateauing of mass education (and therefore less growth in skills), rising inequality, and soaring public debt as forces slowing growth. Perhaps most controversially, he believes there has been a deceleration in the rate of new innovation, with less scope for new technologies to support rapid growth in the future.[3]

Slower long-term growth in the advanced economies would weaken the prospects for sustained growth in developing countries. Although developing countries trade more with one another than ever before, they still depend on rich-world markets to sell their commodities, manufactured products, and services. Investment and finance from the advanced economies power businesses around the world. And, as we have seen, developing countries benefit from technological innovation that originates in rich countries in information technology, health, agriculture, and energy. While developing countries do not rely on rich-world markets as much as they once did, their fates remain intertwined.

The concerns go beyond growth and touch on the broader architecture of the global economy. Since the end of World War II, the global economy has been undergirded by international organizations and institutions such as the International Monetary Fund, the World Bank, and the General Agreement on Tariffs and Trade (GATT), which evolved into the World Trade Organization. These organizations are part of a larger set of international organizations (including the United Nations) that, for all their many faults, deserve some credit for the increase in global prosperity and reduction in conflict during the past seventy years.

These organizations and institutions are showing signs of fraying. One clear example is the failure of the Doha round of global trade talks under the auspices of the WTO. These negotiations began in 2001, with a major objective of improving the trade prospects of developing countries. They stalled in 2008, primarily over disagreements on agriculture import rules and subsidies. The inability to conclude the round is a worrying sign that global trade negotiations will become more difficult in the future. More broadly, as developing countries have progressed in the last several decades, they have begun to demand greater participation and leadership in these organizations, and a louder voice in negotiations and decisions. There is resistance from some in the rich world who just want developing countries to line up and "follow the rules"—even though they had little say in establishing those rules. A failure to incorporate emerging countries will mean that these organizations will begin to lose credibility and effectiveness, which could further weaken global growth.

These issues are coming into focus at the IMF and World Bank. The process by which the heads of these organizations are chosen is outdated and creates issues of legitimacy. By informal arrangement, the president of the World Bank is always an American, and the managing director of the IMF is always a European. In effect, the president of the United States selects the president of the World Bank, and the EU decides who runs the IMF. This arrangement makes little sense. In addition, member voting shares in the IMF and World Bank are outdated and do not reflect the increasing economic weight of developing countries in the global economy. Unfortunately, in 2014 the US Congress failed to pass legislation that would have approved a change in voting shares in the IMF—a change with which all other member countries had agreed after years of discussion.

In frustration, a few weeks later, China announced that it would establish a new investment development bank for Asia—the Asian Infrastructure Investment Bank (AIIB)—that would compete with the World Bank and the Asian Development Bank in providing infrastructure financing to countries across Asia and the Middle East. Almost immediately, Brazil, Russia, India, China, and South Africa (the BRICS countries) announced their intention to form two new organizations: their own development bank (the New Development Bank), to provide funding for infrastructure and other development projects in emerging countries; and a Contingent Reserve Arrangement, to help the BRICS manage liquidity pressures. Tellingly, and with unusual pointedness for a public diplomatic document, the official statement from the BRICS heads of state announcing these new organizations declared:

> International governance structures designed within a different power configuration show increasingly evident signs of losing legitimacy

and effectiveness, as transitional and ad hoc arrangements become increasingly prevalent, often at the expense of multilateralism . . . We remain disappointed and seriously concerned with the current non-implementation of the 2010 International Monetary Fund (IMF) reforms, which negatively impacts on the IMF's legitimacy, credibility and effectiveness.[4]

When the United States and other advanced countries fail to lead, problems emerge and progress stalls. A little competition for the World Bank is not a bad thing, and as Georgetown University's Raj Desai and James Vreeland have argued, greater reliance on regional organizations has certain advantages, since countries typically have deeper economic connections and more shared interests at the regional level.[5] But even in a more regionalized world, global institutions will continue to play a major role in sustaining continued progress. The moves by Beijing and the BRICS show that the traditional international organizations are at risk of losing legitimacy in the eyes of many developing countries.

ECONOMIC HEADWINDS

In addition to these global strains, there are concerns that growth could slow in developing countries because of their own internal challenges. Developing countries that have initiated growth over the last two decades face a difficult test in trying to sustain it: they can't just keep producing the same goods and services. They must continuously change the structure of production and upgrade to new goods and services to create more higher-skilled jobs with better pay for a new generation of workers. In the early stages of economic growth, countries typically rely on natural resources and agriculture, but sustained growth requires moving to higher-skilled manufacturing, industry, and services, which are based on knowledge, innovation, and a deeper stock of physical and human capital.

Stimulating this transition is not easy. It requires new infrastructure, more advanced skills, extensive global supply and marketing networks, and effective policies. It requires strengthening health and education systems and building social safety nets to provide more widespread opportunities and to protect those left behind. The growth strategies that served well at lower income levels no longer apply. As a result, some countries show a burst of growth based on commodities but then get stuck and never make it to middle-income status. Many countries in sub-Saharan Africa, for example, still rely on agriculture and natural resources. Ghana, Senegal, Tanzania, Mozambique, Ethiopia, and Rwanda have all grown rapidly during the last two decades but have yet to diversify significantly to manufacturing and services. If they don't fully make the transition, growth will slow and could drop from the 3 percent per capita rate enjoyed over the last two decades to 1 percent to 2 percent or even less. Their challenge will be all the greater because of underlying demographic dynamics, in which large numbers of youth in sub-Saharan Africa will soon reach working age and will need decent jobs.

Princeton University's Dani Rodrik perceives several obstacles facing low-income countries in making the transition to manufacturing. He sees part of the problem in impediments such as the costs of power, transport, corruption, regulations, and contract enforcement. He also points to more deep-seated issues, including slower global growth, more widespread competition, and changes in technology (robotics, for example) that are causing some manufacturing processes to become more capital intensive, which will make it more difficult for developing countries to initiate sustained rapid growth in basic industries.[6]

If countries make this initial shift to basic manufacturing and services, they typically achieve faster growth that can last for years, or even decades. Workers shift from agriculture to manufacturing, and firms evolve from low-end manufacturing to more sophisticated products as productivity rises, bringing more jobs and higher wages. Deeper global integration brings new ideas and technology, further supporting growth.

At some point, many developing countries face a second major transition. Once most workers have switched to basic manufacturing and services, growth can get hung up again in what economists Homi Kharas of the Brookings Institution and Indermit Gill of the World Bank labeled the "middle-income trap": the difficulty of shifting from low-skilled manufacturing and services (shoes and shirts) to higher-skilled products (electronics and call centers). Investments in education, training, health, and infrastructure can help, but some countries don't make them. Income inequality can worsen if some workers move to high-skilled products but others remain stuck in lower-wage activities.

Harvard economist Lant Pritchett has highlighted both growth accelerations and decelerations, and documented that many developing countries that begin to achieve rapid growth do not sustain it over time.[7] False starts are all too common, and ten or even twenty years of solid growth—as we have seen in many developing countries—does not guarantee that it will continue. The key to long-term development is not generating a burst of rapid growth but building the institutions that can sustain it over long periods. A century ago, Argentina was one of the world's richest countries based on its commodities, but it never switched to high-skilled manufacturing and services, and it has slipped further behind. South Korea and Taiwan have made this transition, but many developing countries have not yet fully done so, including Thailand, Indonesia, Vietnam, India, South Africa, and Brazil.

Why are these changes so hard? Some see the issue as greater competition among developing countries themselves, especially in the future. As more developing countries attempt to move up the production ladder, they will compete among themselves to attract investment and know-how. The first movers in Asia had a big advantage in that they had fewer competitor countries, but today dozens of developing countries are competing against one another. History suggests that this concern is overstated: as economies grow, they compete for investment, but they also become larger markets for one another's goods and services, and become more integrated in global production chains. Hence, the United States, Europe, and Japan all competed with one another in the post–World War II boom, but they also became one another's major markets. Developing countries have followed a similar pattern during the past twenty years: increasingly, they compete with one another, but they also buy and sell one another's products.

Transforming production and finding the right niche in global markets is far from easy. Shifting to new products requires both letting go of the old and investing in the new. It demands that policy makers be willing to accept that factories producing the old products shut down when they can no longer compete, which will mean transitional job losses for some workers and reduced profits for owners (some of whom may be political supporters). It means generating the savings needed to invest in the infrastructure, technology, training, and education and health systems required to move up the ladder. In some situations, it may include moderate subsidies or tariff protection for some industries, as Dani Rodrik has argued. These choices and actions are hard, and require sacrifices and risk taking, alongside competent economic management. As a result, shifting to higher-skilled products will be a significant challenge for many developing countries. If they fail to make the transition, economic growth is sure to slow, and broader development progress will diminish.

POLITICAL HEADWINDS

As we saw in chapter 5, the number of developing-country democracies grew rapidly in the 1990s, but since around 2005, the shift toward democracy has stalled. While some countries have continued to move forward, democracy is reversing direction in several countries. Thailand, Armenia, Pakistan, Uganda, Zimbabwe, Venezuela, and Russia have all taken steps backward, and there are worrying signs in Turkey, Hungary, and even Botswana. The hopefulness that came with the Arab Spring in 2011 has receded. Middle-class protests have spread from Brazil to Turkey to Thailand. The news is not all bad, however: Myanmar, Côte d'Ivoire, and Tunisia have moved forward. Mali, Senegal, Madagascar, and the Philippines, which had taken steps backward, now seem to be (mostly) getting back on track. The protests in Brazil and Turkey are a sign of the strength of democracy, not weakness—they simply would not have been allowed under the old authoritarian regimes. Indonesia, which many people thought would retreat, held successful elections in mid-2014 that continued to strengthen its deepening democracy. Nigeria's successful elections and transition of power in early 2015 may herald a new era. However, the stagnation in the number of democracies is a worrying trend. As Josh Kurlantzick of the Council on Foreign Relations has written, democracy may be in retreat.[8]

In some cases, these pressures stem from the inability of democracies to deliver quickly the kind of progress that citizens expect. Democracy, by design, involves complex decision-making processes that require consensus and power sharing. Slow processes create frustrations, expectations and hopes can outrun reality, and tensions can flare. If growth is uneven and income distribution worsens, the political system can lose legitimacy. The 2008 global financial crisis, and the failures of the United States and Europe to respond effectively, added to disillusionment about capitalism, globalization, and democracy. For many people, the United States and Western Europe aren't attractive models these days. As economic growth slowed in developing countries following the crisis, frustrations surged and protests erupted.

In some countries, deep corruption has been the problem, as elected leaders have used their power to grab what they can with both arms wide open. Partial and superficial democracy—what journalist and author Fareed Zakaria referred to as "illiberal democracy"—has been common: elections without accountability (which is not democracy at all), or concentrated power without adequate checks and balances. Increased corruption in the Philippines under Joseph Estrada and Gloria Macapagal-Arroyo, Thailand under Thaksin, and South Africa under Jacob Zuma have all undermined the credibility of democracy. In these cases, judicial systems, the legislature, the media, and other democratic institutions designed to limit the authority of the executive branch have been unable to do so effectively. In some countries, security has been the issue. The crime epidemic in Central America—perhaps most acute in Honduras—is a clear example. Other reversals are the result of leaders taking advantage of weak institutions to consolidate their own power, as in Russia, Venezuela, Uganda, and Zimbabwe. In almost all of these cases, some of the underlying institutions of democracy—the courts, media, legislature, civil-society groups—were not resilient or strong enough to forestall the reversal. In other words, often the problem was not democracy but the absence of sufficient democracy.

As frustrations build, patience can snap, which can open the door for a return to authoritarianism. In March 2012, soldiers in Mali launched a coup d'état just weeks before presidential elections, reversing two

decades of democratic gains. The coup created the opportunity for sep-
aratist Tuareg and Islamist rebels from the north to seize territory and
towns that the regular army had abandoned to take part in the fun in the
capital, Bamako. Reuters reporters Cheick Dioura and Adama Diarra
described the coup—which soldiers had launched ostensibly because
they wanted more resources to contain the rebels—as "a spectacular
own-goal."[9] A French-led military intervention defeated the rebels in
early 2013, paving the way for fresh presidential elections. A fragile
peace is holding, and Mali is slowly recovering, but the coup was a major
setback.

Democracy is also under attack by fundamentalist Islam. We have
seen that democracy is compatible with Islam in Indonesia, Bangladesh,
Senegal, Turkey, and, most recently, Tunisia, among other countries.
There has been much less progress in Arab countries in the Middle East.
Most worrying is the minority of Muslims who espouse extreme fundamentalism and who are undermining democracy through violence and
terror. In this way, fundamentalist Islamists are similar to Fascists (although the latter claimed ultimate allegiance to country as opposed to
religion), the Nazis, and fundamentalist and reactionary Christian groups
throughout history such as the Ku Klux Klan.

The history of democracy is dynamic—full of global surges forward,
retreats, and new surges forward. Samuel Huntington's classic history
documented that the first wave of democracy ended in reversals between
1926 and 1942 with the rise of Fascism and Nazism. The same pattern
followed the second wave, when the spread of Communism and the
ascent of right-wing dictatorships led to a democratic decline between
1962 and 1974.[10] The third wave has not reversed, but it has plateaued.
The combination of reversals in countries such as Thailand, the lack of
democratic progress in the Middle East, the rise in fundamentalist Islam,
and the tendency of some leaders to slide toward corruption and dictatorship could hold back further progress toward democracy in developing countries.

Then there is China, which provides an attractive alternative for some
countries as a model of authoritarian capitalism. China holds appeal for
some citizens, investors, and political leaders who have misgivings about

the slowness and messiness of democracy, and who are uneasy with political instability, protests, and violence. Vietnam, Rwanda, and Ethiopia, not to mention far less economically successful countries such as Zimbabwe, Sudan, and Turkmenistan, all claim to be following China's example. As long as China continues to make economic progress with little political reform, it provides a quasi-legitimate model for dictators to follow, whether they are interested in broad economic development or not.

RISKS TO GLOBAL HEALTH

The spectacular gains in global health over the last several decades are perhaps the most important advancement of all in developing countries, and one of the greatest triumphs in human history, but they may not last. New disease threats are emerging constantly, and that the world has managed many of these threats in the past does not ensure that it will continue to do so in the future.

The HIV/AIDS pandemic stands as a stark reminder that health progress can be fleeting. The virus simmered, undetected, for decades, then exploded around the planet during the 1980s, leaving millions dead in its wake. Life expectancy in the five most severely affected countries in southern Africa—Botswana, Namibia, South Africa, Swaziland, and Zimbabwe—plummeted from sixty-one years in 1992 to just forty-six years a decade later. The effect on families and communities was devastating.

Similarly, the Ebola virus, first identified in 1976, has almost certainly been around much longer. In the thirty-eight years from 1976 through 2013, its impacts, while devastating to the families and communities involved, were sporadic. Ebola claimed a total of seventeen hundred lives during all those years, with outbreaks occurring only in East Africa and Central Africa, and typically lasting just a few weeks and claiming several hundred victims. The largest outbreak, in Uganda in 2000, killed 425 people.[11] In 2014 the virus exploded into West Africa in countries where it had never been detected. The weak health systems in Guinea, Liberia, and Sierra Leone were overwhelmed. International health organizations and major donors downplayed the threat at first and then seemed incapable of responding. By mid-2015, more than ten thousand people had died and more than twenty-six thousand had been infected. The outbreak is an unspeakable tragedy for the three countries that have been affected most, especially since they were each finally recovering from long civil wars and beginning to make steady development progress. It also showed that the international systems are not in place to stop a sudden epidemic.

At the same time, antibiotics and other antimicrobial drugs are becoming less effective in fighting infections, raising the specter of increased death rates among people with bacterial, fungal, and parasitic infections. Sally Davies, England's chief medical officer, has characterized growing antimicrobial resistance as a "ticking time bomb" and a "catastrophic threat" to citizens around the world, especially since there has been little progress in recent years developing new, more powerful drugs.[12] *Lancet*'s Global Health 2035 Commission warned:

> The antibiotics used for decades to treat tuberculosis no longer work in 20% of patients in some countries. For malaria, just one new drug class—the artemisinins—stands between cure and failure. Even more dangerous, and with greater consequences in the long term, common fatal infections are becoming resistant to first-line penicillins, cephalosporins, and macrolide antibiotics. Yet, since 2000, just ten new antibiotics have been approved in the USA, and only two of these since 2009. The development of antibiotics has decreased steadily since the 1960s, with fewer companies bringing forth ever fewer compounds.[13]

The threats don't end there. The spread of severe acute respiratory syndrome (SARS), the appearance of the H1N1 virus, and similar outbreaks have stoked concerns that the world could soon face a global pandemic similar to the 1918 influenza outbreak. Any kind of major pandemic, or spread of antimicrobial resistance, is sure to have an enormous effect on developing countries, where the resources and expertise to fight new threats are limited.

Finally, an additional emerging health challenge facing developing countries is the increased prevalence of noncommunicable diseases (NCDs) such as cancer, cardiovascular disease, and diabetes. Health expert Thomas Bollyky of the Council on Foreign Relations has shown that with the decline in child death and infectious diseases, NCDs have become the largest cause of death in developing countries. To some extent, this development is a normal part of the epidemiological transition: at very low incomes, infectious diseases such as cholera, diarrhea, malaria, and other parasites and viruses are the biggest killers. As incomes rise and societies are better able to fight those diseases, people live longer and are more likely to be affected by NCDs. This shift seems to be happening rapidly and is disproportionately affecting younger people in developing countries. In part, the increased prevalence of NCDs is due to continued weaknesses in health systems, and in part to rapid urbanization combined with less nutritious diets, greater tobacco use, and exposure to air pollution. More than 8 million people under sixty years of age died of NCDs in developing countries in 2013, and that number is likely to rise. During the next two decades, many developing countries will face the dual burden of continuing to fight infectious and childhood diseases that still affect many people, while building the systems to also fight NCDs.[14]

The combination of these threats means that in the absence of investments in new technologies, strengthening of public health systems, efforts to bolster the effectiveness of global health organizations, and sufficient amounts of foreign assistance and other funding, the great health gains that have been achieved over the last few decades will be at increased risk.

In the years ahead, these obstacles to continued development could reinforce and amplify one another. An inability to create jobs and new economic opportunities will undermine the credibility of weak democracies, increasing the attractiveness of a return to dictatorship. At the same time, political systems with less accountability and voice will permit the reemergence of economic policies geared to favor a narrow group rather than the broader population. An outbreak of new disease, or reduced ability to fight old diseases, will undermine progress in almost every other area of development. Taken together, they raise the possibility that the great surge of development could slow.

Some of these new threats and obstacles will arise, as they have throughout human history, but their emergence does not mean that progress must end, or even decelerate. There was great concern about reduced progress in developing countries after the Asian financial crises of 1997–98, the terrorist attacks of September 11, 2001, the global food crisis of 2007, the worldwide financial crisis of 2008, and the 2009 global H1N1 pandemic. In each case, developing countries rebounded and continued their rapid ascent.

But I have not mentioned the biggest threats of all: growing pressure on the planet from population growth, resource demand, and climate change; growing economic and political tensions from the rise of China; simmering threats from terrorism; and the possibility that these pressures could lead to significant environmental degradation and increases in violence and war. This combination would lead not just to development diminished, but to development derailed and progress reversed. It is to these growing threats that I now turn.

TWELVE

FUTURE 3—
PROGRESS DERAILED:
CLIMATE AND CONFLICT
HALT DEVELOPMENT

The power of population is indefinitely greater than the power in the earth to produce subsistence for man.

—*Thomas Malthus*, An Essay on the Principle of Population, *1798*

When a powerful storm destroyed her riverside home in 2009, Jahanara Khatun lost more than the modest roof over her head. In the aftermath, her husband died and she became so destitute that she sold her son and daughter into bonded servitude. And she may lose yet more. Ms. Khatun now lives in a bamboo shack that sits below sea level about 50 yards from a sagging berm. She spends her days collecting cow dung for fuel and struggling to grow vegetables in soil poisoned by salt water. Climate scientists predict that this area [of Bangladesh] will be inundated as sea levels rise and storm surges increase, and a cyclone or another disaster could easily wipe away her rebuilt life. But Ms. Khatun is trying to hold out at least for a while— one of millions living on borrowed time in this vast landscape of river islands, bamboo huts, heartbreaking choices and impossible hopes.

—*Gardiner Harris*, New York Times, *March 28, 2014*[1]

UP UNTIL TWO DECADES AGO, BANGLADESH WAS REGULARLY WRITTEN OFF AS A DEVELOP-
ment disaster. At the time of its independence in 1971, US secretary of
state Henry Kissinger declared "the place is and always will be a basket case." It seemed, at least for the next two decades, that perhaps he
was right. For those twenty years there was zero economic growth per
person—average income was almost the same in 1990 as it had been in
1970. Extreme poverty was moving in the wrong direction: the share of
people living on less than $1.25 a day jumped from 46 percent in 1981
to 59 percent just nine years later, and the total number of extreme poor
soared from 39 million to 63 million. Disease was widespread, and one
out of seven children did not live to see their fifth birthdays. Millions
died during widespread famines in 1943 and 1974, raising questions as
to whether the country could feed itself. To top it off, Bangladesh was
under brutal military rule until 1990, a period that included two coups
d'état, widespread human rights abuses, and the assassination of President Ziaur Rahman in 1981.

But since 1990, Bangladesh has made remarkable development
gains. Economic growth has averaged 4 percent per person, so average
income *doubled* in real terms in the two decades from 1990 to 2010. The
benefits have been relatively widespread: the share of people living in
extreme poverty not only stopped rising, it turned and dropped sharply
by 19 percentage points in twenty-one years to reach 40 percent in 2011
(and undoubtedly is lower today). Life expectancy grew from fifty-nine
to sixty-nine years, the share of children dying before their fifth birthdays dropped from 14 percent to less than 5 percent, and more than 90
percent of girls are now enrolled in primary school. Bangladesh also has
shifted from dictatorship to democracy—far from perfect, with many
flaws and weaknesses, but a far cry from the military rule of old. The
last two decades have brought a promising beginning on which to build.

All of these gains are under enormous threat. Bangladesh's population has soared from 100 million to a crowded 160 million, which is
roughly equivalent to half the population of the United States living
in an area the size of Illinois. It is one of the most densely populated
countries on the planet. The majority of people are jammed into a flat
flood plain at the mouth of the Ganges River that is a favorite target

for cyclones and floods. As the population has grown, pressures on food and water resources have risen. More people are crowding into already overpacked slums. Fresh water is rapidly being drawn from the water table below the fragile plains, so the land is sinking, increasing the risk of floods.

On top of these pressures come new threats from climate change. Sea levels are already rising, and projections suggest that they may rise anywhere from five to thirteen feet by the end of the century. Even the lower-end estimate of a five-foot increase would be disastrous. Alongside higher seas and rising and more variable temperatures, cyclones in the Bay of Bengal are likely to become stronger and more frequent. Increased salt incursion is turning precious fresh water brackish and laying waste to scarce agricultural land. Like Jahanara Khatun, millions of Bangladeshis face the threat of having their homes washed away, leading not just to substantial human casualties but also to enormous migration to higher ground, creating new slums along the way. As many as 18 million people—more than 10 percent of the population—could be displaced in the next forty years. Rafael Reuveny, a professor in the School of Public and Environmental Affairs at Indiana University at Bloomington, puts it this way: "There are a lot of places in the world at risk from rising sea levels, but Bangladesh is at the top of everybody's list. And the world is not ready to cope with the problems."[2]

Bangladesh is not alone. There is growing concern that the combination of climate change, population growth, and increased resource demand means that developing countries around the world face the prospect of environmental disaster, with increased stress on the land, much greater demand for limited supplies of fresh water, and more flooding in some places alongside greater desertification in others. These growing pressures are exacerbated by the economic successes over the last several decades that have brought so much good news but have also added to growing global resource demand. In particular, tensions are growing around the rise of China, both from shifting global economic and political power and from escalating competition over scarce resources.

So there is a third possible future: development is derailed, and progress stops or even goes in reverse. Climate change and growing environmental stress lead to reductions in agricultural productivity and shortages of fresh water, just as growing urban populations demand more food and water. Food prices rise, leading some nations to withdraw from agricultural trade and keep food supplies at home. Tit-for-tat trade tensions escalate into all-out trade wars, spilling over into trade restrictions on manufacturing and services. Governments facing pressures from citizens unhappy with higher prices and reduced consumption cut back on investment, including on research into new technologies that might help solve some of the problems. Resources are plundered rather than managed properly. Tensions build and conflicts arise both within countries and across borders over competition for energy, food, and water supplies. Confrontations between China and neighboring countries over disputed areas of the South China Sea explode into military conflict, bringing the United States and Japan into the fray. Terrorism spreads and escalates into more sophisticated weapons targeting vulnerable populations in developing countries. Global economic growth slows dramatically, and income growth in developing countries comes to a halt and begins to decline in more countries than not. Global poverty rises, and the changing climate leads to growing health threats and new pandemics. Democracy begins to be reversed, either because some leaders grab the opportunity of slowing progress to seize power, or because others committed to progress are unable to deliver on the promise of greater prosperity and get tossed out. Democracy is seen as a failed experiment, and dictators rise again.

For more than two centuries, people have predicted that the combination of growing population, increased demand for resources, and environmental and ecological damage will lead to famine, war, and a reversal of progress. This view dates back at least to the great English cleric and scholar Thomas Malthus, captured in the quotation at the beginning of this chapter. Malthus argued in 1798 that "the passion between the sexes" was so strong that world population was destined to grow much faster than food supplies. Specifically, he argued that global population would increase geometrically, while food production could grow only arithmetically. The planet could not sustain a rapidly growing population, he believed, and sooner or later population growth would have to be checked by famine, disease, conflict, or another catastrophe. *Malthusian* has been a synonym for predicting global doom ever since.

Let's give Malthus his due: he was no fool. His description captured exactly what had happened throughout human history—up until that point. Agricultural production had not grown particularly quickly, and so more children meant less food per mouth to feed, more overcrowding, and worsening health. From his vantage at the early stages of the industrial revolution and the emergence of democracy, he did not recognize the rapid economic and political changes that were just beginning to unfold. He could not foresee the enormous gains in knowledge and technology that led to the massive advances in agriculture, health, and nutrition that have allowed the world to carry 7 billion people today far more prosperously than the 1 billion that lived then. Nor could he anticipate the changes in governance and the shift toward democracy that allowed human societies to improve their collective decision making and strengthen their ability to hold their leaders accountable. His basic mistake was that he underestimated the human capacity for innovation and change.

At various times since Malthus, others have made similar predictions. One of the more famous is Paul Ehrlich's *The Population Bomb*—written in 1968, when global population reached the unprecedented level of 3.5 billion people—in which he predicted mass starvation and escalating death in the 1970s and 1980s, primarily in Asia.[3] The book begins with this dire warning: "The battle to feed all of humanity is over. In the 1970s hundreds of millions of people will starve to death in spite of any crash programs embarked upon now. At this late date nothing can prevent a substantial increase in the world death rate." Ehrlich, like Malthus before him, is no dummy: he is the Bing Professor of Population Studies in the Department of Biological Sciences at Stanford University and president of Stanford's Center for Conservation Biology. But also like Malthus, he did not appreciate the extent to which the Green Revolution—which was just getting started—would expand Asia's ability to feed itself. He underestimated society's ability to address emerging problems. He has hardly been alone in recent decades in making dire forecasts for the future of the planet.

Fortunately, at least so far, these predictions have not come to pass. Each time that we have been threatened with population pressures and growing resource demand, humans have responded with innovations, technological improvements, new governance structures, and other advances that have helped counter the threat.

However, the past may not be the future. That we have made the sacrifices and investments to build the knowledge that has produced the technologies that have allowed us to advance in the past, and that we have developed more effective institutions of governance and cooperation as the basis of prosperity, does not mean we will make those investments and those hard decisions in the future. It is possible that the predictions that Malthus and Ehrlich and others have made might come to pass. Ehrlich, for one, maintains that he was off only on his timing. The combination of the world's population increasing to 9 billion or 10 billion or 11 billion people; growing demand for energy, water, and other natural resources; and the damage from climate change and ecological distress could derail development, undermine prosperity, and create enormous suffering. The world's poorest countries would bear the greatest costs and suffering, and the great surge of development progress would be a short chapter in history.

SEVEN BILLION AND COUNTING

World population growth accelerated in the aftermath of World War II, and peaked at just over 2 percent annually in the years between 1965 and 1972. Since then, the growth rate has slowed considerably to around 1.2 percent per year, with the decline driven primarily by a massive drop in global fertility rates. In the 1960s, fertility rates hovered around 5 children per adult woman, but today that rate has been halved to 2.5.

Even with a slower rate, world population—estimated at 7.3 billion in 2015—is still growing fast. The latest midrange projections from the United Nations suggest that by 2025, global population will reach 8.1 billion, and it will grow to 9.6 billion in 2050 and 10.9 billion in 2100 (figure 12.1). According to these estimates, within a century, global population will be 50 percent larger than it is today.

FIGURE 12.1: WORLD POPULATION: HIGH, MEDIUM, AND LOW PROJECTIONS

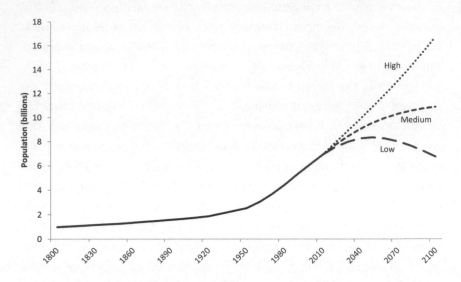

Source: "World Population Prospects: The 2012 Revision," United Nations, Department of Economic and Social Affairs, Population Division, Population Estimates and Projections Section, last modified April 14, 2014.

These estimates are based primarily on the assumption that fertility rates will continue to decline to 2 children per woman. In the UN's high-end projections—which assume that fertility rates remain at 2.5—world population will reach 16.6 billion in 2100. If, on the other hand, fertility rates decline further to around 1.5 children per woman, global population will take a different path: it will reach a peak of 8.3 billion around 2050, and then for the first time since the Black Death in the fourteenth century, global population will begin to decline, falling to 6.8 billion—below the current level—by the end of the century.

Many more people will live in cities. Urbanization goes hand in hand with development as economic activity shifts from agriculture to manufacturing and services. In the United States, for example, the share of people living in urban areas increased from just 6 percent in 1800 to around 80 percent today. The UN projects that the share of people living in urban areas worldwide will increase from about half today to two-thirds by 2050. Half the population of Asia will live in urban areas by

2020, and half the population of Africa will do so by 2035. Virtually all of the expected growth in world population between now and 2050 is expected to be concentrated in the urban areas of developing countries. Far more people will live in megacities with populations greater than 10 million people. In 1970 the world had only two megacities: New York and Tokyo. Today there are twenty-two, and sixteen of the twenty new ones are in developing countries in Asia, Latin America, and Africa.

Greater urbanization means more crowded living spaces, more stress on local water sources, increased air and water pollution, new challenges in creating employment for low-skilled urban workers, and major difficulties in providing adequate water, sanitation, and garbage disposal facilities. With bigger crowds, crime and personal violence tend to rise, as many large cities in developing countries—perhaps most especially in Central America—have found in recent years. In addition, not surprisingly, urbanization creates major environmental stress. Larger and more concentrated energy consumption in urban areas tends to create "heat islands" that can change weather patterns and trap atmospheric pollutants, adding to health risks. And as the citizens of Dhaka in Bangladesh are finding, drawing large amounts of water from under the ground can cause the land to sink, exacerbating the risks of and damage from flooding and other disasters.

HUNGRY FOR RESOURCES

As we have seen, widespread economic and social progress in developing countries has brought enormous improvements in basic welfare for hundreds of millions of poor people around the world. Naturally, as their incomes rise, and as they live longer and healthier lives, they consume more resources—water, food, energy, and minerals. These are sure signs of development progress. After all, a major purpose of increasing the incomes of the world's poorest people is to allow them to meet their basic needs and improve their standard of living.

This raises a huge and obvious concern. The aggregate income of all people living in developing countries could *triple* by 2040 because of larger populations and higher average incomes. In turn, this income growth will generate an enormous surge in demand for basic resources—perhaps the most rapid increase in aggregate demand for the planet's resources in world history. In effect, what is good for individual people around the world may not be good for the planet as a whole.

There are three key areas where there are likely to be significant new pressures on resources: energy, water, and food. The three are inextricably linked: water and energy are needed to produce food, energy is needed to treat and transport water; and water is needed to extract energy and to generate power.

Energy use per person today is more than nine times higher in rich countries than in poor countries. As poor countries continue to develop, the gap will close, and aggregate energy demand will grow. The US Energy Information Administration projects that demand for energy over the next thirty years is likely to increase by 56 percent globally and by 125 percent in developing countries, with demand growing for every major source of energy (figure 12.2). Global demand for electricity is likely to nearly double. Demand for natural gas is expected to rise quickly, especially with its low relative price compared with other fuels in recent years.

Perhaps most troubling from a global resource perspective, demand for coal is likely to increase by almost 50 percent, despite concerns about its environmental impact. Coal is dirty locally and globally, mining is dangerous to workers, and opencast mining rips away topsoil and harms water supplies. Moreover, burning coal exacerbates global warming because of increased emissions of carbon dioxide. But while coal creates problems, so does poverty, and this creates a dilemma for policy makers in developing countries. In many ways, coal is an attractive option for governments focused on growth and poverty reduction. It's cheap, simple to extract and transport, and easy to burn and convert into power. Even if rich countries begin to use less coal, developing countries might use more unless new, cleaner, and cheaper sources of energy are developed that they can adapt. For now, with current technologies and economic trajectories, it's likely that the demand for coal—and other sources of energy—in developing countries will rise rapidly in the coming decades.

FIGURE 12.2: ENERGY DEMAND WILL SOAR

Growth in Global Energy Demand, 2010 to 2040

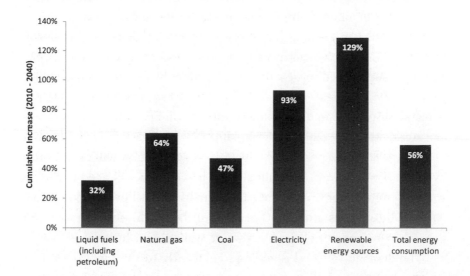

Source: *International Energy Outlook 2013* (Washington, DC: US Energy Information Administration, 2013).

So will the demand for water. As populations grow and become more urbanized, and as manufacturing and industry grow, the demand for water will continue to expand. Under midrange projections, by 2030, global water requirements will grow from 4.5 trillion cubic meters today to 6.9 trillion m³, an increase of more than 50 percent in twenty years. Demand in India alone will more than double to 1.5 trillion m³, driven by increasing demand for rice, wheat, and sugar and growing industrial activity.[4]

Can the earth supply enough fresh water to meet these growing demands, especially in southern Asia, parts of Africa, and across the Middle East? Only 3 percent of the earth's water is salt free, and 70 percent of that is locked in glaciers or icebergs. By some estimates, by the year 2025, around 5 billion people will be experiencing water stress. Shortages of fresh water could seriously undermine human health and basic well-being, curtail agricultural and food production, slow industrial growth, and cause greater ecological damage as people search for more water from new sources. It could also add to growing conflict, as nations—and communities within nations—compete for scarce fresh water.

Then there is food. Can we continue to feed today's 7 billion people, plus another 3 billion more? As incomes grow, demand increases not just for basic grains and staples but also for meat, eggs, dairy products, fish, and other protein, which, in turn, boosts pressure to grow more corn and soybeans to feed more cattle, pigs, and chickens. Producing 1 kilogram of beef requires 7 kilograms of grain. Between now and 2050, the demand for protein in developing countries will likely double. The Food and Agricultural Organization estimates that by 2050, food production must increase by 70 percent. Annual cereal production will need to rise by about 3 billion tons, and annual meat production will need to rise by over 200 million tons. We'll have to be smart about how we do it: agriculture already uses around 40 percent of the earth's ice-free land and more than 70 percent of the fresh water available for human use.[5]

The demand for food is adding significantly to the rapid decline in forest cover around the world. Forests are being cleared about three times faster than new forests are being planted. Just since 2000, the world has lost forest area larger than the total size of Greenland, while an area only one-third that size has regrown. The vast majority of the forest loss was in developing countries. While, much to its credit, Brazil has reduced its rate of deforestation, many other countries have increased their forest loss, including Indonesia, Malaysia, Paraguay, Bolivia, Zambia, and Angola, among others.[6] Forest clearing leads to enormous loss of carbon dioxide: a hectare of tropical forest may contain more than two hundred tons of carbon, but it can all be released in one afternoon in a fire aimed at clearing the land. Some of the deforestation stems from increased demand for paper, pulp, and lumber supplies, but at least in these cases many of the trees are replanted to rebuild future supplies. Most tropical land, once deforested, is converted to agriculture or pasture, and is used to produce soy, beef, palm oil, and other products. The forests are falling to feed us.

During the global food crisis of 2007–08, the combination of rising demand for food, a spike in the price of fertilizers (driven in part by rising fuel prices), a series of major climatic disruptions (including a major drought in Australia, a heat wave in California, floods in India, and a cyclone in Myanmar, all of which undermined food production), and subsidies for biofuels in rich countries (which diverted land from food production into biofuel crops) created a sharp spike in food prices. The price of corn doubled in two years, and the price of wheat reached its highest level in nearly three decades. Prices for basic foods rose 80 percent.

Some farmers and rural laborers in developing countries benefitted from the higher prices, but urban workers and the unemployed were hard hit. Food makes up anywhere from half to three-quarters of people's budgets in developing countries, so the price increase was a big problem for urban consumers. Riots and demonstrations broke out in nearly thirty countries, including Burkina Faso, Cameroon, Egypt, Guinea, Haiti, Indonesia, Mauritania, Mexico, Morocco, Mozambique, Nepal, Peru, Senegal, Uzbekistan, and Yemen.

Ironically, what ended the spike in global food prices was the onset of the global financial crisis, which curtailed global demand for energy, food, and agricultural products. The root causes of the crisis continue, and food prices remain historically high and unusually volatile. Was the crisis simply a prelude to the future?

TOO HOT TO HANDLE

We now come to the real trump card in the deck. As if growing population and increased resource demand were not challenging enough, we face the growing threat of climate change, and the serious potential it creates to derail development in the world's poorest countries. Most of the world's poorest countries have had little to do with the forces behind climate change, yet they are likely to bear the brunt of the damage.

Scientists have reached an unusually strong consensus that climate change is well under way and that global greenhouse gas emissions from human activity are a major contributor. The American Association for the Advancement of Science (AAAS), noting that 97 percent of climate scientists have concluded that human-caused climate change is happening, had this to say in its 2014 report *What We Know: The Reality, Risks and Response to Climate Change*:

The evidence is overwhelming: levels of greenhouse gases in the atmosphere are rising. Temperatures are going up. Springs are arriving earlier. Ice sheets are melting. Sea level is rising. The patterns of rainfall and drought are changing. Heat waves are getting worse, as is extreme precipitation. The oceans are acidifying. The science linking human activities to climate change is analogous to the science linking smoking to lung and cardiovascular diseases. Physicians, cardiovascular scientists, public health experts, and others all agree smoking causes cancer. And this consensus among the health community has convinced most Americans that the health risks from smoking are real. A similar consensus now exists among climate scientists, a consensus that maintains climate change is happening, and human activity is the cause.[7]

According to the Intergovernmental Panel on Climate Change (IPCC), atmospheric temperatures rose by about 0.85°C (about 1.5°F) during the last century, and the first decade of the twenty-first century was the hottest on record. Ocean temperatures have risen even faster. Sea levels have risen by about 0.2 meters over the last century, on average, and in some places, they have risen higher. Atmospheric concentrations of carbon dioxide, methane, and nitrous oxide have increased to levels unprecedented in at least the last eight hundred thousand years. Carbon dioxide concentrations, in particular, have increased by 40 percent since the industrial revolution.[8]

How climate will change in the future, of course, is a matter of extensive debate and uncertainty. The IPCC believes it is "likely" that average global temperatures will rise another 0.7°C this century, bringing the total increase in temperatures to 1.5°C (2.7°F). Under some scenarios, the total increase could reach or exceed 2°C, a point at which many scientists believe the planet could experience irreversible damage.

The issue is not just rising temperatures per se, but greater weather volatility. The contrast between wet and dry seasons in many developing countries will become much greater. Arctic sea ice and snow cover will continue to decrease, and ocean temperatures are likely to continue to rise. Scientists expect increased precipitation in higher latitudes, and decreased precipitation in the tropics and subtropics, with more wide-spread desertification in some areas. Some parts of the world will face much more extreme weather, including more intense hot and cold cycles, and more frequent and severe storms. The changes will be far from uniform. Some countries might see improved climatic conditions and an increase in agricultural productivity—especially in areas where a little warming would be helpful for agriculture, such as northern Europe and parts of Canada.

But for most developing countries—almost all of which are located in the tropics—the opposite will be the case. Just when we need to increase agricultural productivity to meet the growing demands of a larger and wealthier population, climate change is likely to reduce aggregate agricultural productivity and food production, making the challenge all the greater.

The challenges presented by climate change are hard enough for those of us who live in wealthier countries—we may face higher prices for energy, be forced to make adjustments in our choices of housing and automobiles, and otherwise make difficult adjustments in the way we live. Some people in richer countries—such as those who live in the hurricane pathways of the East Coast and the Gulf Coast or the increasingly parched farmlands of the southwestern United States—may be hit by more frequent and more intense natural disasters. Our political system is having enormous difficulties even recognizing the problem, much less addressing it.

The impact will be much greater in the world's poorest countries. For people living on the edge of subsistence, these changes could spell outright catastrophe. Climate change will alter water availability because of changing patterns in droughts, rainfall, and floods. Crop yields will suffer as temperatures rise and become more erratic, agricultural lands near the ocean will be laid to waste by salt incursion, and more urban slum areas will be inundated by flooding. Storms could become more violent and more frequent. In 2013 and 2014, the Philippines was hit by massive typhoons that many believe were caused in part by climate change.

By some estimates, climate change could increase the number of people at risk of hunger by between 30 million and as many as 200 million.[9]

Climate change is also likely to alter disease patterns, increase the intensity of major outbreaks, create greater heat stress, and increase health problems associated with air pollution. *Lancet*'s Global Health 2035 Commission warned that "unless countervailing measures are taken, the death toll and reach of vector-borne infectious disease is likely to increase because of global climate change."[10] Physical infrastructure is more likely to be damaged from storms and changes in soil conditions, so the cost of maintaining infrastructure—not to mention improving it—is likely to rise.

Much of Africa is expected to become hotter and drier, which means increased water stress and lower agricultural yields—in some countries as much as 50 percent lower. Asia faces the prospect of decreased freshwater availability, and a much greater risk of increased flooding. Latin America may see increased desertification, or rapid biodiversity loss, increased water stress, and decreased agricultural productivity. Perhaps the greatest stress will come to people living on small islands, especially flatter atolls such as in the Seychelles, the Maldives, and the Marshall Islands, some of which could disappear because of rising sea levels.

Faced with these issues, many people living in developing countries are likely to leave. I might, if it were me, just as my mother's ancestors left Ireland under the stress of the Great Famine in the middle of the nineteenth century, when more than 1 million people died, and another 1 million fled. Who wants to stick around and watch their family starve? By some estimates, as many as three hundred thousand people or more may emigrate from China and India *each year*, and another two hundred thousand might leave Mexico and Pakistan.

RESOURCE WARS

Growing pressures from population, resource demand, and climate change could also lead to much greater conflict, including all-out war. History is littered with conflicts and wars over natural resources, including invasions to expand into new territories and grab land, colonial and military occupations to extract resources, localized fights over water and grazing rights, and wars to control oil or diamonds. Recent decades are no exception. UN secretary-general Ban Ki-moon observed recently, "Since

1990, at least 18 violent conflicts have been fueled by the exploitation of natural resources such as timber, minerals, oil and gas."[11]

The long war in the Democratic Republic of the Congo, at its heart, is a fight over diamonds and timber, as were the wars in Liberia and Sierra Leone. Disputes over Nigeria's oil resources have led to ongoing violence for years. The conflict in western Sudan's Darfur region was triggered by disputes between African farmers and Arab pastoralist communities over the growing scarcity of water and grazing land. The conflict has claimed hundreds of thousands of lives and displaced an estimated 2 million people. The civil war in Sudan, which has now become a civil war in the new country of South Sudan, is predominantly about control over oil and water. In Peru, disputes among companies, governments, and local communities over mining projects have killed several hundred people over the last decade, as local communities have erupted into protests over the impacts of mining operations on their land, water supplies, and livelihoods. "Land grabs" by large international businesses have caused conflict and controversy throughout sub-Saharan Africa as they displace small farmers and pastoralists and push them onto marginal land. The Middle East—home to 5 percent of the world's population and only 1 percent of its fresh water—is rife with disputes over water. The 1967 Six-Day War between Israel and its neighbors Egypt, Jordan, and Syria was sparked at least partially by conflicts over control of Jordan River water supplies. Turkey, Syria, and Iraq have long-running disputes over the waters of the Euphrates and Tigris Rivers. Ethiopia and Sudan battle over the Nile River. Kazakhstan, Uzbekistan, Turkmenistan, Tajikistan, and Kyrgyzstan all fight over control of the waters originating in the Aral Sea.

Some disputes have simmered for decades and seem primed to erupt into major conflict in the years to come. India and Pakistan have a long history of disputes over the waters of the Indus River and its tributaries. Pakistan's agricultural economy relies on the Indus, but India controls the upstream waters. The two countries signed the Indus Waters Treaty in 1960, and while the treaty has held over the years, it is increasingly challenged. Pakistan is dealing with serious and growing water scarcities, as its increasing population has reduced the amount of water available in its reservoirs. In addition, there is deepening concern that climate change will shrink major glaciers in the Himalayas and reduce water flows in the Indus, meaning there will be less water available for many more people to share. A serious water shortage could be catastrophic for Pakistan. It would undermine not just agricultural production but also health and sanitation, which, in turn, would lead to mounting tensions within the country and with India, which would further complicate their already complicated relationship.

Hostilities could be exacerbated by widening income gaps in some countries, especially if the poor or certain ethnic or religious groups feel excluded from access to water, land, or other resources. Crowded and unsanitary conditions in many urban slums can foment discontent, especially if the pace of economic and social progress does not meet expectations. Tensions can erupt if specific ethnic or religious groups believe that they are not being afforded the same kinds of opportunities as others.

Of all of the consequences of growing pressure on the planet, a resurgence of conflict, violence, and war may be the worst. However, there are two other sources of growing friction and conflict that could have a substantial impact on developing countries: the threat of terrorism, and the rise of China.

WEAPONS OF TERROR

On October 12, 2002, a suicide bomber from the radical Islamist Jemaah Islamiyah movement walked into a pub in Bali, Indonesia, the world's largest Muslim country. He detonated a bomb in his backpack, killing several people and sending dozens more fleeing into the street. There was a second and far more powerful explosion outside the pub twenty seconds later. The blast was enormous. It destroyed nearby buildings, shattered windows several blocks away, and left a crater in the street one meter deep. More than two hundred people were killed and several hundred more badly injured. Just ten months later, a suicide bomber detonated a car bomb outside the JW Marriott Hotel in South Jakarta, killing twelve and injuring 150 more. Two years later, Bali was struck again, with two near-simultaneous suicide bombers killing twenty people and injuring more than one hundred others.

Several orchestrated bomb blasts in Delhi, India, killed 30 people and injured 130 more on September 13, 2008. Just seven days later, a dump truck filled with explosives detonated in front of the Marriott Hotel in Islamabad, Pakistan. The massive explosion left a crater twenty meters wide and six meters deep. At least 54 people were killed and more than 260 were injured. Two months after that, on November 26, 2008, extremists killed at least 166 people and wounded several hundred others in a series of attacks in Mumbai, India.

On February 20, 2004, several hundred soldiers from the extremist Christian group the Lord's Resistance Army (LRA) surrounded the Barlonyo camp for Internally Displaced Persons (IDPs) in northern Uganda—a camp full of people displaced because of earlier LRA violence. They cut off escape routes, burned huts with families inside, and brutally murdered those who tried to escape. More than 200 people were killed, mostly women and children. The attack was one of dozens that the LRA carried out over two decades in its attempt to achieve its goal of ruling Uganda according to the Ten Commandments.[12]

On April 14, 2014, 276 girls were kidnapped from a secondary school in northern Nigeria by the Islamic jihadist group Boko Haram. The group has killed more than 1,000 people in a series of attacks during the last several years, leading the Nigerian government to declare a state of emergency in the state of Borno. Boko Haram has targeted schools, killing hundreds of students and kidnapping girls, purportedly to use them as cooks and sex slaves. More than 10,000 children have stopped attending school as a result of the attacks.

History is full of fundamentalist and terrorist movements that have used violence to instill fear and impose their views, including Fascists, Nazis, Christian crusaders, Stalinists, Basque separatists, Peru's Sendero Luminoso (Shining Path), white supremacist militia groups, the LRA, Hindu nationalists, and Islamic fundamentalists. Today a major threat in many developing countries comes from groups like these that espouse violence and are willing to do great damage to get their way.

Terrorism has not yet occurred on a scale large enough to undermine the great surge, but it could do so in the future. We have seen the big benefits from globalization and the spread of technologies, but there are huge downside risks as well. Globalization allows the rapid spread of ideas and the means for enormous violence, such as the ability to find recipes for chemical weapons on the internet. At least since the invention of the atomic bomb, many have feared that technological advances could destroy us, and that small fringe groups could inflict great damage. Extremist groups could detonate dirty bombs in Islamabad, Lagos, London, or New York; place weapons of mass destruction in shipping containers; or disperse biological agents via drones. Such actions could change everything: trade and investment would falter, the West would pull up a drawbridge, and democracy would be in retreat. Francis Fukuyama has observed that "what is different today is the democratization of the means of violence, whereby very small, stateless groups have the possibility of acquiring weapons of vast destructive power."[13]

TENSIONS AROUND THE RISE OF CHINA

On November 23, 2013, Beijing announced it was establishing an air defense identification zone (ADIZ) in the East China Sea, and that any aircraft flying through it would have to notify Chinese authorities in advance. It's not unusual for a country to establish a zone over its own territory, but China's declared zone reached into and overlapped with zones established by Japan and South Korea already. The alarm bells rang. The United States defied the edict and flew two B-52 bombers straight through the zone without notifying China. Japan sent F-15 jets to intercept two Chinese aircraft. South Korea launched a joint air and sea military exercise and extended its own ADIZ.

China's move was seen as an escalation of the long-simmering dispute over a set of uninhabited islands called the Senkaku by Japan and the Diaoyu by China. Japan has controlled the islands since the 1890s, but in the 1970s, China claimed sovereignty. In part, the friction is driven by the possibility that there may be oil in the waters surrounding the islands. However, the stakes are bigger: China is asserting its power, and the Japan-US alliance is pushing back in a test case of regional authority and strength.

Meanwhile, on May 2, 2014, China National Offshore Oil Corporation parked an oil rig in waters just 120 nautical miles off the coast of

Vietnam, escorted by a flotilla of other ships. The Vietnamese government objected furiously and was joined by widespread global condemnation. Vietnamese workers erupted into anti-Chinese protests, hunted down Chinese workers, and set fifteen foreign-owned factories ablaze. At least twenty-one people were killed.[14] Scores of Vietnamese ships squared off around the rig. China countered that the ships were interfering with its operations. Tensions remain extremely high.

Further to the southwest, China and five other countries continue to clash over sovereignty of the Spratly Islands in the South China Sea; China, Indonesia, and Taiwan battle over a boundary near the Natuna Islands; China has several ongoing arguments with the Philippines about boundary waters; and its decades-old border dispute with India (which led to war in 1962) remains unsettled.

For thirty years, Beijing followed Deng Xiaoping's strategy of concentrating on building the economy, lying low on foreign policy, and staying out of the affairs of other countries. However, as China's economic (and military) might has increased, the government's stance has begun to change. A growing number of policy and military leaders believe it is time for China to take a more forceful role in foreign affairs, and they have support from many Chinese firms investing abroad that want greater protection in risky foreign markets. Whereas for decades China has avoided entering into formal alliances and treaties, preferring to make neither friends nor enemies, there is a growing push to shift course and create such alliances with countries in the region in which China would offer security guarantees (perhaps including a nuclear umbrella) and tighter economic relationships. Chinese president Xi Jinping has been far more assertive internationally than his predecessors, telling President Obama that China wanted "a new type of great-power relationship."

Throughout history, with few exceptions, the rise of a great power has almost always involved war. While China's rise over the last three decades has been remarkably smooth, there are increasing concerns that this could change in the decades to come, especially in a world of heightened resource demand and climate change. The United States—with the exception of the Vietnam War—has held primacy in East and Southeast

Asia since the end of World War II. The combination of its security blanket, protection of shipping lanes, and economic ties has created deep relationships and played an important part in the region's rise. While countries in the neighborhood complain sometimes (often justifiably) about US interference, they recognize the benefits that have accrued from stability and peace. Many of them—Japan, South Korea, Taiwan, the Philippines—look first to the United States to defend their interests, and, given the long histories between them, openly distrust China.

At the same time, China's growing economic and military might, alongside its long history as a major global power (which many Chinese see as the natural and rightful order), mean that it will demand a larger say in regional and global issues. The United States and its regional allies do not want Washington to cede its power and influence, but to some degree, it must do so to accommodate China. For the Western powers, the goal is straightforward: get China to integrate into existing global institutions, follow the accepted international rules, and identify its primary interests as preserving a stable and secure international order. China resists the idea of just following along and joining the Western-led international order that it did not help create and that might not always support its interests.[15]

Conflict is not inevitable. Many people both inside and outside of China believe that the country's ascendancy can continue to be peaceful if China, the United States, Japan, the European powers, and other countries work together in good faith and recognize the need for some rebalancing of power. The key countries have many common interests, most importantly peace and security as a means to continued economic progress. Those common interests may be sufficient to maintain cooperation and refrain from major hostilities, even if there are multiple tensions and flare-ups along the way.

However, it's hardly a given. Many others believe that conflict is likely and perhaps inevitable, a view held by University of Chicago political scientist John Mearsheimer:

> If China continues to grow economically, it will attempt to dominate
> Asia the way the United States dominates the Western Hemisphere.

The United States, however, will go to enormous lengths to prevent China from achieving regional hegemony. Most of Beijing's neighbors, including India, Japan, Singapore, South Korea, Russia, and Vietnam, will join with the United States to contain Chinese power. The result will be an intense security competition with considerable potential for war. In short, China's rise is unlikely to be tranquil.[16]

The impacts of conflict could be enormous. Any of the border disputes could erupt into more violent protests or escalate into military confrontation. The outbreak of one conflict could spill over and spark another, especially if anti-Chinese sentiments spread through the region. Ethnic Chinese around the region would be in danger. The United States and Australia could quickly get involved. Countries would have to choose sides, drawing lines and alliances reminiscent of the Cold War. International organizations would be split. The effects would be greatest in East Asia and Southeast Asia, but they would reach around the world through their effects on trade, finance, and the effectiveness of international institutions and structures.

THE DILEMMA

These are serious threats. Development progress could be derailed or reversed because of intensifying population pressures; rapid increases in the demands for energy, food, and water; climbing temperatures and more volatile climatic conditions; and growing geopolitical tensions from the rise of China. To add to the challenge, the continued success of developing countries amplifies these pressures, since higher incomes and lower poverty increase the global demand for resources (although they also tend to slow population growth). Are the goals of accelerating development and protecting the planet in fundamental conflict?

It seems so, and as a result, some environmentalists are wary about the acceleration in development progress. At the same time, many people in developing countries are suspicious about efforts to protect the environment, which they sometimes see as hypocritical attempts by rich countries to maintain an economic advantage over poor countries. At the extremes of the debate, some people accuse environmentalists of not caring about the global poor, while others accuse those focusing on development as having no concern about burning up the planet.

While there is a clear tension between the goals of sustaining development for the poor and protecting the environment, they need not be in complete conflict. Advancing one does not have to come at the expense of the other. Oxford University economist Paul Collier showed in his 2010 book, *The Plundered Planet: Why We Must—and How We Can—Manage Nature for Global Prosperity*, how progress in the two goals is linked and can be mutually reinforcing. Natural resources are at the core of development efforts: manage them well, and they can power the ascent to prosperity; manage them poorly, and they lead to plunder and poverty. At the same time, poverty and lack of development add to resource exploitation and conflict, and reducing poverty can lead to improved resource management. Sir Nicholas Stern of the London School of Economics has made the point concisely: if we fail at either goal, we ultimately fail at both.

The answer is neither to cut back on development nor to surge ahead with growth at any cost. Stopping, or even slowing, the pace of development would mean maintaining the huge gaps between rich and poor countries, and denying many poor people the chance for progress. That would be both unfair and ethically wrong. Forging ahead and destroying our resources would undermine everyone's future. To paraphrase Collier, if we cut back on development, the world will starve; if we ignore the growing threats to the planet, we may burn.

This dilemma calls for action, not despair. A big lesson from the last two hundred years is that human innovation, resolve, and cooperation have won out over gloom and doom. Achieving continued development progress alongside environmental sustainability will require global leadership, especially from the United States, Europe, Japan, China, and India. It will demand hard choices and investments in innovation, science, and technologies that will generate continued growth in food supplies and new sources of energy. It also will require good governance, sound management, and strong leadership within both international organizations and developing countries.

THIRTEEN
GETTING TO GOOD

The future depends on what we do in the present.
—*Mohandas K. Gandhi*

I BELIEVE THAT DURING THE NEXT TWENTY YEARS, THE GREAT SURGE OF DEVELOPMENT progress can continue. If it does, 700 million more people will be lifted out of extreme poverty, incomes in developing countries will more than double again, childhood death will continue to decline, hundreds of millions of children will get the educations they deserve, and basic rights and democratic freedoms will spread further around the world. China's growth rate will slow gradually rather than abruptly, and it will move—with some disruptions—closer to a more open and democratic society rather than the other way around. India will continue its uneven ascendancy, and the majority of developing countries will continue to achieve moderate or rapid growth. New technologies will help fight diseases, increase agricultural production, and expand cleaner sources of energy. Global governance systems and international organizations will evolve to include developing countries and be more effective in meeting the world's challenges. The world will be a safer, healthier, and more prosperous place.

While I believe this progress can occur, I am far from certain that it will. Achieving it will depend on human choices and action in rich, middle-income, and poor countries alike. The future of developing countries will not be determined by inexorable and impersonal historical, biological, climatological, economic, or political forces set in stone. It will depend, as Mohandas Gandhi observed, on what we do now.

Developing countries will face many challenges in the years to come, some of which are within their control, and many of which are not, including increased competition for scarce resources, growing pressures on food and water supplies, climate change, increasing tensions and possible conflict from changing geopolitical balance and the rise of China, the difficulties in combating terrorism, and the potential for a reversal of democracy. It's easy to be pessimistic about the future. It's also easy to forget that people have despaired about the future of the planet since the earliest civilizations. It may be true that some of the challenges the world faces today are greater than those of the past, but so are the world's capacities to meet these challenges. We can readily see many of the upcoming problems the world faces. It's harder to envision the new innovations, technologies, ideas, governance structures, and leadership that will emerge to tackle them.

In 1981 the economist Julian Simon wrote *The Ultimate Resource* in response to those who believed that the world faced imminent disaster from population pressure and resource constraints. He argued that while people tend to think of resources in terms of land, water, food, and minerals, he believed that the ultimate resource is people themselves—"the human imagination coupled to the human spirit."[1] Since then, we have seen dramatic increases in food production, income levels, and life expectancy, and huge reductions in disease and poverty, driven by innovation, technology, and improved global and local governance.

Innovation means more than just technology: economic and political institutions also must continue to adapt and evolve, including democracy, market capitalism, global governance systems, and ideas around equality, inclusion, and freedom. Those institutions have all changed substantially in the last twenty, fifty, and two hundred years, and they must continue to adapt and become more effective in the decades to come. As British journalists John Micklethwait and Adrian Wooldridge have observed, people have always been cynical of government, and assume that it can never change. This view "ignores the lessons of history: government— and particularly Western government—has changed dramatically over the past few centuries, usually because committed people possessed by big ideas have worked hard to change it."[2]

How do we achieve a future of continued progress for the world's poorest countries? Getting there will require sacrifice, cooperation, compromise, vision, leadership, wisdom, and a lot of hard work, both at the global level and within developing countries. We have seen that three major forces were behind the great surge of development progress during the last twenty years: global conditions and leadership conducive to development, new opportunities driven by technology and market integration, and strong leadership and increased capabilities within developing countries themselves. Going forward, effective actions in all three of these areas will be central for progress to continue.

GLOBAL LEADERSHIP SETS THE STAGE

The world's most advanced countries—especially the United States, those in the European Union, and Japan—will be pivotal for creating the global conditions necessary for continued advancement in the world's poorest countries. In the battle for ideas about how societies should organize themselves, these countries are models for democracy and market capitalism. Their leadership and actions will be central to long-term global peace, security, and prosperity.

First, the world's leading powers need to take care of business at home, for their own benefit, but also to ensure a strong global economy in which developing countries can prosper. The United States urgently needs to regain its economic leadership by making major investments in infrastructure, education, and technology; the US and European countries need to reduce their long-term budget deficits, strengthen their financial systems, and avoid a repeat of the 2008 crisis; and Japan needs to reinvigorate its economy with deep structural reforms, simplification of its regulatory framework, and a strategy to address the challenge of a shrinking workforce (for example, by opening more opportunities for women). The foundations are cracking in the leading economies, and fixing them is crucial to maintaining these countries as vital engines for growth in the world economy.

At the same time, the United States, Europe, and Japan must lead by example on democracy. To their credit, they continue to move forward in some important ways, such as the extension of basic rights and liberties, most recently in the provision of equal rights for gays and lesbians. In other ways, democracy seems to be in danger of decay, with significant risks to both the leading countries themselves and the developing countries that look to them as examples. Samuel Huntington argued two decades ago that "if people around the world come to see the United States as a fading power beset by political stagnation, economic inefficiency, and social chaos, its perceived failures will inevitably be seen as the failures of democracy, and the worldwide appeal of democracy will diminish."[3] The US Congress has not passed a proper budget on time since 1997. Deep polarization, the lack of meaningful debates of substance, the lack of willingness to compromise (one of the hallmarks of democracy), Japan's economic malaise since the 1990s, and the 2008 financial crisis in Europe and the United States have all raised questions about whether Western liberal democracy continues to be attractive and effective. Stanford political scientist Francis Fukuyama observed recently that "American government is hardly a source of inspiration around the world at the present moment."[4] The hope that democracy can continue to spread and deepen in developing countries will be set back if the world's leading democracies are unable to function effectively.

Second, the leading powers, working together with China, India, and other emerging countries, must begin to combat climate change. The central step is no secret: progress will require significantly reducing carbon emissions from the world's largest emitters, rich and poor countries alike. Doing so will no doubt be costly and politically difficult, both within countries and in fostering the international cooperation that will be central to solving the problem. But not acting will be much more costly in the long run. International cooperation will be central: no country will act alone, and developing countries will not switch to low-carbon-emissions electricity and other sustainable technologies without leadership from the United States and other global powers.

There are finally the beginnings of action. In early 2014 the Obama administration raised fuel efficiency standards for cars and trucks significantly, set a goal for reducing emissions by 17 percent by 2020 (relative to 2005), and announced new regulations to reduce power plant carbon emissions by 30 percent by 2030 (which will push power companies to shift from coal to other, cleaner sources of energy). In a demonstration of the impact of global leadership by the United States, the day after it established the new power plant rules, China responded by announcing it would begin to limit its total carbon emissions. Even more important, in November 2014 President Obama and Chinese president Xi Jinping reached agreement on a joint approach to curb carbon emissions. The United States pledged to reduce emissions by 26 percent to 28 percent by 2025 relative to 2005. China agreed to peak its emissions by 2030, and pledged that cleaner energy sources such as solar and wind would account for 20 percent of its energy production by 2030.

An agreement by the world's top two polluters on a joint approach is a significant breakthrough. Harvard University economist and environmental expert Robert Stavins said the accord "is potentially the most important development in international climate negotiations in more than a decade."[5] It provides an impetus for other large emitters—such as the EU and India—to follow suit, and may signal the beginning of the end to a years-long impasse in which developing countries said they would not act until rich countries moved first. Just two weeks after the US-China deal, the Philippines—one of the countries that has been hit worst by climate change, with back-to-back major typhoons in 2013 and 2014—said it was shifting its position from demanding all the action from rich countries to pushing all developing countries to make commitments to reduce the use of fossil fuels.[6]

These steps are long overdue. They show the promise of change and that cooperative action is possible, but they are only the beginning. Much more action will be needed to stem the threat of climate change.

Third, the rich countries must lead on making changes to improve the effectiveness and legitimacy of international institutions and organizations. The United Nations, IMF, World Bank, and other organizations were created in the aftermath of World War II at a time of different global power structures and different kinds of problems. They increasingly face major challenges, as evidenced by the failure of the Doha round of trade talks under the auspices of the WTO, the US Congress's failure to approve the new voting shares and financing arrangements at the IMF, and the creation by China and the BRICS of new development banks. These institutions must evolve to better reflect today's world economic and political relationships and to focus on solving today's most critical challenges. Developing countries must be given the opportunity for greater participation and leadership, and a louder voice in debates, negotiations, and decisions. He Fan, the assistant director of the Institute of World Economics and Politics, in Beijing, put it this way: "China is more suspicious of the existing international institutions because China feels it was not one of the founders. China feels a lack of ownership."[7] If developing countries are not treated more as genuine partners, these organizations will lose their validity and effectiveness.

The shift from the traditional G-7 group of rich countries to the G-20 group that includes several large emerging countries was an important move forward. Taking other steps in this direction won't be easy: larger organizations always make negotiations, consensus building, and decision making more difficult. It was not easy for the United States and the allied powers to work together to create these institutions after World War II, and it was especially difficult for them to include their sworn enemies Germany and Japan alongside the Soviet Union. Developing countries will be willing to work together with rich countries on a shared global agenda only if the rich countries begin to share power and decision making. Nancy Birdsall from the Center for Global Development has noted, "Perhaps ironically, it is through sharing power at the global economic institutions that the United States can best secure the engagement of developing countries in a global agenda reflecting our own values and objectives."[8]

Fourth, perhaps more than any other single factor, the relationship between the United States and China will affect the course of global events and the future of developing countries in the decades to come.

China's economic and political futures are central to the prospects for continued development in part because it is the largest single developing country in and of itself, and in part because it has such substantial influence on the economic and political futures of so many other developing countries. China has built deep trade, financial, and investment relationships around the world. In some countries, China has displaced the United States as the major trading partner, sometimes putting those countries in an awkward position vis-à-vis the two powers. It has also become an important donor in some countries, financing roads, schools, power supplies, and hospitals. Many developing countries' economic interests are tied directly to China's future economic success, and they recognize that China's interests must be respected. At the same time, China's economic rise has allowed it to build its military capacity and project a stronger political role across Asia.

However, China's rise has made many countries—especially its neighbors—nervous about its long-term ambitions. Washington and its regional allies do not fully trust China, but neither does China fully trust the United States. Beijing sees the Obama administration's Asia "pivot" not as a way to deepen ties with China but as an attempt by America to maintain its economic dominance and keep China's regional influence in check. That neither side has full confidence in the other creates the potential for escalating misunderstanding, tension, and conflict, which would have a serious detrimental effect on developing countries in the region and around the world. As James Steinberg of Syracuse University and Michael O'Hanlon of the Brookings Institution have argued, "Given the vast potential costs such a conflict would carry for both sides, figuring out how to keep it at bay is among the most important international challenges of the coming years and decades."[9]

Many people on both sides assume, or at least hope, that increasing economic interdependence among the United States, Europe, and China will trump political and power aspirations, minimizing the chances for conflict. While this may prove to be true, it is hardly assured, since growing economic interdependence also contains the seeds of conflict. It's natural that there will be tensions and disagreements in the years to come. The challenge will be to prevent minor disagreements from escalating into major conflicts. Managing these tensions will depend on building trust and creating open lines of communication between political, military, diplomatic, and economic leaders, and clarity in conveying both areas of agreement as well as major concerns and disagreements. It will require establishing a larger role for China in international organizations and negotiations without jeopardizing the long-term legitimate interests of the United States, Europe, Japan, and other countries. China must take on the greater responsibilities that come with its growing leadership and stature. Just as China wants other countries to honor its legitimate interests, it must honor the legitimate interests of its neighbors and other countries in its border disputes, trade arrangements, military maneuvers, commercial negotiations, and other issues. Managing the peaceful rise of China will be one of the most important global challenges of the next two decades, with profound effects on global development progress.

TECHNOLOGY AND INNOVATION

We live in a period of some of the most dramatic technological changes in history—what Erik Brynjolfsson and Andrew McAfee called "the second machine age."[10] Many view the microprocessor as the single most important invention since the steam engine kicked off the industrial revolution. Advances in information technology, energy, transportation, health, and agriculture have propelled the world economy forward. Developing countries have not fully reaped the benefits of existing powerful technologies, not to mention those of the future. The internet has barely begun to reach many of the poorest countries; its continued spread will create new economic opportunities, reduce costs, and facilitate the exchange of ideas and innovations. Cell phones are more widely available, but their impact in developing countries has not reached its potential. Electricity is hardly a new technology, but there are hundreds of millions of people (and countless small entrepreneurs) who do not yet benefit from being connected full-time. The opportunities for major advancements in agriculture, food, water, and energy are vast, as described by entrepreneur Peter Diamandis and science writer Steven Kotler in their terrific book *Abundance: The Future Is Better Than You Think.*

The challenges are also vast. Global food production must increase by 70 percent by 2050 to meet the growing demand from larger populations and higher incomes, so developing countries will need new technologies to grow more (and higher-quality) food. Global freshwater requirements could increase by as much as 50 percent, creating the need for new technologies to conserve water, tap new sources where feasible, and make large-scale desalinization cost-effective. Energy requirements in developing countries will more than double over the next thirty years, and meeting this demand will be central to raising incomes and reducing poverty. Developing countries need to find cleaner, more abundant, and cost-effective energy sources, including technologies aimed specifically at their particular circumstances (such as small-scale off-grid hydro, solar, or wind sources for remote regions). New advancements in health will be needed to continue to fight disease and halt the spread of antimicrobial resistance. Climate change adds to the urgency and complexity of each of these issues.

Technology alone will not solve these problems. New technologies will bring progress only in conjunction with strong global leadership and effective institutions and governance within developing countries. Some technologies create new challenges. Robotics might eliminate some manufacturing jobs but may create others, just as conveyor belts and automation have done in the past. Not all innovations bring progress, and certain technologies in the wrong hands could bring ruin, such as weapons of mass destruction. But meeting the major global challenges of the next few decades won't be possible without robust investments in new technologies.

These investments will cost money, lots of it, and will require cooperation, astute policy choices, and strong leadership. To some extent, the development of new technologies will be driven by private business and entrepreneurs. Market forces—and in particular higher prices—can be a powerful mechanism to encourage new investment. Rising world energy prices in the 1970s and 1980s sparked an onslaught of research aimed at making energy consumption more efficient and developing new energy supplies. The higher price of fossil fuels was the driving force behind developing more fuel-efficient engines and initial research into solar, hydro, and wind energy. Higher food prices have sparked new research by private businesses into improved agricultural technologies, many of which are helping increase crop yields and farmers' incomes.

But private sector research won't be enough. Market prices do not always create the right incentive, whether it is abating pollution, fighting climate change, or finding a new malaria vaccine. These are all classic "public goods," in which the benefits to society from new innovations can be huge, but the incentives for individual private investors to fund the underlying research are limited. Governments in both rich and poor countries must undertake some of the research directly, such as through the US National Institutes of Health or agricultural institutes in developing countries. They must also fund and subsidize research by universities, nongovernment research organizations, international organizations, and private companies through grants, tax incentives, prizes, awards, and other approaches. Some of the most important technological advances in history have been driven by governments and government funding, from the internet, to vaccines, to the Green Revolution, and the same will be true in the decades to come. More innovations will spring from developing countries themselves—China, India, Brazil, and others—and will have more direct applicability to other developing countries. From all of these sources, stimulating new investments in technology and further expanding the use of existing technologies will be central to continuing the great surge of development progress and improving human welfare in the decades to come.

LEADERSHIP, ACTION, AND INSTITUTIONS IN DEVELOPING COUNTRIES

Whatever the global context and the state of technology, each developing country will hold much of its fate in its own hands. While the specifics differ across countries, continued advancement will require action in three critical areas: building competent state institutions and good governance that strengthens democracy, implementing sound economic strategies, and strengthening education and health systems.

First, sustained progress will require good governance and effective leadership. Increasingly, across the majority of developing countries, political legitimacy depends on delivering both prosperity *and* the freedoms of democracy. The ideas of market-based capitalism and democracy have spread around the world—not yet everywhere, but far more extensively than just two decades ago. The key debates in most developing countries are about how to make those institutions and ideas work better, rather than about their fundamental legitimacy. Individual leaders have made huge differences—for good or bad—in so many developing countries during the last few decades, and effective leadership will continue to be critical.

Individual leadership, while crucial, will not be enough. Continuing to deliver development progress and sustaining it over time will depend on building more competent and effective states and institutions. Economic, political, and social progress—for individuals and for society as a whole—require a state with the capacity to effectively provide security, protect property rights, administer justice, regulate trade and commerce, safeguard basic freedoms, and deliver basic health and education services. Many low-income countries have weak government capacity and ineffective institutions, and so corruption runs amok, courts do not function, sanitation systems do not work, freedoms are suppressed, banks are not well regulated, and children do not learn.

It's easy to blame the countries, as some do, and argue that if they would just decide to fix these institutions, development would take off and they would prosper. The reality is more complex. Building these institutions takes time, effort, leadership, and money. A good court system can't be built overnight, or on the cheap. Poverty itself constrains the ability of many countries to build and strengthen institutions, just as it constrains their ability to fight disease and illiteracy. There is a type of development trap at work here rooted in poor governance that Oxford economist Paul Collier identified in *The Bottom Billion*: a competent state is needed for development, but development is needed to build a competent state.

Fortunately, as we have seen, many developing countries are beginning to climb out of this trap: government competence, institutions, and public sector capacity are much stronger than they were twenty years ago. Democratic institutions, while still fragile, are taking root. The negative reinforcing cycle of the bad-governance trap has begun to turn into a positive reinforcing cycle in which more effective institutions begin to deliver progress, and progress helps build more effective institutions.

To sustain the positive cycle, leaders in developing countries must continue to invest in building capacity and strengthening basic institutions. Consolidating and deepening democracy will depend on governments delivering economic and social progress, including economic growth, better health, and more effective education systems. Leaders must strengthen institutions of accountability, including free and fair elections, an effective legislature, a proficient court system, a free press, and a vibrant civil society. Fighting corruption will require greater transparency, stronger rules on disclosure of assets and conflicts of interest for public officials, more effective penalties for those who steal, and leaders who are honest and are willing to remove officials who violate the public trust. Improved governance entails opening opportunities and reducing barriers to all citizens, including women, by taking steps such as further increasing educational options, reducing gender-based violence, and promoting full property rights for women. In turn, these actions will help bolster the legitimacy of governments, strengthen institutions, and deepen democracy.

Second, in addition to more effective governance, continued progress will require sustained economic growth. Growth strategies must be broadly inclusive and provide increasing opportunities for all citizens, both to ensure widespread progress and for governments to retain their legitimacy. A major challenge for most developing countries will be to diversify their economies to manufacturing and services and upgrade the goods and services they produce. Too many countries remain reliant on a narrow range of natural resources and low-grade manufactured products. The key to long-term economic growth is to gradually shift to a wider array of more highly skilled—and more highly paid—economic activities, a challenge that lies ahead for many countries.

No country has succeeded in sustaining growth without robust public investment. Many developing countries, especially in sub-Saharan Africa, have major infrastructure deficiencies: too few quality roads (especially connecting farms to markets, and markets to ports), inadequate energy supplies, overcrowded port facilities, and growing strains on water supplies. Global interest rates have been at historically low levels since the 2008 global financial crisis, providing an opportunity for emerging markets to finance infrastructure and attract other foreign investment. At the same time, no country (except a few city-states) has initiated and sustained growth without significant investments in agriculture. More extensive farm-to-market roads, appropriate pricing policies, local research into new seeds and fertilizers, and strong extension services will be key to continuing to increase agricultural productivity and provide greater income opportunities for the rural poor. These investments will become even more important in the face of climate change and other environmental stresses that threaten to reduce agricultural productivity in the future.

More extensive trade, and the skills and technologies that come with it, will continue to be a major driver of growth in the decades to come. In a more globalized world, businesses in developing countries will look for opportunities to specialize, find niche markets, and integrate themselves into global supply chains. Financial and insurance markets need further development, since access to finance remains a major constraint for many businesses, especially small ones. In many countries, considerable scope remains for reducing tariff and other trade restrictions. In others, limited amounts of protection may be helpful in some circumstances, especially if tariffs are time limited and applied in sectors where firms can become competitive quickly. Many of the most successful exporters have employed various export platforms, such as export processing zones, which help businesses reduce costs and compete in global markets.

For many developing countries, skilled management of natural resources will be central to sustaining inclusive economic growth. Many countries remain highly dependent on natural resource exports, and are therefore vulnerable to the natural resource "curse." Overcoming the curse requires astute macroeconomic and exchange-rate management; transparency and accountability around production agreements and financial flows; prudent use of the funds generated to finance infrastructure, health, and education; and concerted efforts to diversify the economy and reduce resource dependence. International guidelines for sound management and codes of conduct for both governments and private sector extraction companies can help this process, including those developed by the Extractive Industries Transparency Initiative, Publish What You Pay, and the Natural Resource Governance Institute. In complementary ways, these approaches provide protocols for transparency in budgets, payments, and contracts; mechanisms for public accountability; and best practices for managing resources and the related financial inflows and investments.

Third, long-term development demands sustained investments in education and health. These investments are important in and of themselves as core elements of human development, but they are also critical for building the skills and capacities that are needed to advance other aspects of development. The focus in education increasingly must be on quality. In too many countries, teachers are poorly paid, frequently absent, and insufficiently trained and equipped to create an effective learning environment. The right next steps differ across countries, but improved teacher training, higher pay for skilled teachers, stronger curricula, and more local control over schools will typically help move countries forward. Middle-income countries need to begin to focus more on tertiary education to train more engineers, physicians, teachers, researchers, and other skilled workers that they will need in the future. Schools also must continue to create greater opportunities for traditional marginalized groups, especially women and minorities.

Continuing progress in health calls for building stronger health systems, investing in greater skills and capacity, and funding international research to develop new health technologies. *Lancet*'s Global Health 2035 Commission concluded that most developing countries should focus on building a network of primary health care clinics that are equipped to deliver basic services, complemented by community health care workers at the local level and hospitals at the national level, which will require investments both in infrastructure and in building the skills of health care workers.[11] They must also continue to reduce fertility rates to ease growing population pressures. Doing so will depend on sustaining income growth, reducing infant mortality, introducing institutionalized social security systems (which reduce the need for parents to depend on their children for support in old age), increasing opportunities for women both in schools and in the workplace, and making contraception more widely available. Foreign assistance programs will continue to play an important role in strengthening health systems and fighting disease (see below), but as developing countries continue to grow their economies and collect additional tax revenues, they will be able to provide additional services with their own financing, leading to more sustainable and successful systems.

Finally, developing countries need to continue to build effective social safety nets for the poorest, most vulnerable, and most excluded groups in society. The twin objectives are to provide immediate assistance to the poor and to help them build the capacities and skills they need to participate more fully in the economy. Well-designed social safety net programs take many forms, including unconditional cash or in-kind transfers (food or housing), conditional transfers (based on school attendance or getting vaccinations), and targeted subsidies. Social safety net programs have begun to grow in recent years, but while almost 1 billion people participate in some kind of program, more than 800 million people in need remain uncovered.[12]

STRENGTHENING DEVELOPMENT ASSISTANCE

Foreign assistance will continue to play an important supporting role in sustaining development progress, especially in the poorest countries. In the face of growing challenges, donor governments should provide larger amounts of assistance, while refocusing funds to where they can do the most good, and strengthening their efforts in monitoring and evaluation to make programs more effective. Donors should allocate less funding to countries reaching middle-income status, and more to the poorest countries where the needs remain great and the financing options are limited, and especially to poor countries that combine smart economic policies and reasonably good governance. In other words, more aid should be focused in low-income democracies. Foreign assistance can help these countries spur progress in agriculture, health, education, water, and governance, which, in turn, will help reinforce the credibility of democracy. At the same time, democratically elected governments must play a bigger role in setting priorities, developing strategies, and accounting for results in aid-financed programs.

Focusing more funding on democracies does not imply completely cutting off nondemocracies, but it does imply smaller, more focused programs in the nondemocracies. In countries such as Zimbabwe, it makes little sense to provide large amounts of funding in hopes of wholesale transformation that will not happen in the absence of major political change. But aid-financed programs can still improve the welfare of individual people directly. For example, programs fighting HIV/AIDS and malaria can save many lives, even in the context of poor governance. In both democracies and non-democraries, more money should go directly to poor people as cash transfers, which have been shown to be particularly beneficial in fighting poverty.

In parallel with direct investments in developing countries, aid agencies should provide additional support for research and dissemination of new technologies aimed at addressing pressing development challenges. Doing so will require forging new partnerships with universities, foundations, private companies, and other research facilities, and exploring innovative new financing mechanisms.

Finally, aid agencies must develop innovative ways to work with the private sector and encourage private investment. For too long, aid has been seen as a substitute for missing private capital, aimed at filling "gaps" in savings rather than as a mechanism to stimulate investment. There are many ways that aid agencies can do so. They can help farmers in agricultural cooperatives that produce coffee, fruits, or vegetables to meet the quality and time standards demanded by buyers. They can work with local banks and encourage them to provide loans to promising local enterprises, as USAID's Development Credit Authority does by providing partial loan guarantees. They can help reduce investment risks by financing the costs of due diligence, environmental impact assessments, and other up-front costs that investors must bear long before they decide whether to invest. In all these ways and more, donors can work with private investors to leverage their funds, improve results, and further support broad-based development progress.

This agenda is ambitious. I'm sure some people will read it and conclude that it is too long, and that it is not possible for individuals, organizations, and societies to work together to take the actions and make the sacrifices necessary to continue the great surge. But I'm confident that we can, and that we will, in part because we've done it before.

Think about the agenda of action that was necessary after World War II to forge peace and prosperity and to make the gains that have been achieved around the world since then. The list would have included the following: rebuild Europe and Japan from the ashes of war; keep Fascism and Nazism from reemerging; create a global institution—call it the United Nations—where countries can come together and argue and fight and ultimately find common ground for peace and prosperity; forge cooperation among the Western democracies to push back against the Soviet Union until its eventual—and peaceful—dissolution without sparking World War III; create organizations such as the International Monetary Fund, the World Bank, and the World Trade Organization to help—imperfectly—establish the foundation for greater global economic stability and increased trade; invest hundreds of billions of dollars in new technologies that will make air travel much cheaper and faster, make sea-based shipping much more efficient, reduce air and water pollution in the world's leading economies, develop vaccines that can save millions of lives, invent new seed varieties that will substantially increase global food production, and create handheld supercomputers—call them smartphones—that will allow massive amounts of information to flow around the world instantaneously; completely eradicate smallpox—the world's greatest killer—from the planet and nearly eradicate polio and other major diseases; and create the economic and political foundations for hundreds of millions of the world's poorest people to begin to escape extreme poverty and live in functioning democracies.

Foolhardy. Achieving this agenda would have been seen as impossible, but all of it has been accomplished, and much more. As Nelson Mandela said, "It always seems impossible until it's done."

Twenty years ago, developing countries around the world started a quiet but powerful transformation. The achievements—so far— include a huge reduction in extreme poverty, substantial increases in income, major gains in health and education, a reduction in war, and an unprecedented sweep toward democracy and improved governance. However, there is still a long way to go.

The opportunity is within grasp—with concerted action, committed leadership, and wise choices—for the next two decades to be even better and become the greatest era of progress for the world's poor in human history. The potential gains are huge, not only for the 5 billion people living in developing countries but also for the rest of the world. The emergence of developing countries around the world creates a strong foundation for mutual gain and a more peaceful world. It is time to take advantage of this rare opportunity for reducing poverty and widening the global circle of development, prosperity, and freedom.

APPENDIX

List of 109 Developing Countries

Albania

Algeria

Angola

Armenia

Azerbaijan

Bangladesh

Belarus

Benin

Bolivia

Bosnia and Herzegovina

Botswana

Brazil

Bulgaria

Burkina Faso

Burundi

Cambodia

Cameroon

Central African Republic

Chad

Chile

China

Colombia

Congo, Democratic Republic
   of the

Congo, Republic of the

Costa Rica

Côte d'Ivoire

Cuba

Dominican Republic

Ecuador

Egypt, Arab Republic of

El Salvador

Eritrea

Estonia

Ethiopia

Gabon

Gambia, The

Georgia

Ghana

Guatemala

Guinea

Guinea-Bissau

Haiti

Honduras

Hungary

India

Indonesia

Iran, Islamic Republic of

Iraq

Jamaica

Jordan

Kazakhstan

Kenya

Korea, Republic of

Kosovo
Kyrgyz Republic (Kyrgyzstan)
Lao People's Democratic
  Republic (Laos)
Latvia
Lesotho
Liberia
Macedonia, Republic of
Madagascar
Malawi
Malaysia
Mali
Mauritania
Mauritius
Mexico
Moldova
Mongolia
Morocco
Mozambique

Namibia
Nepal
Nicaragua
Niger
Nigeria
Oman
Pakistan
Panama
Papua New Guinea
Paraguay
Peru
Philippines
Romania
Rwanda
Senegal
Serbia
Sierra Leone
Singapore
South Africa

Sri Lanka
Sudan
Swaziland
Syrian Arab Republic (Syria)
Tajikistan
Tanzania
Thailand
Timor-Leste
Togo
Tunisia
Turkey
Turkmenistan
Uganda
Ukraine
Uzbekistan
Vietnam
Yemen, Republic of
Zambia
Zimbabwe

Note: This group includes all countries in which (1) annual per capita incomes were below $3,000 (in constant US dollars from the year 2000) at some point between 1960 and 2013, (2) populations were greater than 1 million people in 2012, and (3) sufficient data are available for most of the indicators to be included in the analysis.

NOTES

PROLOGUE: NOVEMBER 9, 1989

1. Christopher Wren, "Milestone in Africa: Namibians Vote Their Future," *New York Times*, November 8, 1989, www.nytimes.com/1989/11/08/world/milestone-in -africa-namibians-vote-their-future.html.
2. Nicholas Kristof, "Deng Is Resigning Last Formal Post with China Party," *New York Times*, November 10, 1989, www.nytimes.com/1989/11/10/world/deng-is -resigning-last-formal-post-with-china-party.html?pagewanted=all&src=pm.

ONE: A GREAT TRANSFORMATION

1. *The Ignorance Survey: United States*, question 8 (Stockholm, Sweden: Gapminder, 2013), www.gapminder.org/GapminderMedia/wp-uploads/Results-from-the -Ignorance-Survey-in-the-US..pdf.
2. Charles Kenny, *Getting Better: Why Global Development Is Succeeding—and How We Can Improve the World Even More* (New York: Basic Books, 2012); Matt Ridley, *The Rational Optimist: How Prosperity Evolves* (New York: HarperCollins, 2010); Michael Mandelbaum, *The Road to Global Prosperity* (New York: Simon & Schuster, 2014).
3. Paul Theroux, "Africa's Aid Mess," *Barron's*, November 30, 2013, http://online .barrons.com/news/articles/SB50001424053111903747504579185800700741812.
4. Dambisa Moyo, "Why Foreign Aid Is Hurting Africa," *Wall Street Journal*, March 21, 2009, http://online.wsj.com/news/articles/SB123758895999200083.

5. Daron Acemoglu, Simon Johnson, and James A. Robinson, "The Colonial Origins of Comparative Development: An Empirical Investigation," *American Economic Review* 91, no. 5 (December 2001): 1369–1401, http://economics.mit.edu/files /4123. Acemoglu and Robinson develop these ideas further in *Why Nations Fail: The Origins of Power, Prosperity, and Poverty* (New York: Crown Business, 2012).

6. Abhijit Banerjee and Esther Duflo, *Poor Economics: A Radical Rethinking of the Way to Fight Global Poverty* (New York: PublicAffairs, 2012). For the study on shouting at bus drivers, see James Habyarimana and William Jack, "Heckle and Chide: Results of a Randomized Road Safety Intervention in Kenya," *Journal of Public Economics* 95, nos. 11–12 (December 2011): 1438–46.

7. Jeffrey Sachs, *The End of Poverty: Economic Possibilities for Our Time* (New York: Penguin Press, 2005); Paul Collier, *The Bottom Billion: Why the Poorest Countries Are Failing and What Can Be Done About It* (New York: Oxford University Press, 2007).

8. Amartya Sen, *Development as Freedom* (New York: Anchor Books, 2000), p. 3.

9. For discussions on this topic, see Kishore Mahbubani, *The Great Convergence: Asia, the West, and the Logic of One World* (New York: PublicAffairs, 2013); Charles Kenny, *The Upside of Down: Why the Rise of the Rest Is Good for the West* (New York: Basic Books, 2014); *Smart Power 2.0: America's Global Strategy* (Washington, DC: US Global Leadership Coalition, 2012), www.usglc.org/downloads/2012/12 /USGLC-Smart-Power-Brochure.pdf.

10. The global economy shares are from the World Bank's World Development Indicators and include all low- and middle-income countries, and are calculated based on GDP in purchasing power parity prices. The trade shares are from Constantine Michalopoulos and Francis Ng, "Trends in Developing Country Trade 1980–2010," policy research working paper 6334, World Bank, Development Research Group, Trade and Integration Team, Washington, DC, January 2013, http:// elibrary.worldbank.org/doi/pdf/10.1596/1813-9450-6334.

TWO: BREAKTHROUGH FROM THE BOTTOM

1. Thomas Hobbes, *Leviathan, or The Matter, Forme and Power of a Common Wealth Ecclesiasticall and Civil*, chap. 13. (London: Printed for Andrew Crooke, 1651).

2. The life expectancy, income, and poverty data in this section are drawn from François Bourguignon and Christian Morrisson, "Inequality Among World Citizens, 1820–1992," *American Economic Review* 92, no. 4 (September 2002): 167, 727–44.

3. The PovcalNet database can be found at http://iresearch.worldbank.org /PovcalNet/. The World Bank updates the data regularly; all of the data in this chapter were accessed in October 2014. For a description of the data through 2010, see Shaohua Chen and Martin Ravallion, "An Update to the World Bank's Estimates of Consumption Poverty in the Developing World," World Bank, Development Research Group, March 1, 2012, http://siteresources.worldbank.org /INTPOVCALNET/Resources/Global_Poverty_Update_2012_02-29-12.pdf.

4. Abhijit Banerjee and Esther Duflo, "The Economic Lives of the Poor," *Journal of Economic Perspectives* 21, no. 1 (Winter 2007): 141–67, http://pubs.aeaweb.org /doi/pdfplus/10.1257/jep.21.1.141; Banerjee and Duflo, *Poor Economics: A Radical Rethinking of the Way to Fight Global Poverty* (New York: PublicAffairs, 2012).

5. Daryl Collins et al., *Portfolios of the Poor: How the World's Poor Live on $2 a Day* (Princeton, NJ: Princeton University Press, 2009).

6. Banerjee and Duflo, "Economic Lives of the Poor."

7. Ibid, p. 8.

8. Collins et al., *Portfolios of the Poor*, pp. 89–90.

9. Ariel Fiszbein, Ravi Kanbur, and Ruslan Yemtsov, "Social Protection, Poverty and the Post-2015 Agenda," policy research working paper 6469, World Bank, Human Development Network, Social Protection and Labor Department, Washington, DC, May 2013, www-wds.worldbank.org/external/default/WDSContent Server/WDSP/IB/2013/05/30/000158349_20130530132533/Rendered/PDF /WPS6469.pdf.

10. Pedro Olinto et al., "The State of the Poor: Where Are the Poor, Where Is Extreme Poverty Harder to End, and What Is the Current Profile of the World's Poor?," World Bank, Poverty Reduction and Economic Management Network (Prem), *Economic Premise* 125 (October 2013), http://siteresources.worldbank.org/EXTPREMNET /Resources/EP125.pdf.

11. Laurence Chandy, Natasha Ledlie, and Veronika Penciakova, "The Final Countdown: Prospects for Ending Extreme Poverty by 2030," policy paper 2013-04, Global Economy and Development at Brookings Institution, Washington, DC, April 2013, www.brookings.edu/~/media/research/files/reports/2013/04/ending %20extreme%20poverty%20chandy/the_final_countdown.pdf.

THREE: THE WEALTH OF A NEW GENERATION

1. This description of events in Mozambique is drawn from Steven Radelet, *Emerging Africa: How 17 Countries Are Leading the Way* (Washington, DC: Center for Global Development, 2010).

2. David Smith, "Boom Time for Mozambique, Once the Basket Case of Africa," *Guardian* (UK), March 27, 2012, www.theguardian.com/world/2012/mar/27 /mozambique-africa-energy-resources-bonanza.

3. Ibid.

4. Javier Montanaro, "8 New Trends in Latin America's Mobile Market for 2013," Latin Link, August 13, 2013, http://latinlink.usmediaconsulting.com/2013/08 /8-new-trends-in-latin-americas-mobile-market-for-2013; Roberto A. Ferdman, "Why Apple's First Retail Store in Brazil Is Actually a Really Big Deal," Quartz, October 28, 2013, http://qz.com/140467/why-apples-first-retail-store-in-brazil -is-actually-a-really-big-deal.

5. Coca-Cola Company, "Coca-Cola Continues Strong Investment in China with Opening of 43rd Production Facility," press release, October 24, 2013,

www.coca-colacompany.com/press-center/press-releases/coca-cola-continues -strong-investment-in-china-with-opening-of-43rd-production-facility; Reuters, Adam Jourdan, "Coca-Cola Says to Invest Over $4 Billion in China in 2015– 2017," November 7, 2013, www.reuters.com/article/2013/11/08/us-cocacola -china-idUSBRE9A704H20131108.

6. Reuters, Tiisetso Motsoeneng, and Wendell Roelf, "Wal-Mart Wins Final Go-Ahead for Massmart Deal," March 9, 2012, www.reuters.com/article/2012/03/09/us -massmart-walmart-idUSBRE8280KH20120309.

7. International Finance Corporation, "The Latin American Agribusiness Development Corporation (LADD)," 2009, www.ifc.org/wps/wcm/connect/c025a 1004121d372bcacbcdf0d0e71af/Latin_American_Agribusiness_Development .pdf?MOD=AJPERES.

8. Pedro H. G. Ferreira de Souza, "Poverty, Inequality and Social Policies in Brazil, 1995–2009," working paper 87, International Policy Centre for Inclusive Growth, February 2012, www.econstor.eu/dspace/bitstream/10419/71804/1/687787998 .pdf.

9. For an analysis of the turnaround in sub-Saharan Africa, see Radelet, *Emerging Africa*.

10. "Ethiopian Textile Exports Reach $29 Mn in First Quarter," Fibre2fashion.com, November 7, 2013, www.fibre2fashion.com/news/textile-news/ethiopia/news details.aspx?news_id=155309.

11. "Blooming Desert: An Agricultural Revolution," *Economist*, July 7, 2005, www .economist.com/node/4157659.

12. This paragraph is drawn from Radelet, *Emerging Africa*, and is based on a personal email interview with Masetumo Lebitsa (May 6, 2010), and "Maseru Tapestries and Mats," AfricanCraft.com, last modified July 2006, www.africancrafts.com/artisan .php?sid=329378831151824482389753811690031&id=maseru&pg=intro.

13. De Souza, "Poverty, Inequality and Social Policies in Brazil, 1995–2009."

14. Rachel Heath and A. Mushfiq Mobarak, "Manufacturing Growth and the Lives of Bangladeshi Women," working paper 20383, National Bureau of Economic Research, Cambridge, MA, August 2014.

15. *World Development Report 2013: Jobs* (Washington, DC: International Bank for Reconstruction and Development/World Bank, 2013), pp. 56, 59, http://dx.doi .org/10.1596/978-0-8213-9575-2.

16. Jeffrey R. Vincent et al., "Tropical Countries May Be Willing to Pay More to Protect Their Forests," *Proceedings of the National Academy of Sciences of the United States of America* (*PNAS*) 111, no. 28 (July 15, 2014), doi:10.1073/pnas.1312246111; Partha Dasgupta, *An Inquiry into Well-Being and Destitution* (Oxford: Oxford University Press, 1993).

17. *The Changing Wealth of Nations: Measuring Sustainable Development in the New Millennium* (Washington, DC: International Bank for Reconstruction and Development/World Bank, 2011), http://siteresources.worldbank.org/ENVIRONMENT /Resources/ChangingWealthNations.pdf.

18. Kenneth J. Arrow et al., "Sustainability and the Measurement of Wealth," *Environment and Development Economics* 17 (2012): 317–53, doi:10.1017/S1355770X12000137.

19. Two of the first studies to reach this conclusion were Michael Roemer and Mary Kay Gugerty, "Does Economic Growth Reduce Poverty?," Consulting Assistance on Economic Reform II discussion paper 4, Harvard Institute for International Development, Cambridge, MA, April 1997, http://pdf.usaid.gov/pdf_docs/pnaca655.pdf; and John Luke Gallup, Steven Radelet, and Andrew Warner, "Economic Growth and the Income of the Poor," Consulting Assistance on Economic Reform II discussion paper 36, Harvard Institute for International Development, Cambridge, MA, 1999, www.pdx.edu/sites/www.pdx.edu.econ/files/media_assets/jlgallup/grow_pov.pdf. The most widely read and cited study is by David Dollar and Aart Kraay, "Growth Is Good for the Poor," *Journal of Economic Growth* 7, no. 3 (September 2002): 195–225. An updated version of the latter paper (written with Tatjana Kleineberg) is "Growth Still Is Good for the Poor," policy research working paper 6568, World Bank, Development Research Group, Macroeconomics and Growth Team, Washington, DC, August 2013, http://elibrary.worldbank.org/doi/pdf/10.1596/1813-9450-6568.

20. Dollar and Kraay, "Growth Is Good for the Poor."

21. Branko Milanovic, *The Haves and the Have-Nots: A Brief and Idiosyncratic History of Global Inequality* (New York: Basic Books, 2011).

22. De Souza, "Poverty, Inequality, and Social Policies in Brazil."

23. Branko Milanovic, "Global Income Inequality by the Numbers: In History and Now—An Overview," policy research working paper 6259, World Bank, Development Research Group, Poverty and Inequality Team, Washington, DC, November 2012, http://elibrary.worldbank.org/doi/pdf/10.1596/1813-9450-6259.

24. Ibid., p. 6.

FOUR: MORE CHILDREN NOW LIVE—AND LIVE BETTER

1. Chinua Achebe, *Things Fall Apart* (New York: Anchor Books, 1994), p. 77.

2. *Levels and Trends in Child Mortality Report 2014* (New York: United Nations Children's Fund, 2014), p. 1, http://www.unicef.org/media/files/Levels_and_Trends_in_Child_Mortality_2014%281%29.pdf.

3. *World Malaria Report 2014* (Geneva, Switzerland: World Health Organization, 2014), p. *xii*, http://apps.who.int/iris/bitstream/10665/144852/2/9789241564830_eng.pdf?ua=1; *World AIDS Day Report 2014* (Geneva, Switzerland: Joint United Nations Programme on HIV/AIDS [UNAIDS], 2014), p. 6, www.unaids.org/sites/default/files/media_asset/JC2686_WAD2014report_en.pdf; *Global Tuberculosis Report 2014* (Geneva, Switzerland: World Health Organization, 2014), table CD.1, http://apps.who.int/iris/bitstream/10665/137094/1/9789241564809_eng.pdf?ua=1; *Diarrhoea: Why Children Are Still Dying and What Can Be Done* (New York: United Nations Children's Fund [UNICEF]; and Geneva, Switzerland:

World Health Organization [WHO], 2009), http://whqlibdoc.who.int/publications
/2009/9789241598415_eng.pdf; "Diarrhoeal Disease: Fact Sheet 330," World
Health Organization, last modified April 2013, www.who.int/mediacentre/fact
sheets/fs330/en.

4. At the request of the family, we have changed the names in this section.

5. For an excellent in-depth analysis of these changes, see Angus Deaton, *The Great
Escape: Health, Wealth, and the Origins of Inequality* (Princeton, NJ: Princeton
University Press, 2013).

6. For a terrific account of Snow's dogged determination and sleuthing skills in trac-
ing the origins of cholera, see Steven Johnson, *The Ghost Map: The Story of London's Most Terrifying Epidemic and How It Changed Science, Cities, and the Modern
World* (New York: Riverhead Books, 2007).

7. "Chapter 4: Mortality, 2010-Based NPP Reference Volume," Office for National
Statistics (United Kingdom), March 29, 2012, fig. 4.6, www.ons.gov.uk/ons
/dcp171776_253938.pdf.

8. "Life Expectancy at Exact Age x (ex), for Both Sexes Combined, by Major Area,
Region and Country, 1950–2010," in *World Population Prospects: The 2012 Re-
vision*, United Nations, Department of Economic and Social Affairs, Population
Division, New York, June 2013, http://esa.un.org/wpp/excel-data/mortality.htm.

9. *The State of Food Insecurity in the World 2014: Strengthening the Enabling Environment for Food Security and Nutrition* (Rome, Italy: Food and Agriculture Organization of the United Nations, 2014), www.fao.org/3/a-i4030e.pdf.

10. Richard Horton and Selina Lo, "Nutrition: A Quintessential Sustainable Development Goal," in Maternal and Child Nutrition Series, special issue, *Lancet* 382, no.
9890 (June 6, 2013): 371–72.

11. Thomas Espenshade, Juan Carlos Guzman, and Charles Westoff, "The Surprising
Global Variation in Replacement Fertility," *Population Research and Policy Review*
22, nos. 5–6 (December 2003): 575–83.

12. Ezra Klein, "Bill Gates: 'Death Is Something We Really Understand Extremely
Well,'" *Washington Post*, May 17, 2013, www.washingtonpost.com/blogs/wonkblog
/wp/2013/05/17/bill-gates-death-is-something-we-really-understand-extremely
-well.

13. Richard A. Easterlin, "Why Isn't the Whole World Developed?," *Journal of Economic History* 41, no. 1, The Tasks of Economic History (March 1981): 1–19, www
.econ.ucdavis.edu/faculty/gclark/210a/readings/Easterlin.pdf.

14. *The Growth Report: Strategies for Sustained Growth and Inclusive Development*
(Washington, DC: International Bank for Reconstruction and Development,
2008): p. 2, https://openknowledge.worldbank.org/bitstream/handle/10986/6507
/49860PUB0Box3101OFFICIAL0USE0ONLY1.pdf?sequence.

15. UNESCO Institute of Statistics, online database, http://stats.uis.unesco.org
/unesco/TableViewer/tableView.aspx?ReportId=201.

16. *Learning for All: Investing in People's Knowledge and Skills to Promote Development*
(Washington, DC: International Bank for Reconstruction and Development/World

Bank, 2011), p. 2, http://siteresources.worldbank.org/EDUCATION/Resources /ESSU/463292-1306181142935/WB_ES_ExectiveSummary_FINAL.pdf.

17. "Girls' Education," World Bank, last modified December 3, 2014, www.world bank.org/en/topic/education/brief/girls-education.

18. Robert Barro and Jong-Wha Lee, "A New Data Set of Educational Attainment in the World, 1950–2010," working paper 15902, National Bureau of Economic Research, Cambridge, MA, April 2010, www.nber.org/papers/w15902.pdf.

19. Lawrence Summers, *Investing in All the People*, policy research working paper 905, World Bank, Washington, DC, May 1992, www-wds.worldbank.org/servlet/WDS ContentServer/WDSP/IB/1992/05/01/000009265_3961003011714/Rendered /PDF/multi_page.pdf.

20. Lant Pritchett, *The Rebirth of Education: Schooling Ain't Learning* (Washington, DC: Center for Global Development, 2013). See also Maureen Lewis and Marlaine Lockheed, *Inexcusable Absence: Why 60 Million Girls Are Still Not in School and What to Do About It* (Washington, DC: Center for Global Development, 2006).

21. Deaton, *Great Escape*, p. 105.

22. Dean Jamison et al., "Global Health 2035: A World Converging Within a Generation," *Lancet* 382, no. 9908 (December 7, 2013): 1898–1955.

23. My thanks to David Lindauer for making this point.

24. *Diarrhoea: Why Children Are Still Dying and What Can Be Done;* "Diarrhoeal Disease: Fact Sheet 330."

25. John Bland and John Clements, "Protecting the World's Children: The Story of WHO's Immunization Programme," *World Health Forum* 19, no. 2 (1998): 162–73, http://apps.who.int/iris/bitstream/10665/55604/1/WHF_1998_19%282%29_p162 -173.pdf; "Immunization Coverage: Fact Sheet 378," World Health Organization, last modified November 2014, www.who.int/mediacentre/factsheets/fs378/en.

FIVE: DICTATORS OUT, DEMOCRACY IN

1. O. Henry, "The Admiral," in *Cabbages and Kings* (New York: Doubleday, Page & Company, 1904).

2. Parts of this chapter are drawn from Steven Radelet, *Emerging Africa: How 17 Countries Are Leading the Way* (Washington, DC: Center for Global Development, 2010).

3. Michael Bratton and Nicholas van de Walle, *Democratic Experiments in Africa: Regime Transitions in Comparative Perspective* (Cambridge: Cambridge University Press, 1997), p. 3.

4. Christopher Wren, "Namibian Voting Is Heavy and Eager," *New York Times*, November 11, 1989, www.nytimes.com/1989/11/11/world/namibian-voting-is-heavy -and-eager.html.

5. Rachel Swarns and Norimitsu Onishi, "Africa Creeps Along Path to Democracy," *New York Times*, June 2, 2002, www.nytimes.com/2002/06/02/world/africa -creeps-along-path-to-democracy.html.

6. Samuel Huntington, "Democracy's Third Wave," *Journal of Democracy* 2, no. 2 (Spring 1991): 12, www.ou.edu/uschina/gries/articles/IntPol/Huntington.91.Demo .3rd.pdf. See also Huntington, *The Third Wave: Democratization in the Late Twentieth Century* (Norman: University of Oklahoma Press, 1991).

7. Freedom House, "Freedom in the World Comparative and Historical Data Series, Individual Country Ratings and Status 1973–2015," Freedom House, Washington, DC, https://freedomhouse.org/report-types/freedom-world#.VVUT9PnF9qU; Polity IV Project, "Political Regime Characteristics and Transitions, 1800–2013," Center for Systemic Peace, Vienna, VA, 2014, http://www.systemicpeace.org /polity/polity4.htm.

8. Swarns and Onishi, "Africa Creeps Along Path to Democracy."

9. Philip E. Keefer, Database of Political Institutions (updated January 2013), http:// go.worldbank.org/2EAGGLRZ40; Thorsten Beck, George Clarke, Alberto Groff, Philip Keefer, and Patrick Walsh, "New Tools in Comparative Political Economy: The Database of Political Institutions" *World Bank Economic Review* 15, no. 1 (September 2001): 165–76.

10. Daniel N. Posner and Daniel J. Young, "The Institutionalization of Political Power in Africa," *Journal of Democracy* 18, no. 3 (July 2007): 128, http://www .journalofdemocracy.org/sites/default/files/PosnerandYoung-18-3.pdf.

11. Larry Diamond, *The Spirit of Democracy: The Struggle to Build Free Societies Throughout the World* (New York: Times Books, 2008), p. 256.

12. Thomas Carothers, "The End of the Transition Paradigm," *Journal of Democracy* 13, no. 1 (January 2002): 5–21, www.journalofdemocracy.org/articles-files/gratis /Carothers-13-1.pdf.

13. Steven Pinker, *The Better Angels of Our Nature: Why Violence Has Declined* (New York: Penguin Books, 2011).

14. Ibid., p. 302. The data are from figure 6.4, p. 304.

15. Uppsala Conflict Data Program, "UCDP/PRIO Armed Conflict Dataset, v.4-2014, 1946–2013," June 12, 2014, Uppsala University, Uppsala, Sweden, www.pcr.uu.se /research/ucdp/datasets/ucdp_prio_armed_conflict_dataset. For the underlying research papers, see Lotta Themnér and Peter Wallensteen, "Armed Conflicts, 1946–2013," *Journal of Peace Research* 51, no. 4 (July 2014): 541–54; Nils Petter Gleditsch et al., "Armed Conflict, 1946–2001: A New Dataset," *Journal of Peace Research* 39, no. 5 (September 2002): 615–37.

16. The two data sets are (1) Peace Research Institute Oslo (PRIO), "PRIO Battle Deaths Dataset Version 3.0," October 2009, www.prio.org/Data/Armed-Conflict /Battle-Deaths/The-Battle-Deaths-Dataset-version-30, and (2) the Uppsala Conflict Data Program, Uppsala Conflict Data Program "UCDP Battle-Related Deaths Dataset, v.5-2014, 1989–2013," June 12, 2014, Uppsala University, Uppsala, Sweden, www.pcr.uu.se/research/ucdp/datasets/ucdp_battle-related_deaths_dataset. For the underlying research papers, see Bethany Lacina and Nils Petter Gleditsch, "Monitoring Trends in Global Combat: A New Dataset of Battle Deaths," *European Journal of Population* 21, nos. 2–3 (June 2005): 145–66, doi:10.1007/s10680-005-6851-6.

17. *World Development Report 2011 Conflict, Security and Development* (Washington, DC: International Bank for Reconstruction and Development/World Bank, 2011), http://data.worldbank.org/data-catalog/wdr2011.
18. Paul Collier, *The Bottom Billion: Why the Poorest Countries Are Failing and What Can Be Done About It* (New York: Oxford University Press, 2007), p. 27.
19. Paul Collier, Anke Hoeffler, and Måns Söderbom, "Post-Conflict Risks," working paper 2006-12, Centre for the Study of African Economies, Department of Economics, University of Oxford, August 17, 2006, www.csae.ox.ac.uk/workingpapers/pdfs/2006-12text.pdf.
20. Ellen Johnson Sirleaf, introduction to *Emerging Africa*, by Radelet.
21. For a deeper analysis and discussion of many of the points in this section, see Diamond, *The Spirit of Democracy: The Struggle to Build Free Societies Throughout the World* (New York: Times Books, 2008).
22. Huntington, "Democracy's Third Wave," pp. 30–31.
23. Seymour Martin Lipset, "Some Social Requisites of Democracy," *American Political Science Review* 53, no. 1 (March 1959): 69–105, http://eppam.weebly.com/uploads/5/5/6/2/5562069/lipset1959_apsr.pdf.
24. Huntington, "Democracy's Third Wave," p. 30.
25. Amartya Sen, *Development as Freedom* (New York: Anchor Books, 2000), p. 32.
26. Ibid.
27. For more on this point, see Morton Halperin, Joseph Siegel, and Michael Weinstein, *The Democracy Advantage: How Democracies Promote Prosperity and Peace* (New York: Routledge, 2005).
28. Radelet, *Emerging Africa*.
29. John Gerring et al., "Democracy and Economic Growth: A Historical Perspective," *World Politics* 57, no. 3 (April 2005): 323–64; Daron Acemoglu et al., "Democracy Does Cause Growth," working paper 20004, National Bureau of Economic Research, Cambridge, MA, 2014, www.nber.org/papers/w20004.

SIX: GOOD-BYE COLD WAR, SO LONG COMMUNISM

1. In *Why Nations Fail: The Origins of Power, Prosperity, and Poverty* (New York: Crown Business, 2012), Acemoglu and Robinson argue that institutions are more likely to change at critical moments of world history, and they point to the Black Death, the opening of the Atlantic sea routes, and the industrial revolution as examples.
2. M. W. Van Boven, "Towards a New Age of Partnership (TANAP): An Ambitious World Heritage Project (UNESCO Memory of the World—reg.form, 2002)," VOC Archives Appendix 2, p. 14, http://portal.unesco.org/ci/en/files/22635/11546101681netherlands_voc_archives.doc/netherlands%2Bvoc%2Barchives.doc.
3. For more on this point, see Acemoglu and Robinson, *Why Nations Fail*.
4. "Global 500 2013," *Fortune* (2013), http://fortune.com/global500/2013.

5. George Ayittey, *Africa Betrayed* (New York: St. Martin's Press, 1993); Acemoglu and Robinson, *Why Nations Fail.*

6. Francis Fukuyama, *The End of History and the Last Man* (New York: Free Press, 1992), p. *xiii.*

SEVEN: HELLO GLOBALIZATION, WELCOME NEW TECHNOLOGIES

1. Adam Smith, *An Inquiry into the Nature and Causes of the Wealth of Nations* (London: W. Strahan and T. Cadell, 1776), chap. 7.

2. Frank Viviano, "China's Great Armada," *National Geographic*, July 2005, p. 37.

3. Ibid., p. 52.

4. The figures are drawn from the World Bank's World Development Indicators, and are the sum in each year of the number of patent applications for residents and nonresidents.

5. "ICT Facts and Figures: The World in 2014," International Telecommunication Union, last modified April 2014, www.itu.int/en/ITU-D/Statistics/Documents /facts/ICTFactsFigures2014-e.pdf.

6. Constantine Michalopoulos and Francis Ng, "Trends in Developing Country Trade 1980–2010," policy research working paper 6334, World Bank, Development Research Group, Trade and Integration Team, Washington, DC, January 2013, http:// elibrary.worldbank.org/doi/pdf/10.1596/1813-9450-6334.

7. The total trade figures are from the World Development Indicators. For the exports of manufactures, see ibid.

8. World Development Indicators, data for all low- and middle-income countries for "Immunization, DPT (% of Children Ages 12–23 Months)."

9. *World Development Report 2013: Jobs* (Washington, DC: International Bank for Reconstruction and Development/World Bank, 2012), p. 59, http://siteresources .worldbank.org/EXTNWDR2013/Resources/8258024-1320950747192 /8260293-1322665883147/WDR_2013_Report.pdf.

10. Theodore H. Moran, *Beyond Sweatshops: Foreign Direct Investment and Globalization in Developing Countries* (Washington, DC: Brookings Institution Press, 2002).

11. Drusilla Brown, Rajeev Dehejia, and Raymond Robertson, "Is There a Business Case for Improving Labor Standards? Some Evidence from Better Factories Cambodia," in *Workers' Rights and Labor Compliance in Global Supply Chains: Is a Social Label the Answer?*, ed. Jennifer Bair, Marsha A. Dickson, and Doug Miller (New York: Routledge, 2013).

12. Theodore H. Moran, "Foreign Investment and Supply Chains in Emerging Markets: Recurring Problems and Demonstrated Solutions," working paper 14-12, Peterson Institute for International Economics, Washington, DC, December 2014, www.iie.com/publications/wp/wp14-12.pdf.

13. *The Growth Report: Strategies for Sustained Growth and Inclusive Development* (Washington, DC: International Bank for Reconstruction and Development/World Bank on behalf of the Commission on Growth and Development, 2008), p. 2,

https://openknowledge.worldbank.org/bitstream/handle/10986/6507/449860 PUB0Box3101OFFICIAL0USE0ONLY1.pdf?sequence.

14. Erik Brynjolfsson and Andrew McAfee, *The Second Machine Age: Work, Progress, and Prosperity in a Time of Brilliant Technologies* (New York: W. W. Norton, 2014).

15. "History of Containerization," World Shipping Council, www.worldshipping.org /about-the-industry/history-of-containerization.

16. Daniel Bernhofen, Zouheir El-Sahli, and Richard Kneller, "Estimating the Effects of the Container Revolution on World Trade," working paper 4136, Center for Economic Studies and the Ifo Institute, February 2013, http://ssrn.com/abstract =2228625. See also "Why Have Containers Boosted Trade So Much?," *Economist*, May 21, 2013, www.economist.com/blogs/economist-explains/2013/05 /economist-explains-14.

17. Prabhu Pingali, "Green Revolution: Impacts, Limits, and the Path Ahead," *Proceedings of the National Academy of Sciences of the United States of America (PNAS)* 109, no. 31 (July 31, 2012): 12302–8, doi:10.1073/pnas.0912953109.

18. Ibid.

19. "The Drought Tolerant Maize for Africa Project: Six Years of Addressing African Smallholder Farmers' Needs," International Maize and Wheat Improvement Center (CIMMYT), http://dtma.cimmyt.org/index.php/about/background.

20. Feliz Nweke and Steven Haggblade, "The Cassava Transformation in West and Southern Africa," in Steven Haggblade and Peter Hazell, eds., *Successes in African Agriculture: Lessons for the Future* (Washington, DC: International Food Policy Research Institute; and Baltimore: Johns Hopkins University Press, 2010, published for the IFPRI).

21. American Association for the Advancement of Science, "Statement by the AAAS Board of Directors on Labeling of Genetically Modified Foods," news release, October 20, 2012, www.aaas.org/sites/default/files/AAAS_GM_statement.pdf.

22. *A Decade of EU-funded GMO Research 2001–2010* (Brussels: European Union, 2010), p. 16, http://ec.europa.eu/research/biosociety/pdf/a_decade_of_eu-funded _gmo_research.pdf.

23. Rob Paarlberg, "The World Needs Genetically Modified Foods," *Wall Street Journal*, April 14, 2013, www.wsj.com/articles/SB1000142412788732410520457838 0872639718046.

24. *Diarrhoea: Why Children Are Still Dying and What Can Be Done* (New York: United Nations Children's Fund [UNICEF]; and Geneva, Switzerland: World Health Organization [WHO], 2009); "Diarrhoeal Disease: Fact Sheet 330," World Health Organization, last modified April 2013, www.who.int/mediacentre /factsheets/fs330/en.

25. Ruth Levine and the What Works Working Group, with Molly Kinder, *Millions Saved: Proven Successes in Global Health* (Washington, DC: Center for Global Development, 2004).

26. UNAIDS, *World AIDS Day Report 2014*, http://www.unaids.org/sites/default /files/media_asset/JC2686_WAD2014report_en.pdf.

27. *Global Report: UNAIDS Report on the Global AIDS Epidemic 2013* (Geneva, Switzerland: Joint United Nations Programme on HIV/AIDS [UNAIDS], 2013), www.unaids.org/en/media/unaids/contentassets/documents/epidemiology/2013/gr2013/UNAIDS_Global_Report_2013_en.pdf.

28. Peter Howitt et al., "Technologies for Global Health," *Lancet* 380 (August 4, 2013): 507–35, http://apsredes.org/site2012/wp-content/uploads/2012/08/Technologies-for-Global-Health.pdf.

29. Sarah Arnquist, "In Rural Africa, a Fertile Market for Mobile Phones," *New York Times*, October 6, 2009, www.nytimes.com/2009/10/06/science/06uganda.html?_r=0.

30. "Mobile Marvels: A Special Report on Telecoms in Emerging Markets," *Economist*, September 24, 2009, p. 1, www.economist.com/node/14483896.

31. Robert Jensen, "The Digital Provide: Information (Technology), Market Performance and Welfare in the South Indian Fisheries Sector," *Quarterly Journal of Economics* 122, no. 3 (August 2007): 879–924; Jenny Aker, "Information from Markets Near and Far: Mobile Phones and Agricultural Markets in Niger," *American Economic Journal: Applied Economics* 2, no. 3 (July 2010): 46–59, http://sites.tufts.edu/jennyaker/files/2010/09/aker_nigercell.pdf..

32. "Aponjon," Mobile Alliance for Maternal Action, www.mobilemamaalliance.org/mama-bangladesh.

33. Marshall S. Smith and Rebecca Winthrop, "A New Face of Education: Bringing Technology into the Classroom in the Developing World," working paper 1, Brooke Shearer Series, Brookings Institution, Washington, DC, January 2012, www.brookings.edu/research/papers/2012/01/education-technology-winthrop.

EIGHT: LEADERSHIP, CIVIL SOCIETY, ACTION—AND A BIT OF LUCK

1. Margaret Keck, *The Workers' Party and Democratization in Brazil* (New Haven, CT: Yale University Press, 1992), as quoted in Acemoglu and Robinson, *The Origins of Power, Prosperity, and Poverty* (New York: Crown Business, 2012), p. 456.

2. Francis Fukuyama, *The End of History and the Last Man* (New York: Free Press, 1992), p. 220.

3. Larry Diamond, *The Spirit of Democracy: The Struggle to Build Free Societies Throughout the World* (New York: Times Books, 2008), p. 4.

4. *The Growth Report: Strategies for Sustained Growth and Inclusive Development* (Washington, DC: International Bank for Reconstruction and Development/World Bank on behalf of the Commission on Growth and Development, 2008): p. 2, https://openknowledge.worldbank.org/bitstream/handle/10986/49860PUB0Box3101OFFICIAL0USE0ONLY1.pdf?sequence.

5. Jessica Achberger, "Belgian Colonial Education Policy: A Poor Foundation for Stability," Ultimate History Project, www.ultimatehistoryproject.com/belgian-congo.html.

6. Andrea Alfieri, Channing Arndt, and Xavier Cirera, "Mozambique," in *Distortions to Agricultural Incentives in Africa*, ed. Kym Anderson and William A. Masters

(Washington, DC: International Bank for Reconstruction and Development/ World Bank, 2009).

7. Samuel Huntington, *The Third Wave: Democratization in the Late Twentieth Century* (Norman: University of Oklahoma Press, 1991), p. 258.

8. Ethan Kapstein and Nathan Converse, *The Fate of Young Democracies* (Cambridge: Cambridge University Press, 2008), p. *xv*.

9. Adam Smith, *An Inquiry into the Nature and Causes of the Wealth of Nations* (London: W. Strahan and T. Cadell, 1776), bk. 1, chap. 3, and bk. 3, chap. 4.

NINE: FOREIGN AID: BLESSING OR CURSE?

1. Richard Carter and Kamini N. Mendis, "Evolutionary and Historical Aspects of the Burden of Malaria," *Clinical Microbiology Reviews* 15, no. 4 (October 2002): 564–94, table 3.

2. John L. Gallup and Jeffrey Sachs, "The Economic Burden of Malaria," *American Journal of Tropical Medicine and Hygiene* 64, nos. 1–2 (2001): 85–96.

3. Richard A. Feachem and the Malaria Elimination Group, "Shrinking the Malaria Map: A Guide on Malaria Elimination for Policy Makers," Global Health Group/ UCSF Global Health Sciences, University of California, San Francisco, April 2009, p. 13, www.malariaeliminationgroup.org/sites/default/files/fileuploads/AGuideon MalariaEliminationforPolicyMakers.pdf.

4. "Our History—Our Story," Centers for Disease Control and Prevention, last modified April 26, 2013, www.cdc.gov/about/history/ourstory.htm.

5. "Malaria: The Panama Canal," Centers for Disease Control and Prevention, last modified November 9, 2012, www.cdc.gov/malaria/about/history/panama_canal .html.

6. *Global Malaria Action Plan for a Malaria-Free World* (Geneva, Switzerland: Roll Back Malaria Partnership, 2008), www.rollbackmalaria.org/gmap/gmap.pdf.

7. Christopher Murray et al., "Global Malaria Mortality Between 1980 and 2010: A Systematic Analysis," *Lancet* 379, no. 9814 (February 2012): 413–31.

8. *World Malaria Report 2014* (Geneva, Switzerland: World Health Organization, 2014), p. *x*, http://apps.who.int/iris/bitstream/10665/144852/2/9789241564830 _eng.pdf?ua=1.

9. Feachem and Malaria Elimination Group, "Shrinking the Malaria Map," p. 13.

10. *World Malaria Report 2014*, p. *xii*.

11. Ruth Levine and the What Works Working Group, *Case Studies in Global Health: Millions Saved* (Sudbury, MA: Jones and Bartlett, 2007).

12. "Afghanistan: Education," United States Agency for International Development (USAID), last modified February 9, 2015, www.usaid.gov/afghanistan/education.

13. Peter Roeder and Karl Rich, "Conquering the Cattle Plague: The Global Effort to Eradicate Rinderpest," in *Millions Fed: Proven Success in Agricultural Development*, ed. David J. Spielman and Rajul Pandya-Lorch (Washington, DC: International Food Policy Research Institute, 2009).

14. John P. Brennan and Arelene Malabayabas, "International Rice Research Institute's Contribution to Rice Varietal Yield Improvement in South-East Asia," Australian Centre for International Agricultural Research (ACIAR) Impact Assessment Series #74, 2011, http://aciar.gov.au/files/node/13941/international_rice_research _institute_s_contribu_39069.pdf.

15. Bill Gates, speech to the United Nations General Assembly, September 25, 2008, http://www.gatesfoundation.org/media-center/speeches/2008/09/bill-gates -speaks-at-the-united-nations.

16. Ellen Johnson Sirleaf, introduction to *Emerging Africa: How 17 Countries Are Leading the Way* (Washington, DC: Center for Global Development, 2010) by Steven Radelet.

17. For example, see "American Public Vastly Overestimates Amount of U.S. Foreign Aid," WorldPublicOpinion.org, November 29, 2010, www.worldpublicopinion .org/pipa/articles/brunitedstatescanadara/670.php.

18. Angus Deaton, *The Great Escape: Health, Wealth, and the Origins of Inequality* (Princeton, NJ: Princeton University Press, 2013).

19. Jeffrey Sachs, "The Case for Aid," Foreign Policy online, January 21, 2014, www .foreignpolicy.com/articles/2014/01/21/the_case_for_aid.

20. Peter T. Bauer, *Dissent on Development: Studies and Debates in Development Economics* (London: Weidenfeld and Nicolson, 1971).

21. Thad Dunning, "Conditioning the Effects of Aid: Cold War Politics, Donor Credibility, and Democracy in Africa," *International Organization* 58, no. 2 (Spring 2004): 409–23, doi:10+10170S0020818304582073; Sarah Bermeo, "Foreign Aid and Regime Change: A Role for Donor Intent," *World Development* 39, no. 11 (November 2011): 2021–31; Simone Dietrich and Joseph Wright, "Foreign Aid Allocation Tactics and Democratic Change in Africa," *Journal of Politics* 77, no. 1 (January 2015): 216–34, doi:10.1086/678976. Erasmus Kersting and Christopher Kilby find a significant positive relationship between aid and democracy from 1972 to 2011 ("Aid and Democracy Redux," *European Economic Review* 67 [April 2014]: 125–43). In a well-known earlier study, World Bank economist Stephen Knack found no positive relationship between aid and democracy through 2000, but he also found no evidence that aid undermined democracy or supported nondemocracies ("Does Foreign Aid Promote Democracy?," *International Studies Quarterly* 48, no. 1 [March 2004]: 251–66).

22. Peter Boone, "Politics and the Effectiveness of Foreign Aid," *European Economic Review* 40, no. 2 (February 1996): 289–329; Craig Burnside and David Dollar, "Aid, Policies, and Growth," *American Economic Review* 90, no. 4 (2000): 847–68; Burnside and Dollar, "Aid, Policies, and Growth: Revisiting the Evidence," policy research working paper 3251, World Bank, Washington, DC, March 2004, http:// elibrary.worldbank.org/doi/pdf/10.1596/1813-9450-3251; Raghuram Rajan and Arvind Subramanian, "Aid and Growth: What Does the Cross-Country Evidence Really Show?," *Review of Economics and Statistics* 90, no. 4 (November 2008): 643–65.

23. Michael Clemens et al., "Counting Chickens When They Hatch: Timing and the Effects of Aid on Growth," *Economic Journal* 122, no. 561 (June 2012): 590–617.
24. Henrik Hansen and Finn Tarp, "Aid and Growth Regressions," *Journal of Development Economics* 64, no. 2 (April 2001): 547–70; Robert Lensink and Howard White, "Are There Negative Returns to Aid?," *Journal of Development Studies* 37, no. 6 (August 2001): 42–65; Sandrina Berthault Moreira, "Evaluating the Impact of Foreign Aid on Economic Growth: A Cross-Country Study," *Journal of Economic Development* 30, no. 2 (December 2005), 25–48, www.jed.or.kr/full-text /30-2/J02_702.PDF; Channing Arndt, Sam Jones, and Finn Tarp, "Aid, Growth, and Development: Have We Come Full Circle?," *Journal of Globalization and Development* 1, no. 2 (2010); Markus Brükner, "On the Simultaneity Problem in the Aid and Growth Debate," *Journal of Applied Econometrics* 28, no. 1 (January /February 2011): 126 50.
25. Sebastian Galiani et al., "The Effect of Aid on Growth: Evidence from a Quasi-Experiment," policy research paper 6865, World Bank, Development Research Group, Human Development and Public Services Team, and Finance and Private Sector Development Team, May 2014, www-wds.worldbank.org/external/default /WDSContentServer/IW3P/IB/2014/05/13/000158349_20140513161349 /Rendered/PDF/WPS6865.pdf.
26. Joseph Stiglitz, *Globalization and Its Discontents* (New York: W. W. Norton, 2002), p. 5; Martin Ravallion, "On the Role of Aid in *The Great Escape*," *Review of Income and Wealth* 60, no. 4 (December 2014): 973; Paul Collier, *The Bottom Billion: Why the Poorest Countries Are Failing and What Can Be Done About It* (New York, Oxford University Press, 2007), p. 100; Lawrence Summers, quoted on the ONE website, www.one.org/us/press/condoleezza-rice-lawrence-summers-sheryl-sandberg-join -one-board-of-directors-2; Arndt et al., "Aid, Growth, and Development," p. 23.

TEN: FUTURE 1—PROGRESS EXPANDED: A NEW AGE OF GLOBAL PROSPERITY

1. Angus Maddison, *The World Economy: A Millennial Perspective* (Paris: Organization for Economic Cooperation and Development, 2001).
2. *World Economic Outlook: Legacies, Clouds, Uncertainties* (Washington, DC: International Monetary Fund [IMF], October 2014), p. 188, www.imf.org/external /pubs/ft/weo/2014/02/pdf/text.pdf; Lant Pritchett and Lawrence Summers, "Asiaphoria Meets Regression to the Mean," working paper 20573, National Bureau of Economic Research, Cambridge, MA, 2014.
3. Dwight Perkins, "China's Growth Slowdown and Its Implications," analysis brief, National Bureau of Asian Research (NBR), November 4, 2013, www.nbr.org /publications/analysis/pdf/brief/110413_Perkins_ChinaSlowdown.pdf.
4. Barry Eichengreen, Donghyun Park, and Kwanho Shin, "When Fast Growing Economies Slow Down: International Evidence and Implications for China," working paper 16919, National Bureau of Economic Research, Cambridge, MA, March 2011, www.nber.org/papers/w16919.pdf.

5. See, for example, Jong-Wha Lee and Kiseok Hong, "Economic Growth in Asia: Determinants and Prospects," working paper 220, Asian Development Bank, Manila, Philippines, September 2010, www.adb.org/sites/default/files/publication /28424/economics-wp220.pdf.

6. Raghuram Rajan, "Why India Slowed," Project Syndicate, April 30, 2013, www .project-syndicate.org/commentary/the-democratic-roots-of-india-s-economic -slowdown-by-raghuram-rajan.

7. "Looking to 2060: Long-Term Global Growth Prospects," economic policy paper 3, Organisation for Economic Co-operation and Development (OECD), Paris, France, November 2012, www.oecd.org/eco/outlook/2060%20policy%20 paper%20FINAL.pdf; *World Economic Outlook*; Pritchett and Summers, "Asiaphoria Meets Regression to the Mean."

8. *World Economic Outlook.*

9. Jean Chateau et al., "Long-Term Economic Growth and Environmental Pressure: Reference Scenarios for Future Global Projections," environment working paper, Organisation for Economic Co-operation and Development (OECD), Paris, France, September 26, 2012, www.oecd.org/officialdocuments/publicdisplaydocumentpdf /?cote=ENV/EPOC/WPCID%282012%296&docLanguage=En.

10. Homi Kharas, "The Emerging Middle Class in Developing Countries," working paper 285, Organisation for Economic Co-operation and Development (OECD) Development Centre, Paris, France, January 2010, www.oecd.org/dev/44457738 .pdf.

11. Kishore Mahbubani, *The Great Convergence: Asia, the West, and the Logic of One World* (New York: PublicAffairs, 2013).

12. Laurence Chandy, Natasha Ledlie, and Veronika Penciakova, "The Final Countdown: Prospects for Ending Extreme Poverty by 2030," policy paper 2013–14, Global Economy and Development at Brookings Institution, Washington, DC, April 2013, www.brookings.edu/~/media/research/files/reports/2013/04/ending %20extreme%20poverty%20chandy/the_final_countdown.pdf.

13. Dean Jamison et al., "Global Health 2035: A World Converging Within a Generation," *Lancet* 382, no. 9908 (December 7, 2013): 1898–1955.

14. John Gerring et al., "Democracy and Economic Growth: A Historical Perspective," *World Politics* 57, no. 3 (April 2005): 323–64, http://faculty.washington.edu /apbond/research/Demo%20growth%20%28World%20Pol%29.pdf.

ELEVEN: FUTURE 2—PROGRESS DIMINISHED: STUCK MUDDLING THROUGH

1. Joshua Kurlantzick gives an excellent account of political changes in Thailand in *Democracy in Retreat: The Revolt of the Middle Class and the Worldwide Decline of Representative Government* (New Haven, CT: Yale University Press, 2013), and my narrative follows his. The quote from James Kelly comes from his speech "U.S.-Thai Relations After September 11, 2001," to the Asia Foundation in Bangkok on March 13, 2002, http://avalon.law.yale.edu/sept11/kelly_002.asp.

2. For a series of articles in which Summers lays out his views on secular stagnation, see his webpage: http://larrysummers.com/secular-stagnation.

3. See also Robert Gordon, "Is U.S. Economic Growth Over? Faltering Innovation Confronts the Six Headwinds," working paper 18315, National Bureau of Economic Research, Cambridge, MA, August 2012, www.nber.org/papers/w18315 .pdf.

4. Press Information Bureau, Government of India, Prime Minister's Office, "Sixth BRICS Summit—Fortaleza Declaration," July 16, 2014, paragraphs 5 and 18, http://pib.nic.in/newsite/PrintRelease.aspx?relid=106712.

5. Raj Desai and James Vreeland, "Global Governance in a Multipolar World: The Case for Regional Monetary Funds," *International Studies Review* 13, no. 1 (March 2011): 109–21.

6. Dani Rodrik, "An African Growth Miracle?," Ninth Annual Richard H. Sabot Lecture, Center for Global Development, April 2014, http://www.cgdev.org/sites /default/files/2014-Rodrik-Sabot-lecture.pdf; Dani Rodrik, "The Past, Present, and Future of Economic Growth," working paper 1, Global Citizen Foundation, Geneva, Switzerland, June 2013, www.gcf.ch/wp-content/uploads/2013/06/GCF _Rodrik-working-paper-1_-6.17.131.pdf.

7. Lant Pritchett, "Understanding Patterns of Economic Growth: Searching for Hills Among Plateaus, Mountains, and Plains," *World Bank Economic Review* 14, no. 2 (May 2000): 221–50; Ricardo Hausmann, Lant Pritchett, and Dani Rodrik, "Growth Accelerations," working paper 10566, National Bureau of Economic Research, Cambridge, MA, June 2004, www.nber.org/papers/w10566.pdf.

8. Kurlantzick, *Democracy in Retreat.*

9. Reuters, Cheick Dioura and Adama Diarra, "Mali Rebels Assault Gao, Northern Garrison," *Huffington Post*, March 31, 2012, www.huffingtonpost.com/2012/03 /31/mali-rebels-assault_n_1393415.html.

10. Samuel Huntington, "Democracy's Third Wave," *Journal of Democracy* 2, no. 2 (Spring 1991): 12, www.ou.edu/uschina/gries/articles/IntPol/Huntington.91.Demo .3rd.pdf/.

11. "Ebola Virus Disease Fact Sheet, No 103," World Health Organization, last modified September 2014, www.who.int/mediacentre/factsheets/fs103/en.

12. Michael McCarthy, "Resistance to Antibiotics Is 'Ticking Time Bomb'--Stark Warning from Chief Medical Officer Dame Sally Davies," *Independent* (UK), March 11, 2013, www.independent.co.uk/news/science/resistance-to-antibiotics -is-ticking-time-bomb—stark-warning-from-chief-medical-officer-dame-sally -davies-8528469.html.

13. Dean Jamison et al., "Global Health 2035: A World Converging Within a Generation," *Lancet* 382, no. 9908 (December 7, 2013): 1898–1955, pp. 1941–1942.

14. Mitchell E. Daniels Jr., Thomas E. Donilon, and Thomas J. Bollyky, *The Emerging Global Health Crisis: Noncommunicable Diseases in Low- and Middle-Income Countries* (New York: Council on Foreign Relations, 2014), www.cfr.org/diseases -noncommunicable/emerging-global-health-crisis/p33883?co=C007301.

TWELVE: FUTURE 3—PROGRESS DERAILED: CLIMATE AND CONFLICT HALT DEVELOPMENT

1. Gardiner Harris, "Borrowed Time on Disappearing Land: Facing Rising Seas, Bangladesh Confronts the Consequences of Climate Change," *New York Times*, March 28, 2014, www.nytimes.com/2014/03/29/world/asia/facing-rising-seas-bangladesh-confronts-the-consequences-of-climate-change.html.
2. Ibid.
3. Paul Ehrlich, *The Population Bomb* (New York: Sierra Club/Ballantine Books, 1968).
4. *Charting Our Water Future: Economic Frameworks to Inform Decision-Making* (Washington, DC: Water Resources Group, 2009), www.mckinsey.com/client _service/sustainability/latest_thinking/charting_our_water_future.
5. Food and Agricultural Organization of the United Nations, "2050: A Third More Mouths to Feed," news release, September 23, 2009, www.fao.org/news/story/en /item/35571/icode.
6. M. C. Hansen et al., "High-Resolution Global Maps of 21st-Century Forest Cover Change," *Science* 342, no. 6160 (November 15, 2013): 850–53, www.sciencemag .org/content/342/6160/850.
7. *What We Know: The Reality, Risks and Response to Climate Change* (New York: American Association for the Advancement of Science, 2014), p. 6, http://what weknow.aaas.org/wp-content/uploads/2014/07/whatweknow_website.pdf.
8. "Climate Change 2013: The Physical Science Basis—Headline Statements from the Summary for Policymakers," Intergovernmental Panel on Climate Change (IPCC), last modified January 30, 2014, www.climatechange2013.org.
9. Nicholas Stern, "How Climate Change Will Affect People Around the World," chap. 3 in *Stern Review: The Economics of Climate Change* (London: Government of the United Kingdom, 2006), http://webarchive.nationalarchives.gov.uk /20100407172811/http://www.hm-treasury.gov.uk/stern_review_report.htm.
10. Dean Jamison et al., "Global Health 2035: A World Converging Within a Generation," *Lancet* 382, no. 9908 (December 7, 2013): 1898–1955.
11. United Nations, "Secretary-General Urges Recommitment to Safeguarding Natural Resources in Message on International Day for Preventing Exploitation of Environment in Armed Conflict," news release, November 1, 2012, www.un.org /press/en/2012/sgsm14615.doc.htm.
12. "Survivors Recount Barlonyo Massacre," *New Vision*, February 20, 2010, www.arlpi .org/february-20-2010-survivors-recount-barlonyo-massacre; USAID, "Uganda— Complex Emergency Situation Report #3, Fiscal Year 2006," September 15, 2006, www.ecoi.net/file_upload/225_1158910756_uganda.pdf.
13. Francis Fukuyama, *The End of History and the Last Man* (New York: Free Press, 1992), p. 353 of the afterword of the 2006 edition.
14. Kate Hodal and Jonathan Kaiman, "At Least 21 Dead in Vietnam Anti-China Protests over Oil Rig," *Guardian* (UK), May 15, 2014, www.theguardian.com/world /2014/may/15/vietnam-anti-china-protests-oil-rig-dead-injured.

15. For more discussion on these points, see Mark Leonard, "Why Convergence Breeds Conflict: Growing More Similar Will Push China and the United States Apart," *Foreign Affairs*, September/October 2013, pp. 92–95, www.foreignaffairs.com/articles/139650/mark-leonard/why-convergence-breeds-conflict.

16. John Mearsheimer, *The Tragedy of the Great Power Politics*, rev. ed. (New York: W. W. Norton, 2014), from the excerpt published as "Can China Rise Peacefully?," *National Interest*, October 25, 2014, http://nationalinterest.org/commentary/can-china-rise-peacefully-10204.

THIRTEEN: GETTING TO GOOD

1. Julian Simon, *The Ultimate Resource* (Princeton, NJ: Princeton University Press, 1981).

2. John Micklethwait and Adrian Wooldridge, "The State of the State: The Global Contest for the Future of Government," *Foreign Affairs*, July/August 2014, p. 119.

3. Samuel Huntington, "Democracy's Third Wave," *Journal of Democracy* 2, no. 2 (Spring 1991): 15–16, www.ou.edu/uschina/gries/articles/IntPol/Huntington.91.Demo.3rd.pdf/.

4. Francis Fukuyama, "At the 'End of History' Still Stands Democracy," *Wall Street Journal*, June 6, 2014, www.wsj.com/articles/at-the-end-of-history-still-stands-democracy-1402080661.

5. Alan Neuhauser, "U.S., China Reach Historic Climate Accord," *U.S. News and World Report*, November 12, 2014, www.usnews.com/news/articles/2014/11/12/us-china-reach-historic-climate-change-accord.

6. Coral Davenport, "Philippines Pushes Developing Countries to Cut Their Emissions," *New York Times*, December 8, 2014, www.nytimes.com/2014/12/09/world/americas/philippines-pushes-developing-countries-to-cut-their-emissions-.html.

7. Jane Perlez, "U.S. Opposing China's Answer to World Bank," *New York Times*, October 9, 2014, http://www.nytimes.com/2014/10/10/world/asia/chinas-plan-for-regional-development-bank-runs-into-us-opposition.html.

8. Nancy Birdsall, ed., *The White House and the World: A Global Development Agenda for the Next U.S. President* (Washington, DC: Center for Global Development, 2008), p. 28. See also Nancy Birdsall, Christian Meyer, and Alexis Sowa, "Global Markets, Global Citizens, and Global Governance in the 21st Century," working paper 329, Center for Global Development, Washington, DC, September 2013, www.cgdev.org/publication/global-markets-global-citizens-and-global-governance-21st-century-working-paper-329-0.

9. James Steinberg and Michael O'Hanlon, "Keep Hope Alive: How to Prevent US-Chinese Relations from Blowing Up," *Foreign Affairs*, July/August 2014, p. 107.

10. Erik Brynjolfsson and Andrew McAfee, *The Second Machine Age: Work, Progress, and Prosperity in a Time of Brilliant Technologies* (New York: W. W. Norton, 2014).

11. Dean Jamison et al., "Global Health 2035: A World Converging Within a Generation," *Lancet* 382, no. 9908 (December 7, 2013): 1898–1955.

12. *The State of Social Safety Nets 2014* (Washington, DC: International Bank for Reconstruction and Development/World Bank, 2014), www-wds.worldbank.org/external/default/WDSContentServer/WDSP/IB/2014/05/12/000350881_20140512111223/Rendered/PDF/879840WP0FINAL00Box385208B00PUBLIC0.pdf.

ACKNOWLEDGMENTS

This book has been taking shape for a long time, and I am deeply indebted to the many people who have influenced the major ideas and provided extensive assistance along the way. Chief among them is the late Carol Lancaster, dean emeritus of the Edmund A. Walsh School of Foreign Service at Georgetown University until she passed away far too early in 2014. It was Carol who offered me the opportunity to join the Georgetown faculty in 2012 and teach, research, and write about development. She enthusiastically encouraged me to write this book, and gave me much guidance to get me started. She was a mentor, teacher, colleague, and friend whom I greatly miss, and who inspires my work and the work of countless of her former colleagues and students every day.

Several friends and colleagues read all or parts of this manuscript, and I owe them all a great debt. Most important, my longtime friend and collaborator David Lindauer of Wellesley College read every line of every chapter, sometimes more than once, and provided exceptionally insightful comments and critiques. He made this a far better book. Charlie Kirkwood also read the entire manuscript, and, as usual, vastly clarified my thinking. Many other colleagues read all parts of the drafts and provided helpful ideas and suggestions, including Steve Block, Duncan Boughton, Steve Cashin, Laurence Chandy, Michael Clemens, Kemal Dervis, Larry Diamond, Jamie Drummond, Kim Elliot, Frank Fukuyama, Tom Hart, George Ingram, Homi Kharas, Ruth Levine, Sarah Lucas, Ted Moran, Dwight Perkins, Martin Ravallion, Sonal Shah, Liesbet Steer, Ernesto Talvi, Jeff Vincent, and Eric Werker.

My trio of superb research assistants at Georgetown—Anna Bonfert, Mallory Plaks, and Taylor Salisbury—did a huge amount of work in building the foundation for this book. They hunted down data, compiled them into comprehensible form, created the graphs, checked all the source documents, and read drafts of the chapters. Wouter Takkenberg provided able assistance in whipping the chapters into shape. I would have been quite lost without them. They built on the work of my former colleagues at the United States Agency for International Development, who put together early versions of some of the graphs and helped me formulate some key ideas: Rachel Bahn, Suzannah Dunbar, Sarah Lane, Jerrod Mason, Anastasia de Santos, and David Trichler.

I have benefitted greatly from far-reaching support from my friends and colleagues at Georgetown throughout the production of this book. Upon my arrival at the university, Carol Lancaster pointed me to Carole Sargent, our director of scholarly publications. Carole spent many hours discussing various ideas and approaches for the book, helped me to write an initial outline and proposal, and provided steady support along the way. Georgetown's president, John J. DeGioia, and Tom Banchoff, Joe Ferrara, Gail Griffith, Jennifer Long, Clare Ogden, and Jim Reardon-Anderson have been especially supportive and welcoming. My longtime friend Steve Cashin makes all things possible at Georgetown, in Liberia, and around the world, and is always available with creative ideas and contagious enthusiasm. I am grateful for the support and encouragement of the strong team at the Global Human Development (GHD) Program, including Ann Van Dusen, Gillette Hall, Janice Hoggs, Indhika Jayaratnam, Shareen Joshi, François Kabore, Maureen Lewis, Katherine Marshall, Susan Martin, Charlie Udomsaph, and Holly Wise. I owe a lot to my students, from whom I constantly learn and who are always there to (diplomatically) correct my mistakes.

The Coca-Cola Foundation has been especially supportive of the GHD program, alongside Amre Youness, Caroline Heinz-Youness, and Donald McHenry. Their financial support, partnership, internship program, and other forms of collaboration have been central to my work and to the advancement of our program. I am deeply honored that my chair at Georgetown is named for the great Donald McHenry, former US ambassador to the United Nations and longtime professor at Georgetown and director of the Coca-Cola Company.

I am grateful to the Hewlett Foundation for the generous support they provided for this book, and especially for the guidance I received from Teresa Dunbar, Ruth Levine, and Sarah Lucas. At the Brookings Institution, I received encouragement and support from Kemal Dervis, Yamillett Fuentes, Homi Kharas, Aki Nemoto, and Kristina Server.

A big thanks goes to Don Fehr of Trident Media Group, my excellent literary agent, who provided skillful guidance and assistance along the way. Ben Loehnen, my editor at Simon & Schuster, infused a terrific balance of constructive critique and strong support to vastly improve the manuscript. I am indebted to Jonathan Karp, Simon & Schuster's president and publisher, who showed great confidence and enthusiasm from the very beginning. Brit Hvide kept the entire project on track with great patience and aplomb, and Ciara Robinson's attention to detail as production editor brought the text to a whole new level. My thanks also go to Thomas LeBien, now with Harvard University Press, who believed in this project, provided some great ideas, and helped get it launched.

Last, and most of all, I could not have written this book without the love and encouragement of my family. Meghan and Sam have learned to put up with my quirky ways and to make sure I never take myself or my work too seriously. Carrie read multiple drafts of the entire book, and in doing so she made it far better. She has deep expertise in global development, and she fixed many of my mistakes and often knew what I was trying to say before I did. Far more important, she was incredibly patient, understanding, and supportive. I could not have done this, or much of anything else, without her.

INDEX

Page numbers in *italics* refer to figures.